THE RESTORATION LAND SETTLEMENT IN COUNTY DUBLIN, 1660–1688

THE RESTORATION LAND SETTLEMENT IN COUNTY DUBLIN, 1660–1688

A HISTORY OF THE ADMINISTRATION OF THE ACTS OF SETTLEMENT AND EXPLANATION

L. J. ARNOLD

IRISH ACADEMIC PRESS

This book was set in 10.5 on 12 Times
by Koinonia Ltd, Manchester for
Irish Academic Press,
Kill Lane, Blackrock, Co. Dublin.

A catalogue record for this title
is available from the British Library.

ISBN 0-7165-2503-8

ACKNOWLEDGEMENT

Publication of this work has been
made possible by a grant in aid
from the Esme Mitchell Trust.

Printed in Ireland
by Betaprint, Dublin.

Contents

To the memory of my mother and father

Preface

The Restoration land settlement in Ireland was one of the most significant events in the remarkable revolution in land ownership in the early modern period whereby the ownership of most of the land passed into the hands of the British. In the broadest sense its history can be said to have spanned the period from the Restoration of Charles II to the Glorious Revolution, although much the greater part of the work involved in the settlement coincided with Ormond's first viceroyalty.

The settlement was regulated by two statutes of parliament, the one familiarly called the Act of Settlement, passed in 1662, the other the Act of Explanation, passed in 1665, both of which became the principal legal instruments upon which land tenure in Ireland was to rest for over two centuries. While the salient features of the land settlement have been known for some time, a detailed examination of the subject has attracted the attention of relatively few historians, with the result that for the most part the topic has remained one of the major unresolved problems facing historians of seventeenth century Ireland.[1] This was primarily due to the statistical uncertainties to which W. F. T. Butler drew attention in his pioneer work, *Confiscation in Irish History* (1917), but it was also due to the uncertainties surrounding various political, legal, and administrative aspects of the settlement. The attempt has been made here to resolve some of the questions raised by Butler, county Dublin (hereafter referred to as simply 'Dublin') being used as a case study.

The development of the settlement in Dublin has been examined against a background of the history of the settlement as a whole. This approach presented certain difficulties in the organization of the book, since the Restoration land settlement, reflecting as it did the realities of the Cromwellian settlement, was based to a considerable extent on county and regional considerations. The attempt has been made to resolve this problem by treating in more general terms those aspects of the settlement that had no significant bearing on Dublin (for example, the settlement of the adventurers and soldiers), while at the same time exploiting those aspects that had application not only for Dublin but for the country generally (for example, the proceedings of the courts of claims). The limits imposed by this approach, however, has precluded any attempt to provide a definitive synthesis of the settlement as a whole, a task which must await the resolution of the remaining statistical uncertainties.

The method employed has been, first, to establish a sound statistical foundation by the extraction of quantitative data from contemporary sources concerning land ownership in Dublin for the years 1641 and 1663–9, and, second, to fill out the narrative by describing the fortunes of various landed families from the county as they were affected by the settlement. In doing so it has been necessary to take the study back beyond 1660 through the Cromwellian settlement to the sixteenth century.

The book is for the most part based on manuscript sources that have not previously been used by historians who have attempted to deal with the subject. Chief among these, and forming the principal basis for the statistical framework, are the Books of Survey and Distribution (consulted but not fully exploited by Butler), which record in detail, barony by barony, the ownership of Irish land in the seventeenth century. Other important manuscript sources, used both as supporting statistical evidence and as a basis for the narrative, include the records of Submissions and Evidence in the trial of the innocents in the first court of claims; the Entry of Warrants of the commissioners of the second court of claims; the Prendergast manuscripts; John Lodge's summaries of entries on the Irish Chancery rolls; the Civil Survey; the Down Survey; and various volumes of the Carte manuscripts. These sources indicate that the dispossessed Catholic proprietors of Dublin were restored to a far higher proportion of their land than were their co-religionists throughout the country generally, a fact that can be attributed primarily to their greater political influence.

I am pleased to acknowledge my gratitude to the staffs of the various libraries in which I have worked: the National Library of Ireland, especially Philip and Seamus MacCann; the Library of Trinity College, Dublin, especially Paul Pollard, formerly Keeper of Early Printed Books and W. E. Mackey, formerly research librarian; the Royal Irish Academy; the King's Inns, Dublin; the Pearse Street Public Library, Dublin; the Public Library, Armagh; the British Library and Public Record Office, London; the Bodleian Library, Oxford. Shortly before the typescript of this book was submitted to the publisher the Public Record Office of Ireland at the Four Courts in Dublin was closed and its function transferred to what is now called the National Archives in Bishop Street. I have decided, however, to retain the old designation of P.R.O.I., partly for sentimental reasons but also as a method of expressing my gratitude to the staff of that institution for its help over the course of many years.

The Esme Mitchell Trust made a very generous subvention towards the cost of publishing this book, and I wish to express my thanks to the trust advisers for their help. I would like to thank the Irish Nationwide Building Society, who also contributed to the cost of publication, and the American Philosophical Society of Philadelphia, who some years ago provided me with a generous grant in aid of my research.

My thanks are also due to a number of scholars who offered their assistance at various stages in my research, especially Paul Levack of Fordham University, who first pointed me in the direction of seventeenth century Ireland, and the late R. C. Simington, who provided me with sound advice at an early point in my work. At a later stage I am pleased to acknowledge the help of Aidan Clarke, Michael Millerick, Michael Adams, and the Rev Donal Cregan, C.M., who very kindly read the entire typescript and offered a number of useful suggestions. The map and graph were drawn by Albert Hill and Brian Abrams, under the direction of Dr Robert Gardula.

The debt I owe to Robert Hunter of the University of Ulster can hardly be exaggerated. His aid proved indispensable and he applied his usual surgical standards of attention to a reading of the typescript, saving me from various errors. I must reserve my deepest sense of gratitude, however, to the late Gerald Simms, under whose gentle guidance this work emerged some years ago as a research project in Trinity College, Dublin. He was in many ways an ideal supervisor; kind, extremely conscientious, generous with his time and above all practical in his approach. I learned much from his wise counsel and will continue to mourn his passing. I owe a special word of appreciation to my wife Helen, who was largely responsible for the preparation of the typescript and whose encouragement and moral support was so essential in seeing the project to a conclusion.

Abbreviations

Abstract	G. Hatchell, *Abstract of grants of lands . . . under the Commission of Grace . . . 1684–1688.*
Ainsworth, Reports	Sir John Ainsworth's Reports on manuscripts in private custody, N.L.I.
Anal. Hib.	*Analecta Hibernica.*
Bagwell *Stuarts*	R. Bagwell, *Ireland under the Stuarts*
Ball, *Judges*	F. E. Ball, *The Judges in Ireland*
B.L.	British Library
Bodl.	Bodleian Library, Oxford
Butler, *Confiscation*	W. F. T. Butler, *Confiscation in Irish History*
Cal. Carew MSS.	*Calendar of Carew Manuscripts*
Cal. Claren. S. P.	*Calendar of Clarendon State Papers*
Cal. fiants Ire., Ed. VI.	*Calendar of fiants Ireland, Edward VI*
Cal. fiants Ire., Eliz.	*Calendar of fiants Ireland, Elizabeth*
Cal. fiants Ire., Hen. VIII	*Calendar of fiants Ireland, Henry VIII*
Cal. pat. rolls Ire., Hen. VIII—Eliz.	*Calendar of patent and close rolls of Chancery in Ireland, Henry VIII to 18th Elizabeth*
Cal. pat. rolls Ire., Jas. I	*[Calendar of] Irish patent rolls, James I*
Cal. S. P. Dom.	*Calendar of State Papers, Domestic*
Cal. S. P. Ire.	*Calendar of State Papers, Ireland*
Cal. Treas. Bks.	*Calendar of Treasury Books*
Carte, *Ormond*	T. Carte, *Life of James, first Duke of Ormond* (1851 edition.)

Commons' jn.	*Journals of the House of Commons*
Commons' jn., Ire.	*Journals of the House of Commons of the Kingdom of Ireland*
Decl.	Declaration (Act of Settlement)
D.K. Rep. 19	19*th Report of the Deputy Keeper of the Public Records of Ireland* (Appendix v)
D.N.B.	*Dictionary of National Biography*
Firth and Rait, *Acts*	C. H. Firth and R. S. Rait, *Acts and Ordinances of the Interregnum*
G.E.C., *Baronetage*	G. E. C[okayne], *Complete Baronetage*
G.E.C., *Peerage*	G. E. C[okayne], *Complete Peerage*
Gilbert, *Cal. Anc. Recs. Dublin*	J. T. Gilbert, *Calendar of the Ancient Records of Dublin*
Gilbert, *Contemp. Hist.*	J. T. Gilbert, *A Contemporary History of Affairs in Ireland, from A.D. 1641 to 1652*
Gilbert, *Ir. Confed.*	J. T. Gilbert, *History of the Irish Confederation and the War in Ireland, 1641–1653*
Gilbert, *Jacobite Narrative*	*A Jacobite Narrative of the War in Ireland 1689–91* (facsimile edition, intro. J. G. Simms, 1971)
H.M.C.	Historical Manuscripts Commission
I.H.S.	*Irish Historical Studies*
I.M.C.	Irish Manuscripts Commission
Inq. Cancell, Hib. Repert.	*Inquisitionum in Officio Rotulorum Cancellariae Hiberniae Asservatorum Repertorium*
Inst.	Instructions (Act of Settlement)
I.R.C.R.	*Reports of the Commissioners appointed . . . to execute the measures . . . respecting the public records of Ireland . . .* vol. iii, 1821–5
Lib. Mun. Pub. Hib.	R. Lascelles, *Liber Munerum Publicorum Hiberniae*
Lodge, *Peerage*	J. Lodge, *The Peerage of Ireland*
Lords' jn.	*Journals of the House of Lords*
Lords' jn., Ire.	*Journals of the House of Lords of the Kingdom of Ireland*

N.I.	Northern Ireland
N.L.I.	National Library of Ireland
P.C.	P.R.O., Privy Council Registers
Prendergast, *Cromwellian Settlement*	J. T. Prendergast, *The Cromwellian Settlement of Ireland*
Prendergast, *Restoration to Revolution*	J. T. Prendergast, *Ireland from Restoration to Revolution, 1660–1690*
P.R.O.	Public Record Office, London
P.R.O.I.	Public Record Office, Ireland
P.R.O.N.I.	Public Record Office, Northern Ireland
R.I.A.	Royal Irish Academy
R.S.A.I.J.	Journal of the Royal Society of Antiquaries of Ireland
Russell and Prendergast, *Carte Manuscripts*	C. W. Russell and J. P. Prendergast, *The Carte Manuscripts in the Bodleian Library, Oxford.*
S. & D.	Books of Survey and Distribution (Quit Rent set, P.R.O.I.)
S. & E.	Submissions and Evidence, court of claims, 1663

Glossary of Terms

Adventurer	A person who subscribed money to support an army to suppress the Irish rebellion of 1641 on the security of lands to be confiscated from Irish landlords.
Article men	Those who claimed the benefit of the terms of the peace treaties of 1646 and 1649.
Cautionary reprisal	Provisional compensation in anticipation of future circumstances or needs; sometimes referred to as a grant *de bene esse*.
Concealed land	Land secretly detained from the crown by people having no title or faulty title.
Custodian	A temporary grant.
Deficiency	Adventurers' subscription money remaining to be satisfied in Irish land.
Discovery	The pointing out of land liable to seizure by the crown.
Ensignmen	Those who served under the ensigns of Charles II in exile and were named to be restored to their estates in the Act of Settlement.
Fee-farm	A permanent lease held by a fixed rent without limitation to a class of heirs.
Forty-nine officers	In the context of the Cromwellian settlement the term refers to those Protestant officers who fought in Ireland for the parliamentary cause before 5 June 1649, the date marking the day on which the first order of the council of state in England was issued for trans-

porting troops to Ireland under Cromwell. After the Restoration the term refers to those Protestant officers who, having served the royalist cause in Ireland until 5 June 1649, subsequently received no satisfaction for their arrears under the Cromwellian settlement. Unless otherwise noted, the term will be used in the latter sense.

In remainder	Right of succession following the demise of a holder.
Incumbrance	A charge or mortgage on real or personal estate, the incumbrancer being the person entitled to enforce the charge or mortgage.
Innocent	Those who proved in the court of claims of 1663 that they had never been in rebellion against Charles I or II since 22 October 1641.
Jointure	An annuity guaranteed to the bride by the father of the groom if she survived her husband.
Letteree	Persons restored to their estates by virtue of letters of Charles II; sometimes referred to as 'mero-motu' men.
Nocent	Those found not innocent in the court of claims of 1663 of having been in rebellion against Charles I or II since 22 October 1641.
Nominees	Thirty-six individuals singled out by name in the Declaration of 30 November 1660 as meriting royal favour, to be restored to their estates without having to be put to further proof; fifty-six people so-named in the Act of Settlement; fifty-four so-named to be restored to their principal estates and 2,000 adjacent acres in the Act of Explanation.
Overplus	That proportion of land in excess of the amount to which a proprietor was legally entitled.
Portion	The part of an estate descending to an heir.
Proviso-men	Those to whom land was to be restored by proviso in the Acts of Settlement or Explanation.

Quoad hoc	Limited to; this far and not further.
Reprise	To compensate.
Savings clause	A reservation or exception to the provisions of a patent.

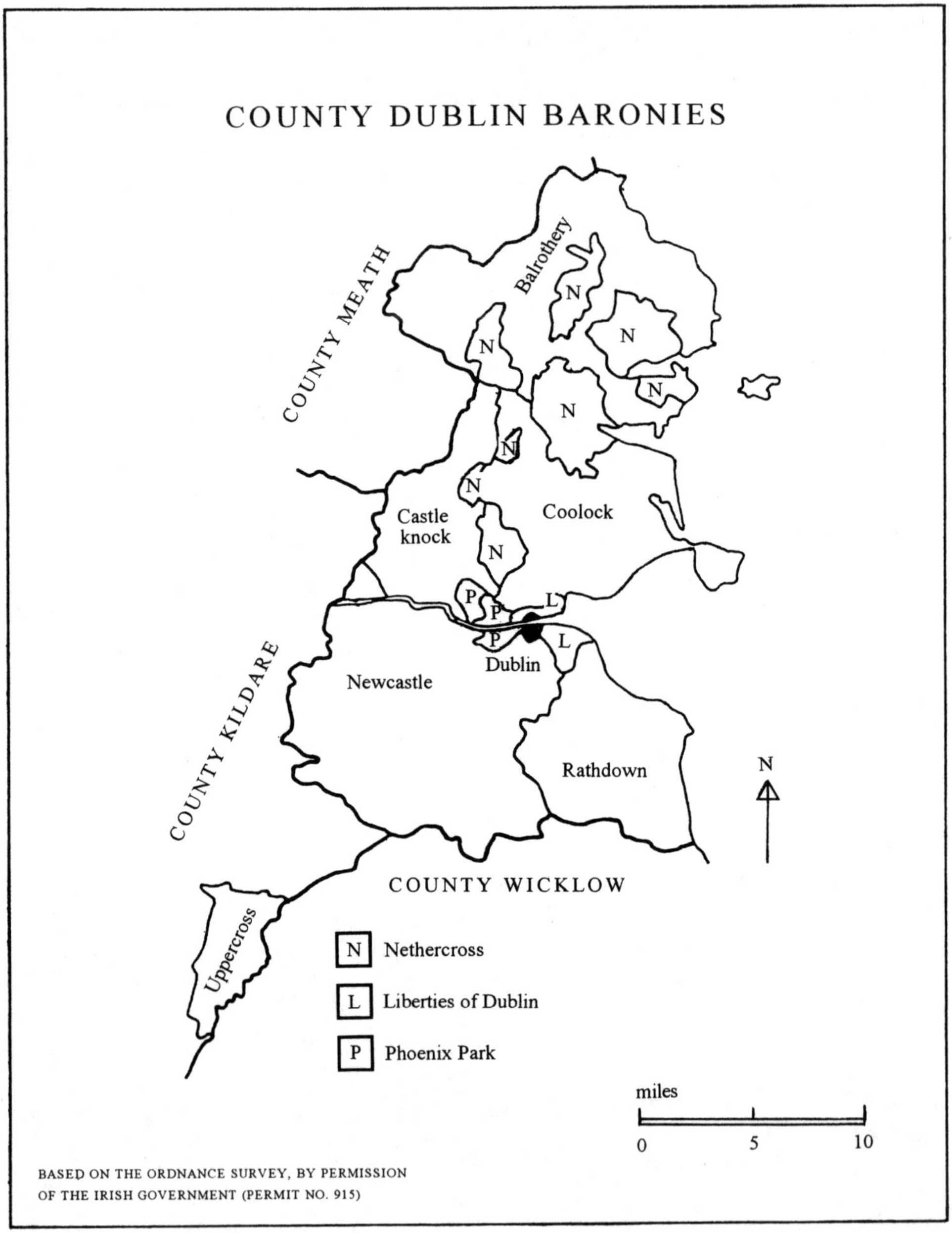
COUNTY DUBLIN BARONIES
COUNTY MEATH
Balrothery
N
N
N
N
N
N
N
N
Castle knock
Coolock
P
P
P
L
L
Dublin
Newcastle
COUNTY KILDARE
Rathdown
N
COUNTY WICKLOW
Uppercross
N Nethercross
L Liberties of Dublin
P Phoenix Park
miles
0
5
10
BASED ON THE ORDNANCE SURVEY, BY PERMISSION
OF THE IRISH GOVERNMENT (PERMIT NO. 915)

CHAPTER I

Dublin from Reformation to Restoration

Anyone examining a list of Dublin landlords in the year 1641 would be struck by the relative absence of names of Old Irish origin, for the county, and the Pale in general, had for centuries been in the hands of the Old English and, since the sixteenth century, of both the Old and New English. Most of the Old English proprietors—the Barnewalls, the Talbots, the Luttrells, the Nottinghams—still predominantly Catholic in 1641, had long family antecedents in the county, in many cases extending back to the original Norman colony. It could be written of them in 1604 that the Old English were 'nobleman and gentlemen descended of English, who are civil men and have continued their obedience to the crown, and retained the English habit and language since the ... conquest of Henry the Second, and they do commonly marry within themselves and in England, and not with the mere Irish. ...'[1]

It is significant that this assessment of the Old English could be written at a time of such moment in Irish history, for the battle of Kinsale several years earlier had marked the beginning of the process of the final extinction of the Old Irish political system, and the 'Flight of the Earls' several years later was effectively to prepare the way for the plantation in Ulster. Effective English administrative control over the entire country was now inevitable and Dublin city, hitherto the nominal centre of royal authority in the country, emerged as the actual centre.

The influx of the New English into Ireland can properly be said to have coincided with Henry VIII's attempt to extend English authority throughout the country following the destruction of the house of Kildare. An important element in this attempt was Henry's policy of 'surrender and regrant', whereby various Old Irish magnates were persuaded, upon submitting to the king and acknowledging his authority, to surrender their lands and receive them back from the crown under the English feudal principles of primogeniture and entailment, thus invalidating the traditional Old Irish proprietary system based on the principles of tanistry and gavelkind. This policy, together with the introduction of reform religious legislation in the Irish parliament of 1536–7, along with the start of the monastic dissolutions several years later, marked the start of the process of English penetration which led, a century later, to the total subjugation of the country under Cromwell.

But the Henrician revolution had little immediate effect, especially in those regions of Ireland beyond English control. In view of the ease with which the reform legislation was enacted in the Irish parliament, it would appear that the changes were initially regarded, at least in Leinster, as involving no doctrinal innovations, rather that it was a matter of church reorganisation. At any rate, the religious divisions in the country did not become pronounced until later in the century and, with the exception of the suppressions of the monasteries, implementation of the new legislation was gradual. Moreover, a large proportion of the spoils which accrued from the dissolutions was distributed to the Catholic gentry, which had the effect of attaching them even closer to the crown.

It naturally followed that Henry's expansionist policies would lead to an increasing tendency toward the appointment of English-born officials, or their retainers, to the higher legal, ecclesiastical, military, and administrative posts. From these positions of political power the New English administrative families began to attain the status of landed proprietors. In Dublin this was not the result of any form of plantation; it was instead primarily the consequence of normal commercial transactions or of the monastic suppressions.

Typical of the new breed of English office seekers who began to arrive in Ireland at this time was Sir John Alen, first cousin of the archbishop of Dublin of the same name. Alen rose from clerk of the council to master of the rolls (in 1553) and, finally (in 1538), to the lord chancellorship. Another was Sir William Brabazon, who had earlier acted as financial advisor to both Wolsey and Cromwell and, later, to the king. Brabazon, who had also acted as surveyor of dissolved monastic property in England, arrived in 1534 as vice-treasurer and was soon engaged, with Alen, in the dissolutions of the religious houses in Ireland.[2]

Also closely connected with the dissolutions were various prominent Old English members of the administration and judiciary, notably the master of the rolls, Thomas Cusack; the chief justice of the king's bench, Sir Gerald Aylmer, the chief justice of the common pleas, Sir Thomas Luttrell; the chief baron of the exchequer, James Bath; and the solicitor-general, Patrick Barnewall, all of whom shared in the spoils.

Barnewall, who had earlier been one of the most vociferous opponents of the dissolutions, later (after a visit to London) became one of its most enthusiastic proponents. As a result, he seems to have obtained the largest share of the former monastic property in the county, amounting in all to some 600 acres, consisting principally of the convent of Gracedieu in Balrothery barony, which he purchased from the crown in 1541. Gracedieu for a time became Barnewall's chief seat, but he later demolished the house, using the stones to build a new residence at Turvey a short distance away.[3]

Among the new English, a large proportion of the dissolved monastic land was originally granted to a handful of prominent individuals, including Alen and Brabazon. Alen, who in 1539 had petitioned the crown for a grant of the Augustinian abbey of Thomas Court, just outside the city walls, was instead granted Palmerstown in Newcastle barony, part of the holdings of the Hospital of St. John the Baptist Without Newgate.[4] Thomas Court was eventually sold by the crown to Barbazon. Both properties were still in the possession of the descendants of Alen and Brabazon in 1641.[5] Sir John Travers, master of the ordnance, received a crown lease for Monkstown in Rathdown barony, situated on the coast a few miles south of the city, together with nearby Cornellscourt in the same barony, both former monastic properties.[6]

The Hospital of St. John of Jerusalem in Kilmainham parish in Newcastle barony was from the first reserved for the use of the crown. In 1541 it was proposed that the principal house might be a suitable viceregal residence; indeed, Lord Deputy Grey seems to have been living there in 1536.[7] At any rate, the suggestion was adopted and the last prior, the 'loyal, old, and ailing soldier, and an Englishman to boot', Sir John Rawson, an influential member of the Irish privy council who surrendered the hospital to the crown in 1541, was retired on a pension and given a title of Viscount Clontarf, the name of a parish several miles to the north of the city on the coast, a preceptory of the order, to which Rawson had intended to retire. Shortly before his surrender, however, Rawson made a ninety-nine year lease of Clontarf to Mathew King, another Englishman described as a 'clerk of the check of the army'.[8] Kings's descendants still held Clontarf in 1641.

Leases from the crown of suppressed monastic land were usually set at twenty-one or thirty-one years and in many cases various individuals obtained reversionary leases for the same land, that is, leases to take effect on the expiry of those in force. As a result, while at the time of the first distribution large blocks of former monastic land were leased to a relatively small number of people, by the middle of Elizabeth's reign the distribution was more widely based, and by the early seventeenth century most of the major proprietors in Dublin were in possession of some suppressed monastic property.[9]

The history of the disposition of the dissolved lands of the Cistercian abbey of the Blessed Virgin Mary (St. Mary's abbey), the greatest monastic proprietor in the county, can be used to illustrate this process. In 1541 the abbey church itself, which was situated north of the river Liffey at a point approximately opposite Dublin Castle, was converted into an arsenal and placed under the command of Sir John Travers.[10] In 1544 most of the rest of the abbey's land in the county, amounting to perhaps 10,000 acres, was leased for twenty-one years to Walter Peppard, who was appointed royal steward of the abbey's possessions. Shortly later, however, a series of reversionary grants, including one to the earl of Desmond, were issued to half a dozen people for much the same land.[11]

In 1552 Peppard, now a gentleman usher to Edward VI, obtained a fresh lease, again for twenty- one years (from the termination of his lease of 1544), of all the abbey's lands 'excepting such proportions as were granted by Henry VIII'. In Elizabeth's reign reversionary leases (some for fifty or sixty years) for many of the same parcels were issued to a variety of people, both Old and New

English, including the earl of Ormond.[12] Finally, in 1603, all the abbey's lands in the county except 'such parts . . . as were granted . . . before 28 August 17th Elizabeth', were granted by James I to John Wakeman of Gloucestershire. But Wakeman was only a front-man for Sir James Hamilton (and Sir Arthur Chichester), the Scots planter in Ulster. In 1610, therefore, Wakeman disposed of the Dublin land to Hamilton and his mercantile associate, Sir James Carroll, later mayor of Dublin. Despite a regrant in 1622 (there was some dispute about Wakeman's grant), neither Hamilton nor Carroll held an estate in Dublin in 1641, and the land contained in their grant was held by at least six different proprietors.[13]

The attainder of several proprietors in the sixteenth century led to the forfeiture of substantial estates in Dublin. Thus, two proprietors, John Burnell and William Bath, were attainted for complicity in the Geraldine rebellion. Burnell's estate included Balgriffin in Coolock barony, which had been granted in 1545 to Con O'Neill, first earl of Tyrone. Following Con's death in 1559 Balgriffin was inherited by Brian O'Neill (who claimed the title of second earl), Con's grandson by his illegitimate son Mathew, who had died the previous year. The inheritance was challenged by Con's eldest legitimate son, Shane, himself attainted (posthumously) in 1569, and Balgriffin was eventually sold, probably by Hugh O'Neill, the third earl, to a member of the Bath family. A John Bath was living on the estate in 1596 and his title was confirmed in 1615.[14] John Bath's son, James, held the estate in 1641.

William Bath was attainted 'treasonable words spoken in the time of Thomas Fitzgerald's rebellion'.[15] Bath's estate in Dublin contained about 500 acres, mostly in Kilbride parish in Newcastle barony.[16] In 1538 the entire estate was granted to chief justice Sir Gerald Aylmer, who had been very active in promoting Henry's policies. But in 1563, after it had been found that Bath's attainder might have been obtained under questionable circumstances, his son Thomas was allowed to sue for recovery. As a result, an agreement was reached between James Aylmer, Gerald's cousin and heir, and Thomas Bath, by which James surrendered part of the estate, but in 1641 the Aylmer's still held a portion of the old Bath estate in the county.[17]

A third important forfeiture occurred in 1585 with the attainder of James Eustace, Viscount Baltinglas, for complicity in Desmond's rebellion.[18] Most of the escheated Baltinglas estate in Dublin (some 2,000 acres) was leased to a half dozen individuals including a son of the earl of Bedford and a Daniel Kelly, 'In consideration of his service in slaying the traitor Desmond'.[19] The forfeiture did not, however, include the lands which came to Baltinglas by this marriage to a granddaughter of Sir John Travers. Thus, Monkstown, *inter alia*, was restored to Lady Baltinglas shortly after her husband's attainder.[20] In 1597 another large segment of the forfeited Baltinglas estate in Dublin—some 1,000 acres in Uppercross barony—was leased to John Hoey, an English soldier and gentleman usher to Lord Deputy Sir William Russell. Hoey obtained a new lease in 1605 and his descendants still held the land in 1641.[21]

Probably the most prized segment of the Baltinglas estate in Dublin, however, was Rathfarnham in Newcastle barony, situated a few miles south-west of the city. Several years after the attainder the property was assigned to Thomas Coppinger, a member of a well-known Cork family, 'in consideration of the great injury he sustained in the rebellion of the earl of Desmond'.[22] But Coppinger only held the estate for a few months. Although the precise evidence for the transaction is wanting, we know that Rathfarnham was acquired by Lord Chancellor Sir Adam Loftus; he 'builded his house' there in 1583.[23]

Rathfarnham, however, represented only a minor portion of the large estate which Loftus had acquired in the county by the time of his death in 1605. He had arrived in Ireland about 1550 as chaplain to Lord Deputy Essex. Showing remarkable political and social acumen, he became successively archbishop of Armagh, archbishop of Dublin, and (in 1581) lord chancellor. Moreover, through the marriages of his many (possible twenty) children with 'divers of the ablest possessioners in the English Pale and borders adjacent', he allied himself with some of the most prominent landed families in the country.[24] The archbishop's grandson and heir, also Sir Adam, appears to have inherited his business and social talents, for by 1641 he had accumulated nearly 8,000 acres in Dublin, the largest individual holding in the county. Loftus's name appears frequently in the land records of the first half of the seventeenth century, and we occasionally get a glimpse of the nature of his operations, as in 1614 when we hear of the king's 'disapprobation . . . of Sir Adam Loftus, being one of his council, intermeddling in buying litigious titles or estates.[25]

Besides the New English who arrived as appointees to administrative posts, Elizabethan and Jacobean Ireland also attracted many place-seekers and fortune hunters, often the impoverished younger sons of the English gentry. A prototype was Sir William Parsons, depicted by Carte as 'plodding, assiduous, and indefatigable, greedy', a characterization that could no doubt be applied to many of his contemporary New English emigrants.[26] He was not long in Ireland before he had replaced (in 1602) his uncle Sir Geoffrey Fenton as surveyor-general, an office which obviously afforded Parsons a unique chance to acquire land. Moreover, it is not without significance that he acted as a member on various commissions of inquiry concerning land titles, including one of 1606 which was entrusted to 'inquire within the county of Dublin . . . of the possessions of the several late dissolved abbeys . . . which have come or ought to have come to the hands of his majesty'.[27] Even more significant was his membership, together with Sir Richard Bolton, Sir Adam Loftus, Sir Gerard Lowther, Sir George Radcliffe, and Sir James Ware, on Wentworth's commission for defective titles of 1634, a position from which, it has been suggested, it may have been possible to acquire land 'on cheap terms'.[28] All the members of this commission were New English, all were closely associated with Wentworth's administration, and all acquired estates in Ireland, including Dublin, Parsons alone having by 1641 obtained some 1,700 acres in the county.

The Protestant New English penetration into the proprietorship of Dublin had reached such proportions that by 1641 thirty-nine of them had acquired 20,732 acres, or nearly 16 per cent of the total land area of the county. Only six of them held two-thirds of this total, the greatest landowner being Sir Adam Loftus, grandson of the Elizabethan chancellor who had arrived in Ireland only about eighty years before. At the same time twenty-two Old English and Old Irish Protestants held another 12,596 acres, which, taken together with the land held by the New English, meant that sixty-one Protestants held 33,328 acres, or 25 per cent of the land of the county. By including all the land held by the church and Trinity College—9,600 acres—the Protestant interest generally in 1641 held nearly 43,000 acres, or about 32 per cent of the land, a figure which tells us something of the gradualist success of the Reformation in Dublin.

The same year found 173 Old English Catholics in possession of 67,487 acres and twenty-five New English and Old Irish Catholics holding 6,861, in total 74,348 acres, or 56 per cent of the land of the county. The twenty greatest Catholic proprietors held, between them, about 43 per cent of the Catholic total, and, it is worth noting, that the only landlord of Old Irish ancestry who held a substantial estate in the county in 1641 was Barnabas O'Brien, earl of Thomond, a Protestant, the result of a series of grants of dissolved monastic lands obtained by his ancestors in the sixteenth and early seventeenth centuries.[29]

II

Such was the state of land ownership in Dublin on the eve of the great rebellion which broke out in the north on 22 October 1641, an event which marks a distinct dividing line in the history of the country. Before 1641 the New English colonialist thrust was directed primarily against the Old Irish Catholics; after 1641 it was to be religion, not ancestry, that was the deciding factor. As such, all Catholic landlords in the country were threatened. The final episode in the English reconquest of Ireland, initiated a century before by Henry VIII, was about to begin. Ironically, the reconquest was to coincide with the destruction of the English monarchy, and when the new plantation of Ireland was complete it took a form no one could have contemplated in 1641.

With the outbreak of the rebellion the Old English gentry of Dublin, like their co-religionists throughout the Pale in general, faced a difficult choice. Although by long tradition loyal to the crown, they came to see that only by an alliance with the Old Irish insurgents from the north, and by supporting the king's prerogatives against the ambitions of the English parliament, could they hope to have their grievances redressed. This decision, however, was not arrived at until several months after the rebellion was under way. Although a few of the Catholic gentry were involved in the rebellion from the start, most of them were reluctant to be associated with it. Indeed, the alliance was only made possible by the declared loyalty of the insurgents to the crown and their professed determination to protect the royal prerogative against the incursions of the English and Scottish Puritans.

Though the professed justification of both the Catholic gentry and the Old Irish insurgents in taking up arms was in general similar, the approach of both parties in the conduct of the rebellion diverged considerably from the start, caused in part by certain traditional racial and religious animosities, but principally by the threat to the security of their estates which the Catholic gentry foresaw in a Puritan victory over the king. Many of the Old Irish, on the other hand, had already lost their estates as a result of earlier confiscations and, with less to lose, were consequently more anxious to continue the war. The Old English gentry were correspondingly more inclined to come to terms with the king; they regarded their association with the insurgents as 'an alliance rather than a union, and were determined to insist upon their continued independence and freedom of decision.'[30] This divergence of approach was to be a marked feature of the entire rebellion, and accounts to a considerable extent for the final Cromwellian success.

Although by the summer of 1642 the rebellion had spread throughout the country, the government had already recovered the military initiative, at least in the Pale. Moreover, following Charles's proclamation, in January, condemning the rebellion and calling on the rebels to lay down their arms, a number of the Catholic gentry went to Dublin city in order to submit. But most of them were imprisoned and several, including James Barnewall, were interrogated under torture.[31] The growing alienation of the Catholics and the government finally led to the expulsion, in June, of forty-one Catholic members of parliament.[32] By the end of the year hundreds of individual Catholics had been outlawed, some 350 from Dublin alone, including many of the landowners, among them Lords Gormanston and Trimleston, Walter Cheevers, Philip Hore, Nicholas Hollywood, George King, John Talbot of Malahide, and Robert Preston.[33]

A change in the complexion of the rebellion of a far reaching nature had meanwhile been assured by events in England, where on 19 March 1642 the king gave his assent to the so-called Adventurers' Act, providing for the setting aside of 2,500,000 acres of land in Ireland which, it was anticipated, would be forfeited as a result of the rebellion and used as a form of repayment to those who advanced ('adventured') money to the crown for suppressing the rebellion.[34] The consequences of this enactment was to crystallize the opposition of the Old English Catholics and to solidify their alliance with the Old Irish insurgents. It also tended to reduce the principles for which the rebellion was being waged to a choice of either gaining a convincing victory and thus preserving their religion and estates or, failing this, to lose both. Indeed, Charles had foreseen this possibility even as he assented to the act when he remarked, 'without taking time to examine, whether this course may not retard the reducing of that kingdom by exasperating the rebels, and rendering them desperate of being received into grace if they shall return to their obedience.'[35]

Another consequence of the hardening attitude of the Irish government and the English parliament was an increased awareness on the part of the rebels that some form of revolutionary governmental machinery was necessary in order to conduct the course of the rebellion. Accordingly, the 'Confederate Catholics of Ireland' convened at Kilkenny in June 1642 and a provisional government was established, composed of representatives of the Old Irish and Old English, with a president, a general assembly and a supreme council consisting of an equal number of representatives from each province. Several months later the English civil war erupted and the Confederate cause in Ireland could now be identified more closely with the royalist cause in England. Charles, therefore, was anxious to conclude a peace treaty with the Confederates in order to secure the forces of the Dublin government for service in England. With this in mind, in early 1643 the marquess of Ormond, recently made lieutenant-general of the army, was instructed to treat with the Confederates.

Although a one-year truce was agreed to in September 1643, negotiations for a final settlement dragged on for several years, during which the situation in Ireland grew extremely confusing, characterized by a series of combinations entered into by the different interests, the Old English and Old Irish, the Protestant royalists and parliamentarians, the Ulster Scots. The truce of 1643 had been extended several times until, finally, a peace treaty was concluded in March 1646, whereby in return for military aid Charles made various concessions to the Confederates. The effectiveness of the treaty was vitiated, however, by the opposition of Giovanni Battista Rinuccini, the papal nuncio, who had the treaty condemned at a synod in Waterford in 1646 . Early the following year the general assembly of the Confederates, dominated by Rinuccini's supporters, formally rejected the treaty.

Following the rejection of the treaty by the Confederates, Ormond surrendered Dublin city to the parliamentary commissioners in June 1647 and, shortly later, withdrew from Ireland. But he returned the following year when there seemed a chance to form a new royalist alliance. As a result, a peace treaty with the Confederates, given urgency by the forthcoming trial of Charles I, and differing only marginally from that of 1646, was concluded in January 1649. The Confederacy, however, was formally dissolved and the centre of authority devolved to Ormond. But attempts to negotiate with the parliamentary party in Dublin city failed, and in August 1649 Ormond's defeat at Rathmines in the suburbs of the city at the hands of Colonel Michael Jones was a severe blow to royalist morale and signalled the beginning of the end of the Stuart cause. Several weeks later Cromwell landed at Dublin city with his Ironsides. The war dragged on for several more years but by the time Cromwell returned to England in May 1650, following his swift and decisive campaign, the issue was no longer in doubt. Ormond sailed for France in late 1650, and by 1652 the parliament was in effective control of the entire country.[36]

III

With the country virtually subdued, in August 1652 the Commonwealth proceeded to pass an act for the settling of Ireland, a remarkable document which set out to describe which people, or classes thereof, were to forfeit their estates either in whole or part. A preamble to the act declared that it was not the intention of the parliament to 'extirpate that whole [Irish] nation', and that the lowest *stratum* of society (the landless labourers) was to be pardoned for life and estate. The upper ranks, however, were classified according to the degree of their guilt in the rebellion.

Five classes of people were declared to be exempt from pardon for life and estate, the first being those who had abetted the rebellion before the first meeting of the general assembly of the Confederates at Kilkenny on 10 November 1642. Also exempt from pardon were all priests who had been involved in the rebellion, along with 105 prominent individuals, including most of the principal Catholic proprietors of the country, but also including a handful of Protestants headed by Ormond. Under the fourth class of the condemned were all those who since 1 October 1641 had been guilty of the murder of civilians; the fifth class exempted from pardon were those who refused to lay down their arms within twenty-eight days from the publication of the act.

All proprietors who fell within these qualifications were to forfeit from a fifty to two-thirds of their estates, according to the degree of their 'delinquency', unless they were able, in the case of the Protestants, to prove that they had manifested 'good affection' to the parliament during the rebellion, or, in the case of the Catholics, to 'constant good affection'. Moreover, such persons were threatened with the possibility of being obliged to accept, in lieu of the proportion of their estates that remained to them, other lands of equal value elsewhere in 'such other places within that nation, as shall be judged most consistent with public safety'.[37]

In the event little 'Protestant land' was expropriated under the Cromwellian settlement, the major exception being the vast Ormond estate. But it needs to be noted that until 1654 the Protestant royalists, like their English counterparts, faced the threat of confiscation. In that year the threat was averted, but they were now required to pay composition fines in order to keep their estates. Henry Cromwell, who became lord deputy in 1657, realized however that the scheme was unenforceable (and possibly dangerous) and he unofficially dropped the composition policy.[38]

The parliament had already been formulating a more comprehensive scheme for the future settlement of Ireland even before the passing of the Act of Settlement of 1652, involving the transplanting of all delinquent proprietors into Connacht and Clare, where they would receive land equivalent in value to the proportion of their forfeited estates that they had been allowed to keep. The forfeited land in ten counties in other areas of the country was to be set aside for the satisfaction of the claims of the adventurers and Cromwellian soldiers, with the rest of the forfeited land reserved for the use of the government. Instructions based on this scheme had already been issued when, in September 1653, the Act of Satisfaction, giving legal sanction to the whole plan, was passed by parliament.[39]

It was intended that all transplanters were to have removed themselves beyond the Shannon river by 1 May 1654, but this proved to be impossible because of the administrative complexities involved in the scheme.[40] As a result, hundreds of temporary dispensations were *per force* granted. Permission to delay departure was often granted on grounds of illness or infirmity or to harvest crops. Thomas Luttrell, proprietor of a large estate west of Dublin city, managed to remain on his land for a time because he had obtained a favourable decree from the Cromwellian commissioners. But the decree stated that Luttrell had shown 'good affection' toward the parliament and not 'constant good affection'. According to J. P. Prendergast, Luttrell was permitted to occupy the stables and till the land until he, too, was finally transplanted in 1655.[41]

Some proprietors, like Christopher Russell of Seatown in Dublin, refused to go and were imprisoned.[42] Others sought relief in the regular law courts. Indeed, as late as 1656 Mary Taylor, a widow from Swords parish in Dublin, was in the court of exchequer pleading not to be dispossessed of her land, having, as she said, 'no other habitation'. Her plea appears to have been based on the grounds that she held her land independently of her late husband as a jointure dated prior to 1641. The case was referred to the recorder of Dublin and a counsellor for a decision. But the plea proved futile and her estate was confiscated. The following year a Mary Bermingham attempted to save her estate by claiming in court that she was a Protestant. But the court heard a report that her brother, John, from whom she claimed the land, was a Catholic and a delinquent and that 'it is but lately since the petitioner turned Protestant and had formerly been a constant Papist'. Mary's case was to be dismissed unless she could 'show good reason otherwise'.[43]

Owing to the expense incurred by his Irish campaign, in September 1649 the council of state ordered Cromwell to rent all forfeited land in Ireland 'to best advantage', the proceeds to be used to pay the army.[44] As a result of this order some Catholics were able to remain for a time on their estates as tenants to the Commonwealth. One of these was John Talbot, who was still living on his demesne at Malahide in late 1654, paying rent to the Commonwealth, but only 'for this year ... and no more'. He was later transplanted.[45] Another was Katherine Plunket, who was paying rent to the Commonwealth for an estate in Balrothery barony, as was Robert Caddell, who was holding a small parcel of land in the same barony 'from the Commonwealth'. Caddell was a physician and his presence may have been found useful to the authorities. He later (in 1666) claimed that they had been 'compelled' to serve in the regiment of the Cromwellian officer, Colonel Thomas Sadleir.[46]

At least twenty Dublin landlords were transplanted, most of them prominent Old English Catholics.[47] But the estates of the transplanters only represented a relatively small proportion of the land held by the Catholics of Dublin 1641. What was the fate of the others? A check of continental army lists during the Interregnum would reveal the names of some; it was the policy of the Commonwealth to assist the transportation of Catholic commanders and their regiments for service in other countries. A few of the more eminent Catholics, such as Richard Talbot and Richard Bellings, joined the exiled Stuart court. Others served as officers under the king's ensigns abroad; their services were later acknowledged under the Restoration settlement.[48] Of course a good many of the more obscure landlords simply disappear from recorded history.

A handful of Catholic proprietors from Dublin managed to avoid the expropriation of their estates. It is not always possible to ascertain how they were able to accomplish this, but their proximity to the city obviously afforded them greater opportunity to display their services on behalf of the parliament than would normally be the case. In January 1654 commissioners were appointed to sit at Loughrea in Galway for the purpose of allotting land to the transplanters.[49] But it has been pointed out that the Catholics of the Pale were allowed, for a short time, to present their claims to constant good affection to a similar court in Dublin city. Although it was soon ruled that no Catholic could submit such a claim to this court, a few may have obtained favourable decrees before the ruling went into effect.[50]

Robert Ussher may have been one such claimant. Ussher, a Catholic whose estate was not sequestered, acted as an informant for the parliamentary forces shortly before the battle of Rathmines; it is recorded that he 'daily informed Michael Jones [the parliamentary commander] of the transactions in the [royalist] camp'.[51] John Connell also escaped sequestration, but we only know that it was due to his 'good faith with the Commonwealth'.[52] James, Robert, and Martin Dillon, James Barnewall, James Humphrey, Katherine Stronge, and James Meagh also eluded sequestration of their estates, as did Edward Taylor, who obtained a decree of constant good affection.[53] Barnewall and Connell may have saved their land by successfully claiming to be Protestants.[54]

Some of the Catholic proprietors made their way to England in hopes of preserving their estates or evading transplantation. This explains the presence in London in 1654 of Sir Richard Barnewall. He apparently based his plea on the articles of agreement (which he had signed) for the surrender of Kilkenny in 1652. The Irish parliamentary commissioners, however, in a letter to Cromwell, urged rejection of the claim. They called Barnewall 'one of the most eminent delinquents in Ireland' and warned that allowing his claim would set a dangerous precedent because 'to enjoy his estate and not to be transplanted, the same rule binds us to admit all others to enjoy their estates, who have not been greater delinquents than he, most Irishmen of estate being by articles to have the same conditions touching their estates. . . .' Barnewall's plea was, therefore, rejected and he was transplanted in 1656 despite the fact that he had been excepted from pardon for life and estate in the Act of Settlement.[55] But he continued to battle against his fate. Although transplanters were normally forbidden to travel beyond the borders of Connacht and Clare, in 1657 the court of exchequer ordered the authorities at Athlone to issue a license to Barnewall, for fourteen days, permitting him to travel 'free of arrest' to Dublin, where he was to appear in court as plaintiff. No evidence exists as to the nature of this petition, but it can safely be surmised that it had something to do with his confiscated estate or the one to which he had been transplanted.[56]

While Barnewall was in England he may have met Colonel Oliver Fitzwilliam, son and heir of Lord Merrion, proprietor of one of the most valuable estates in Dublin. Fitzwilliam had in fact been in England for some time, having first arrived in November 1649 (while Cromwell was campaigning in Waterford), hoping to secure protection for his Irish estate from the council of state. Shortly after his arrival, however, he was arrested on charges of complicity in the rebellion. But a few days later he was released and ordered to leave the country within eight days, 'notwithstanding any of his pretended protections.' This order Fitzwilliam somehow managed to evade, but only until the following year when he and his wife were issued a pass to repair to France. Fitzwilliam's wife was back in England in the summer of 1651, however, at which time she was successful in persuading the council to allow her husband to return to England. Fitzwilliam was back by November and, after posting sureties for good behaviour, over the course of the next several years was engaged in negotiations for the preservation of his Irish estate.[57]

Although the precise nature of these negotiations remain obscure, two principal factors in the case are conspicuous; first, the Fitzwilliam estate in Dublin had been heavily mortgaged before 1641, and, second, in 1647 Fitzwilliam had married Eleanor, the sister of John Holles, second earl of Clare, and of Denzil, the famous Presbyterian MP, both of whom were closely identified with the cause of parliament. The importance of these two factors in the deposition of the Fitzwilliam estate during the Interregnum can best be illustrated by tracing the legal and political complexities surrounding one important segment of the estate, the townland of Merrion in Rathdown barony, situated immediately south of the city on the coast.

Merrion was mortgaged for £1,000 in 1636 to the earl of Cork. When Cork died in 1643 the mortgage was inherited by his youngest son, the eminent scientist Robert Boyle. But in 1652 it was redeemed for £2,000, the money for which came from Eleanor's marriage portion. The portion (£6,000) had been forfeited as a result of Fitzwilliam's attainder and turned over to Clare, but in 1647, by ordinance of parliament, it was placed in the hands of Denzil Holles in trust for Eleanor and her children. Once the redemption of the mortgage had been negotiated, however, a private agreement was reached between Fitzwilliam and Boyle, under which Boyle undertook to convey Merrion (for £700, part of Eleanor's portion) not to Fitzwilliam but to a group of trustees acting, with Denzil Holles, on Eleanor's behalf.

By these means Fitzwilliam appeared to have built a tidy legal shelter to protect Merrion from confiscation; indeed, he seems to have attempted to protect his entire estate in this manner, using his wife's money to redeem the mortgages in the name of the trustees. But there was considerable confusion surrounding the exact status of Merrion (and the rest of the estate), especially after the enactment of the Act of Settlement in 1652, and the evidence indicates that Merrion did in fact proceed through the technical process of sequestration the following year.

Meanwhile, however, the influence of the Holles family was exerted on Cromwell, and by early 1654 the Protector, after reading a report on the case, was persuaded that Eleanor's trustees should be restored. In August he approved an ordinance exempting from sequestration the lands settled on the trustees. Yet there were complaints in 1655 that Eleanor had not received the full benefit of the ordinance. In 1657 Denzil Holles and the trustees stated that they hoped to 'repurchase the mortgaged lands', and that the state's interest . . . may be sold to them', but in 1658 Eleanor was still engaged in redeeming the mortgages.[58] If it is true, therefore, as Clarendon maintained, that Fitzwilliam 'enjoyed the possession of his whole estate' until the Restoration, it could only have been so during the final months of the life of the Commonwealth.[59] At any rate, Fitzwilliam's apparent success in evading the expropriation of his estate accounts, in part, for the animosity directed against him after the Restoration by many of his co-religionists.

Under the provisions of the Act of Satisfaction of 1653 Dublin was designated as one of the counties reserved for the use of the government, and within the county Castleknock barony was selected to be set aside to satisfy the claims of maimed soldiers and the widows and orphans of soldiers.[60] On various occasions over the course of the following three years Balrothery and Coolock baronies were also singled out for the same purpose. In fact, however, the plan never materialized. In 1654 the council of state reported unfavourably on the whole project, finding the claimants 'in exceeding low condition' and unlikely to derive any benefit from the scheme. They recommended instead that the forfeited land in the three baronies be sold for 'ready money'. The next year the lord deputy and council were informed that the plan was impractical, largely because of the small amounts of land to which the claimants were entitled. The commissioners were empowered to satisfy the claimants in cash rather than land. A few weeks later orders were given to investigate means by which the state might buy the debentures of the soldiers who were entitled to this land. Although the Irish council was in 1656 reminded to 'take care' that the arrears of the maimed soldiers, or their widows and orphans, were to be satisfied 'either in land or money to the full value', there is no evidence that any land in the country was ever used for this purpose.[61]

Ultimately, most of the better forfeited estates in the three baronies, and indeed in the county generally, were set out, under long term leases from the Commonwealth or by outright grant, to a variety of prominent Protestant individuals. The majority were Cromwellians but a good number were New

English, who by about 1655 had begun to benefit by the resurgence of their influence in the government of Henry Cromwell.

In 1658 the Protector himself, Richard Cromwell, held some 450 acres in Coolock barony that had been forfeited by a branch of the Nugent family. This land Cromwell leased to Edward Roberts, the auditor-general.[62] The manor of Clontarf in the same barony was granted in 1653 to John Blackwell, a favourite of Oliver Cromwell's who had adventured £2,350. Blackwell,treasure at war under the Commonwealth, was mentioned by name in the instructions of the Act of Satisfaction to be allotted whatever lands he should 'make choice of' in Dublin, Kildare, and Cork. He chose 2,000 acres in Dublin.[63] Other forfeited estates in Coolock barony were set out to people of similar status. Miles Corbet, the regicide, was given a lease of the ancient demesne at Malahide, which had been in continuous occupation by a branch of the Talbot family since the twelfth century.[64] In 1649 the corporation of Dublin city granted to Colonel Michael Jones a sixty-one year lease of the townland of Clonturk, which had been held from the corporation before 1641 by Robert Bath. A short time later, as a reward for his victory over Ormond in the battle of Rathmines, Jones was granted the major portion of the forfeited estate of James Bath, including Balgriffin.[65] In 1659 the townland of Artaine was in possession of Charles Lambart, earl of Cavan, not however as a result of the Cromwellian confiscation but by virtue of a grant from Charles I in 1647, based on the attainder of Nicholas Hollywood, the former Catholic owner.[66]

Sir Charles Coote, a prominent New English figure with a bloodthirsty military reputation (among the Catholics), was granted Lord Gormanston's demesne at Gormanstown in Meath, which included some 600 contiguous acres in Balrothery barony in Dublin.[67] Some years after the Restoration an inquisition revealed that Edmund Ludlow, another regicide, had been in possession of about 3,000 acres in Dublin under the Commonwealth, about half of which was also situated in Balrothery.[68] Luke Nethervill of Corballis, son of Nicholas, first Viscount Nettervill (and a brother-in-law of Roger Moore), had held a substantial estate in his own right in the same barony. Luke, who played a prominent role as a colonel in the rebel army, was killed in the rebellion and the estate was passed to his widow, Margaret, who later married Sir Richard Bolton, the Irish lord chancellor, who was in possession at his death in 1648. Thereafter the estate was confiscated and, by virtue of a parliamentary ordinance, granted to Ann, widow of Sir Simon Harcourt who died in the royalist cause at the siege of Carrickmines in 1642. Ann took as her second husband Sir William Waller, a cousin of Sir Hardress Waller, the regicide. In the Civil Survey, Ann, now Lady Waller, is entered as the proprietor of Luke Nettervill's forfeited estate, including Corballis.[69]

Luttrellstown in Castleknock barony, the ancient seat of the Luttrell family, was leased by the Commonwealth to another regicide, Colonel John Hewson. The Act of Satisfaction stipulated that the arrears of Hewson, who succeeded Michael Jones as governor of Dublin in 1650, were to be satisfied out of forfeited land in a 'convenient place contiguous to his . . . command'.[70] Thomas Hooke, mayor of Dublin city in 1654, received a lease of the former estate of Philip Hore, most of which was situated in the same barony. Hooke, who was one of the commissioners engaged in the surveying of the country prior to the settlement, received his lease by order of Cromwell in 1650 for providing £948.4s worth of provisions for the 'Protestant army'. The lease stated that the estate was to be held until the loan, plus interest, had been recovered. By 1657 he had recovered most of the principal, but the interest had reached £806.18s, nearly equal to the amount of the original loan. Late that year, therefore, Hooke was given a fresh lease by the Commonwealth for twenty-one years of over 1,000 acres of Hore's land, including his chief seat at Kilsallaghan.[71]

The other baronies in the county seem also to have been given over to similar purposes. Colonel Hierome Sankey, one of Cromwell's more effective military commanders and later governor of Tipperary, occupied the former seat of the Segrave family at Cabragh in Nethercross barony.[72] In August 1654 an ordinance was issued for a grant of Irish land to Robert Hammond, Cromwell's cousin (and John Hampden's son-in-law), recently appointed a member of the council of state for Ireland and formerly governor of the Isle of Wight during Charles' confinement there in 1648. Hammond died, however, shortly after his arrival in Ireland, but the grant, consisting of nearly 2,000 acres in Nethercross, held in 1641 by six different Catholic proprietors, was confirmed to his heirs in 1657.[73]

Virtually the entire forfeited estate of William Sarsfield, most of which was located in Newcastle barony, and including the manor of Lucan, was in 1656 granted to Sir Theophilus Jones, a leading New English figure, former royalist officer (and a brother of Colonel Michael Jones) under Lord Conway, who after 1649 had rendered valuable military service on behalf of the Commonwealth.[74] Templeogue, in the same barony, which was the seat of yet another branch of the Talbot family, was included in the grant to John Blackwell. But Blackwell sold the estate before 1660 to Sir John King, another prominent New English figure, who held Templeogue at the Restoration.[75]

The Commonwealth reserved for its own use all church land and tithes, and directions were given that these lands were to be carefully distinguished and set aside in each county and barony. In Dublin however, it has been earlier provided, by act of parliament of 1650, that the land of the archbishop of Dublin and the dean and chapter of St. Patrick's Cathedral should be vested in trustees for the purpose of endowing Trinity College.[76] The fact that the endowment of the college was indeed carried out in this manner can be substantiated from entries in both the Civil Survey and the Books of Survey and Distribution.[77]

These examples provide some idea of the nature of the Cromwellian land settlement in Dublin. It is doubtful if the surviving sources will ever permit a fully satisfactory description, although it is now possible to account for perhaps half of the land in the county that was liable for confiscation. Included in this total would be the estates of at least eleven Catholic proprietors who evaded sequestration. If we can accept the entire Fitzwilliam estate as falling within this category, which is a doubtful supposition, the total amount of unsequestered Catholic land in the country may have reached 5,000 acres, a proportion far higher than would be the case in other counties.[78] The results of research to date, expressed on a map, would show a patchwork effect, with some baronies showing fuller results than others.

It is clear that many of the better forfeited estates in the county had attracted some of the more eminent figures of the Interregnum, including five regicides, Miles Corbet, John Hewson, Edmund Ludlow, Hardress Waller, and John Jones. This in fact may have worked to the advantage of a few of the dispossessed Catholic landlords, since some of the regicides abandoned their estates at the Restoration leaving them open for immediate repossession by their former owners. Indeed, in May 1660 the parliamentary commissioners ordered the estates of the regicides to be sequestered.[79] We know that by this time a number of the exiled and transplanted Catholics had drifted back. There is evidence that some of the transplanters, probably from the more remote regions of the country, had been in the habit of making illegal trips back to their confiscated estates in order to claim exactions from their former tenants.[80] Thus, in September 1660 a petition from 'multitudes' of Protestants complained of 'Irish officers of quality flocking hither out of other countries', who were 'daily seizing upon our long enjoyed possessions; not only labouring forcibly to detain them from us, but unjustly demanding arrears of rent'.[81] The so-called 'Census' of Ireland *c.*1659 shows at least twenty-five former Catholic proprietors back in the county.[82] Their return naturally caused apprehension among the Protestants. The apprehension was so widespread that the Irish General Convention, a coalition of New English and some conservative Cromwellians who had deposed the republican leadership in late 1659, felt it necessary to issue a declaration, in May 1660, for 'preserving the peace and quieting possessions'.[83] The primary purpose of the Convention, however, was to welcome the restoration of the Stuart monarchy and to formulate plans for the preservation of the Cromwellian settlement.

CHAPTER II

The Scheme of the Restoration Land Settlement to 1662

I

No more perplexing problem faced the restored Stuart monarchy than that of an Irish settlement, the complexities of which led Ormond to make the sardonic remark that if all the contending parties were to be satisfied there would have to be 'new discoveries made of a new Ireland, for the old will not serve to satisfy their engagements. It remains then to determine which party must suffer in the default of means to satisfy all; or whether both must be proportionally losers.'

Clarendon foresaw so many difficulties in attempting to reconcile the conflicting claims of half a dozen antagonistic interests that he begged the king to exempt him from any role in the settlement. All the parties, he said, 'filled the king's ears with specious discourses on their behalf', with the result that Charles, 'almost confounded how to begin', and 'unable positively to deny any one party that which they desire', vacillated and, characteristically, began to make promises to both sides.[1]

Even before the Restoration, in April 1660, the Irish General Convention, led by the two pre-eminent figures in the country, Roger Boyle, Lord Broghill, and Sir Charles Coote, had dispatched an advanced contingent of agents to attend the English Convention Parliament in order to protect the existing settlement. The agents were instructed to petition the king for, *inter alia*, an exclusively Protestant Irish parliament and for an act of oblivion for all Protestants, subject to parliamentary exception.[2] Since any form of a future land settlement would ultimately be contingent upon the composition of the Irish parliament, the immediate concern of the agents focused upon the possibility that an act of indemnity, then being drawn up, might be so comprehensive as to include in its benefits the dispossessed Catholic landlords of Ireland. In May 1660 Lord Aungier reported to Ormond that a 'knot' of agents representing the Protestant landed interest of Ireland were attending the Convention Parliament. They were primarily concerned, he said, with their 'new purchases' and 'refuse to think themselves secure in a parliament which shall be called in Ireland except they can exclude out of the act of indemnity . . . all those who have had any hand in the rebellion, under which notion they would comprehend promiscuously all of the Popish religion who have been either sequestered, or in arms. This work is driven hard. . . .'[3]

An important function of their work involved the deliberate exploitation of the latent fears which existed among the members of the parliament concerning the Catholics of Ireland. Extravagant stories of rebellion and the forcible repossession of Protestant estates were pressed on the members, most of whom were predisposed to accept such news from Ireland. The agents succeeded in their work to such an extent that three days after Charles entered London, on 29 May 1660, a royal proclamation declared that the rebellion of 1641 had not yet been suppressed; all 'Irish rebels' then in England or travelling (without a license) between England and Ireland were to be tried as traitors. Meanwhile, the adventurers were to remain undisturbed on their estates until 'order is taken in parliament.'[4]

The agents obviously hoped that the proclamation would obstruct the efforts being made by the Irish Catholics to organize a court lobby. But their designs were frustrated because agents representing the Catholics were in London at least a month before the king's arrival. An address to Ormond, then in Breda, from twenty-one of these agents requesting justice for their co-religionists, was dispatched from London on 6 May 1660. Most of the signatories to the address were dispossessed lords and gentry of the Pale, including six who claimed Dublin estates, Lords Nettervill, Barnewall, and Fitzwilliam, together with John Seagrave, Nicholas Plunket, and Thomas Aylmer.[5]

Hopes ran high at the Restoration among the dispossessed Catholic landlords. The peace which had been concluded in 1649 between Charles and the Confederates had, in addition to granting a full pardon, expressly provided that all Catholics who had submitted to the articles of the treaty should be restored to their possessions and that all treasons and other offences committed since 1641 should be covered by an act of oblivion.[6] Moreover the king's declaration from Breda in April 1660 had promised a general pardon to all his subjects except those who the parliament specified.[7] As late as July 1660, in a speech to the House of Lords, Charles expressed the hope that the Irish Catholic royalists would obtain the benefit of this mercy: 'They have shown much affection to me abroad' he said, 'and you will have a care for my honour, and of what I have promised to them.'[8]

But while it was generally recognized that the king would be obliged in some manner to acknowledge the claims of certain dispossessed Catholic royalists, circumstances did not warrant the rather euphoric mood which permeated their party. The Stuart restoration was an act of political expediency that had been promoted largely by the army of the Commonwealth. Charles was in fact committed to maintaining, in broad outline, the existing Irish settlement. Moreover, the army in Ireland contained a high proportion of radical officers.[9] Charles in effect had already acknowledged the realities of the situation when, in March 1660, he wrote to Coote declaring that 'whatever you shall promise and undertake in my name, and on my behalf, that is in my power to perform, . . . I do give my . . . word to make good.'[10]

Yet for most of Charles's reign the dominant figure in Ireland was Ormond, who was made a duke in 1661. A Protestant (almost alone among his immediate family), the head of an ancient and illustrious house, his immense prestige derived not only from his enormous estates and ancient lineage but also from his unwavering loyalty to the Stuart cause, certified by having spent ten years in exile with the king. He would therefore appear to have been ideally placed to undertake a compromise settlement that would go a long way toward satisfying the claims of the Catholics while at the same time maintaining the Protestant interest. However, while his disdain and contempt for the Cromwellian planters was well known, it was also known that Ormond favoured a policy of supporting the restoration of the Old English Catholic gentry at the expense of the Old Irish. He was in fact distrusted by a significant number of Catholics, especially the former adherents of Rinuccini, who regarded Ormond as having betrayed the Catholic cause, especially by his surrender of Dublin city to the English parliamentary commissioners in 1647.

As a result, the Catholic party turned instead for leadership to Richard Talbot, a cadet member of a distinguished Old English Catholic family from Carton in Kildare. Talbot, who as a young man survived Cromwell's sack of Drogheda in 1649, had been taken into the duke of York's exiled household in Flanders and while there became a great favourite of the duke's. In the restored Stuart court Talbot, whom James created a gentleman of the bedchamber, was depicted by the courtier Gramont as a charming and physically impressive, but rather superficial scatterbrain with a faulty memory. His later reputation suffered as a result of the excoriations of various Whig historians, especially Macaulay, who heaped vitriolic abuse on Talbot.[11] In view of his subsequent career we may accept these interpretations with the caution they deserve, but there is little doubt that his impulsive and irascible temperament earned him a greater degree of enmity than would normally be the case. Ormond's relationship with Talbot (and his brother Peter, a Jesuit and later titular archbishop of Dublin) was mercurial, as it was with another of the principal Catholic agents, Sir Nicholas Plunket, a brother of the first earl of Fingall and an eminent lawyer who had played an important role in the Catholic Confederation.[12]

The Catholic cause was also being served by the Marquis de Ruvigny, the French special envoy and a Huguenot, who was exerting himself, even before his arrival in England, in an effort to prevent the exclusion of the dispossessed Irish Catholics from the benefits of the act of indemnity, partly in the hope of promoting a reciprocal policy toward his co-religionists at home.[13] But neither the exertions of Ruvigny nor the solicitations of the Catholic agents were sufficient to deter Charles, in August, from assenting to an act of indemnity which excluded from its provisions, including the restoration to their estates, of any Catholic who had participated in the 'plotting, contriving, or designing' of the Irish rebellion of 1641, excepting only those who might subsequently be named in an act for the settlement of the country.[14] The proscription of the Catholics of Ireland did not go unnoticed in France. When Ruvigny arrived in England in September he carried with him a letter to Charles expressing Louis XIV's concern for the excluded Catholics.[15]

II

It was only after the passing of the act of indemnity that Charles began to turn his attention to the vexing problem of an Irish settlement. Three general proposals were put forward by the various landed interests of Ireland. The first, sponsored by Broghill (now earl of Orrery), Sir John Clotworthy, and the other agents of the General Convention, proposed that the adventurers and soldiers be confirmed in the estates they held on 7 May 1659, excepting only those adventurers who were to be dispossessed in order to accommodate the restoration of Ormond and a handful of other eminently deserving royalists, following which any undisposed forfeited land still in the king's hands might be applied toward satisfying the so-called ''49 officers'.[16] This proposal was opposed not only by the Catholic agents but also by Coote (now earl of Mountrath), who objected to the blanket confirmation in their estates of all the adventurers and soldiers without distinction , since many of them had opposed Charles's restoration. The proposal was also opposed by some of the Old English Protestant royalists, led by Sir Maurice Eustace, the new lord chancellor, who suggested instead that the king 'look upon . . . as his own' the entire province of Connacht (along with several other countries in Munster) title to which had been found for Charles I by Strafford's strong-armed inquisition before 1641, and to which neither the adventurers, under the Adventurers' Act of 1642, nor the soldiers, under the Act of Settlement ten years later, could pretend legal title. Eustace also suggested that a close examination of the Cromwellian settlement would reveal widespread abuses in the allotment of land to the adventurers, which, he added, had not been based on the English acreage measure, as provided for in the Adventurers' Act, but on the Irish measure, which was considerably larger. Eustace then called for correction of abuses in the so-called 'doubling ordinances' of 1643 and 1647, by which adventurers and army officers who paid in an additional fourth of their original subscriptions were to receive, in Irish rather than English measure, double the amount of land due to them under their original subscriptions. By this approach, Eustace maintained, enough land would accrue to the king to enable him to satisfy all who had any title to land in the country.

The Catholic agents proposed that, once having been restored to their estates, a third of their yearly incomes might be applied, for five years, to satisfy the claims of the adventurers and soldiers. They also asked that a general indemnity be granted to all Catholics, and they flavoured their request with the suggestion that, once having resumed their seats in an Irish parliament, they would be prepared to grant a supply to the king. The Catholic proposals were in turn rejected by Orrery, mainly on the grounds that if granted they would fall far short of satisfying Protestant claims, and partly on the principle that a settlement so favourable to the Catholics would only tend to encourage them to rebel again, leading to the eventual destruction of the entire Protestant settlement, since the English would never again advance money or serve as soldiers to suppress another rebellion.[17]

The discussions thus reached an impasse, and it was not until November that a formula was devised and embodied in the 'Gracious Declaration of 30 November 1660'. Carte maintains that the Declaration was issued after Orrery, Clotworthy, and Sir Audley Mervin had persuaded the king, who by this time was at a loss to know which way to turn, to accept the contents of a report which purported to show that the supply of forfeited land in Ireland was sufficient enough, even after the soldiers and adventurers had been confirmed in their holdings, to satisfy the claims of all the dispossessed Catholics whom the king wished to see restored.[18] Carte's interpretation is substantiated by Clarendon, and also by Sir Maurice Eustace, who said that although Charles had had good intentions toward the 'poor natives', he had been 'too much abused by some who carried on the declaration by making his majesty believe that there was land enough forfeited to reprise [i.e., compensate] the adventurer and soldier and great surpluses for himself to dispose of'.[19]

The Declaration of 30 November 1660 enunciated the broad principles upon which the settlement was to be based. These were, first, the general confirmation to the adventurers and soldiers of the land they held on 7 May 1659, with the major exception of the land held in 1641 by the church; second, the payment of the arrears of the '49 officers, to be derived from funds realised from undisposed forfeited land in Wicklow, Longford, Leitrim, and Donegal, and out of similar land in Connacht and Clare, within a mile of the Shannon river, and including undisposed forfeited houses in walled towns within those areas, together with the income arising from the redemption of mortgages on undisposed forfeited estates not already in the possession of adventurers or soldiers. Finally, provision was made for the restoration of certain classes of dispossessed proprietors, chiefly those Catholics who were able to prove, before the commissioners appointed to execute the Declaration, that they had been innocent of having participated in the rebellion. Those found innocent were to be restored to their estates immediately, without having to wait until the Cromwellian occupant had first been reprised with land of equal value. The Cromwellian occupant who was removed in order to accommodate the restoration of the innocent claimant was, however, to have first priority in the allocation of reprisals. (He was to be 'forthwith' reprised.) 'Innocents' who had accepted land as transplanters were also to be restored, providing they first surrendered their transplanters' estates to the crown.

Thirty-six individuals, called 'nominees', were singled out by name as especially meriting the king's favour and were therefore deemed worthy of restoration without having to be put to further proof. Two hundred and twenty-four 'ensignmen' who had served under the king's flag abroad were also singled out by name as entitled to restoration, as well as those claiming as 'articlemen', i.e., those who had fought with the Confederate Catholics but had submitted to, and observed the terms (or 'articles') of the peace treaties of 1646 or 1649. But the nominees and the ensignmen were to be restored only after the Cromwellian planter had first been reprised, and those claiming as articlemen who had remained in Ireland during the Interregnum and had been allocated land as transplanters were to forfeit all claim to restoration. Those claiming as articlemen who had obtained decrees for land as transplanters, but had in fact never been allocated such land, were to be 'otherwise satisfied'. Preference was to be shown to articlemen who had never accepted land as transplanters but had instead joined the king as ensignmen abroad.[20]

To the dispossessed Catholic proprietor the value of the decree of innocence became immediately apparent, deriving from the principle that his estate had never been legally forfeited.[21] The Protestants, on the other hand, appeared to have been tolerably satisfied with the provisions of the Declaration since it seemed to confirm the essential features of the existing settlement. Moreover, a long and complex set of Instructions to the commissioners appointed to implement the Declaration, drawn up in the months following its publication, were clearly designed to obstruct the restoration of the Catholic claimants. By the terms of these Instructions, dated 19 February 1661,[22] no Catholic was to be restored as innocent who:[23]

> at, or before the cessation [of 1643] were of the rebels party, nor any, who . . . enjoyed their estates . . . in the rebels quarters [unless] expelled from [English quarters] and driven into quarters of the rebels; . . . nor such as entered into the Roman-Catholic confederacy . . . before . . . the [peace of 1649] . . . nor such as at any time adhered to the nuncio's [Rinuccini's] . . . party . . . ; nor such who derived their titles to their estates from any who died guilty of any of the aforementioned crimes; nor such as pleaded the articles of peace for their estates; nor such as being in [royalist quarters] held correspondency with, or gave intellegence to . . . [the rebels]; nor such as before [the peace of 1646 or 1649] sat in any of the Roman-Catholic assemblies or councils . . . ; nor such as empowered agents . . . to treat with any foreign papal power . . . for bringing into Ireland foreign forces, or were persons who acted in such negotiations. . . .

The Catholic cause had already suffered a setback with the appointment, in late 1660, of Lord Chancellor Eustace, Mountrath, and Orrery, as joint lords justices pending the arrival of Monck, the lord lieutenant. Eustace, like Ormond, was inclined to support the restoration of individual members of the Old English Catholic gentry, but his age and physical infirmities (he died in

1665), together with his old-fashioned courtly bearing, prevented him from exerting a proportionate degree of influence with the more adroit and assertive Orrery and Mountrath, the most formidable opponents of Catholic claims, and with whom Eustace was not on friendly terms. Moreover, the thirty-six commissioners who were appointed to carry out the provisions of the Declaration and Instructions, who began their hearings on 20 March 1661, were not a group who would inspire much confidence among the Catholics. They were all prominent Protestants and mostly New English; included were many of the king's Irish council, several members of the judiciary, Orrery and Mountrath, Sir William Petty and others who had been associated with the Commonwealth regime in Ireland, the very people Charles needed to conciliate.[24]

A proclamation issued by the commissioners on 1 April called for all claimants to submit their claims 'at once'.[25] But little progress was made, partly because the commissioners, many of whom were holding the expropriated estates of the Catholics, felt little incentive to alter the existing settlement. Moreover, a judicial opinion ruled that the Declaration lacked the force of law. Aungier told Ormond that the commissioners were 'labouring under such difficulties for want of a law to warrant their proceedings . . . the judges having declared their opinion that the Declaration . . . is only an act of state [and] is no safe and justifiable rule to walk by in the disposing of men's estates'.[26] Eustace said that the work of the commissioners was at a standstill because its members 'do not know what course to take, having no rule of law to go by but his majesty's Declaration, which, as they say, is not warranted by law, for they take it for granted that his majesty has no legal title to any lands in Ireland but of such who had been indicted and . . . outlawed. . . .'[27]

Despite the legal uncertainties surrounding the Declaration, a number of people submitted claims to the commissioners.[28] But the Irish courts were refusing to enforce their decisions and it soon became apparent that it would be necessary to provide the Declaration with statutory authority. As a result, Charles was reluctantly persuaded to summon an Irish parliament, which finally assembled on 8 May 1661,[29] following which the draft of a new bill, based on the Declaration, was drawn up by a joint committee of both houses and, in August, transmitted to England where the final form of the bill was to be determined by the committee on Irish affairs within the privy council. At the same time delegates representing both houses of the Irish parliament, led by Orrery, along with agents of the dispossessed Catholic proprietors, departed for England prepared to present their arguments concerning the new bill. Catholic objections to the bill were read in council in early September, following which discussion was referred to the committee on Irish affairs, which first met on 6 November.[30]

The king, meanwhile, was being inundated with hundreds of petitions from the dispossessed Catholic landlords of Ireland—including many from Dublin—pleading to be restored to their estates, and in many instances Charles directed the Irish authorities to restore the petitioners.[31] But the royal instructions were often confused and contradictory, reflecting the irresolution and agitation that surrounded the whole question of the settlement within the English court. The confusion was compounded by the king's policy of issuing letters providing for grants of land to various (mostly English) courtiers, mainly those who had been active in promoting his restoration. The whole procedure was largely perfunctory and, given the lack of legal machinery to enforce the instructions, it is small wonder that the royal letters were largely ineffective.

As a representative example it is sufficient to cite a royal letter which arrived in Ireland in February 1661 for a patent to be issued to the earl of Meath for Loughlinstown in Rathdown, the order being based on a grant which Meath had obtained in 1647 following the attainder of James Goodman, the forfeiting Catholic proprietor of 1641. Meath had been evicted from the estate during the Interregnum and, since he was still not back in possession in April 1661, another letter from Charles arrived demanding that Meath's patent be issued immediately, 'in spite of anything you may have heard from us to the contrary'. The lords justices replied, however, that they had been unable to comply with the instructions 'inasmuch as Loughlinstown was before [on 6 April 1661] given by grant under the great seal to Sir William Domville, the king's attorney-general'. Meath was left to petition the English privy council, pleading for an investigation into the 'sinister means' by which Domville had acquired his grant.[32]

The confusion and uncertainty arising from the royal instructions appear less surprising when seen in the light of a letter which Charles directed to the Irish General Convention one month after the publication of the Declaration of 30 November 1660, in which he declared that it had not been his intention to 'prejudice the public or intrench on what justly belongs to any adventurer or soldier'. He would 'leave it wholly to your discretion to govern yourselves in complying with those letters as you shall find expedient', providing however that they acted within the terms of the Declaration and, from time to time, explained to the king why they did not see fit to make grants according to his letters. Several months later secretary of state Sir Edward Nicholas stated that the king was indeed anxious to preserve the existing settlement despite any letter which may have been 'wrung from him by great importunity'.[33]

There existed, nevertheless, a deep and widespread sense of insecurity among the Protestant landlords, especially those who had purchased confiscated estates from the original grantees. They were horrified by the prospect of Catholics regaining the wealth and political power which would allow them to make another attempt at rebellion. The insecurity was reflected in the Irish House of Commons, many members of which had bought such estates. The journals of the House between the opening of parliament in May 1661 and January 1663 contain at least sixty references to members being 'disturbed' in their possessions, often with the co-operation of the sheriffs, although this should not always be taken to mean that in every case the dispossessed Catholic proprietor was the culprit.[34] Thus, the Irish secretary of state, Sir Paul Davies, had in 1658 obtained a lease from the Commonwealth of certain lands in Dublin in return for surrendering the office of clerk to the privy council. Part of the lease included some 170 acres in Newcastle that had been sequestered from the Denn family. Shortly after the opening of parliament Davies complained that he was being disturbed by the Denns, one of whom had mowed several acres of his land and had carried off the hay, while threatening to kill anyone who attempted to stop him and warning the tenants not to pay rent to Davies.[35] The insecurity felt by the members finally led them to issue an order, as an assertion of their parliamentary rights and privileges, threatening prosecution of any sheriff who, without permission of the Commons, dispossessed any of the members.[36]

This rising spirit of anxiety was exacerbated by Lord Gormanston's rash act of 30 April 1662 when, in a night assault with a force of 120 men, he forcibly repossessed Gormanstown castle, his ancient family seat in Meath, the demesne of which extended into Dublin. Several people were killed in the assault, sentries were placed on the castle walls, and when the sheriff arrived with a *posse comitatus* to remove Gormanston he was shot at and forced to withdraw.[37] A week later Sir Francis Hamilton and Sir James Cuffe, trustees for the earl of Mountrath (d. 1661), to whom the estate had been granted under the Commonwealth, entered a petition in the Commons calling for Gormanston's removal. The Commons responded with an order to the sheriff of Meath to restore Hamilton and Cuffe, both members of the house. But Gormanston had meanwhile petitioned the House of Lords, justifying his actions by virtue of his parliamentary privileges as a peer, whereupon the Lords permitted him to remain in possession until a report could be made on the petition. On three separate occasions the Commons sent deputations to the Lords requesting them to permit the sheriff to execute the order for restoring Hamilton and Cuffe.

It was not until 22 September that the Lords heard the report, which stated that Gormanston had gained possession by means that were contrary to the privileges of parliament and that he was not a peer, not having sat in parliament and his father having been outlawed.[38] The contest became more complex when in the same year Mountrath's widow married a Dr Robert Reading, who submitted the dispute to the king's bench. But the court would not consider the case until the following term and, meanwhile, Gormanston remained in possession while the sentries patrolled the walls of the castle.[39]

In a very few instances the restoration of the dispossessed proprietor was accomplished with far less drama. Ormond's exalted status earned him almost immediate restoration; he was thus back in possession of his estates in Dublin six months after the Restoration. A handful of the Old English Catholics also appear to have been restored at an early stage; Thomas Luttrell, for example, whose demesne lands had been occupied by a regicide, was restored by 1661.[40] For the most part, however, the Protestants in command of sequestered estates were hard to dislodge. In some instances the sheriffs, probably with the threat of prosecution by the Commons in mind, refused to execute the warrants calling for the restoration of the former proprietor; in other cases the Cromwellian planter simply refused to obey the warrant to vacate.[41]

Even the royal favourites who obtained writs for grants of land encountered stiff resistance. In late 1660 Sir George Lane, clerk of the council in Whitehall (and son-in-law of Sir Edward Nicholas), for many years private secretary to Ormond and for ten years secretary to Charles's council in exile, obtained a writ for a grant of Philip Hore's former estate, including his chief seat at Kilsallaghan in Castleknock. Lane was still not in possession the following year, however, because, as we have already seen, Thomas Hooke, a Dublin city alderman and former mayor, claimed the land by right of a lease from the Commonwealth.[42] Clearly, the Cromwellian occupants had every intention of standing fast until a final settlement, which they had every reason to believe would be favourable to them, had been sanctioned by parliament.

Although most of the evidence derives from Protestant sources, it nevertheless seems apparent that in the discussions in England on the final form of the bill of settlement the Catholic agents presented a rather inept performance, characterized by a tone of arrogance and reckless desperation. Ormond, whose patronage had been scorned by the Catholics, referred to their lack of skill and their habit of 'instructing the king and his council in what was good for them, and recriminating others'. Michael Boyle, bishop of Cork, who was acting as agent for the House of Lords, remarked in a similar vein, accusing the Catholic agents of raising objections which contained nothing by 'vindication of themselves and crimination of us, as if the rebellion of Leinster were an act rather enforced on them by a rude multitude out of the north, whose power they could not resist. . . .'

During a meeting of the privy council in 1661, the king passed a note to Clarendon asking his opinion whether it was 'fit to call in the Irish [Catholic agents] as they desired last night?' Clarendon, replying by the same method, advised against it: 'all will come to nothing if you call them in', he said. 'I cannot imagine, with any justice, how I can refuse to hear them since they desire it', Charles replied. 'Have you not heard them?', Clarendon answered. 'If you do call them, the other side must be called too, and then we are in till morning. If you are tender hearted on their behalf I pray leave them to the House of Commons, and their work is done. They are mad and do not understand their own interest. Sir Nicholas Plunket is desperate and would make all others so too'. To this, Charles replied: 'For my part, rebel for rebel, I had rather trust a Papist rebel than a Presbyterian one. . . .'[43]

Even if Charles harboured a residue of sympathy for the Catholic cause, he was by force of circumstance reluctantly committed to maintain in general form the Cromwellian settlement. Moreover, if the Catholic cause was desperate at the start of the discussions it became hopeless at the end when, in March 1662, Plunket caused personal offence to the king by acknowledging the authenticity of his signature affixed to a letter, handed to the king by Orrery, which authorized the offer of Ireland, in 1647, to various foreign Catholic powers in exchange for military aid. As a result, Plunket was banished from court, all further addresses from the Catholic agents to the council were prohibited, and Charles declared that the 'English' should enjoy their estates, 'the Irish having clearly forfeited them'. Council hearings ended on April 3 and later the same month the bill of settlement was carried to Ireland by Bishop Boyle. It passed both houses of the Irish parliament in May and was given the royal assent on 31 July 1662.[44]

III

Based on the scheme as adumbrated in the Declaration of 30 November 1660 and the Instructions which followed, the Act of Settlement[45] was accurately described, in the eighteenth century, as 'so many private bills, which passed with similar formality to that which is usual upon separate proceedings of that nature. . . .'[46] To the Declaration and Instructions was added a preamble, part of which was devoted to a strongly worded anti-Catholic interpretation of recent Irish history, but also containing provision for the vesting on the king, as trustee for the purposes of the act, all land confiscated since 23 October 1641 as a consequence of the rebellion, with the general exception of the land held on that date by Trinity College, Dublin and the church, together with the land of Protestants and Catholics who were able to prove, in a court to be established for the purpose, that they had been innocent of having participated in the rebellion.[47]

Much the greater part of the act, however, was given over to the Declaration and Instructions, within which provision was made for some 400 individuals. Twenty new names were added to the original thirty-six who had been singled out in the Declaration as especially meriting royal favour. Among these fifty-six nominees appear the names of nine with proprietary interests in Dublin, viz., the earls of Westmeath and Fingall, Lords Gormanston, Nettervill, Trimleston, and Dunsany, along with Sir Richard Barnewall, Richard Bellings, and John Talbot of Malahide. Included among the list of 221 ensignmen were four claimants to Dublin estates, Nicholas Plunket, John Talbot of Belgard, Christopher Russell, and John Harold.[48] Thomas Luttrell was one of the few Catholics who was able to secure a separate proviso in the act providing for his restoration without previous reprisals.[49]

While nearly all the Catholic claimants mentioned in the act were treated in the aggregate, most of the prominent Protestant claimants to Dublin estates obtained individual provisoes. Ormond, not unexpectedly, was generously provided for; his name appears in no less than sixteen different clauses, one of which prescribed that forfeited land in Kildare and Dublin, 'or one of them', be allotted to him in satisfaction of a large debt he had incurred in the royal service.[50]

Ormond's secretary, Sir George Lane, was mentioned in ten different provisoes. Lane was confirmed in the grant he had received of Philip Hore's estate, provided, however, that royal title could be found. Lane's name also appears, along with those of Bishop Boyle, Lord Chancellor Eustace, and Colonel Edward Vernon—all of whom had obtained grants of large amounts of land between 1660 and 1662—in a proviso which confirmed all royal grants and letters patent issued both before and after 30 November 1660, against the claims of all persons whose rights were not protected by the act.[51]

This clause was intended to protect individuals like Vernon, a 'loyal and orthodox' royalist officer from Staffordshire who had fought in both England and Ireland. He was active in royalist conspiracies during the Interregnum, for which he was imprisoned in 1655. Released in 1656 on the plea that his mother was dying, on condition that he voluntarily return to the Tower in two months, he instead escaped to the exiled Stuart court, where he is described as having earned 'great promises of favours'. He is said to have landed at Dover with Charles in 1660 and soon arrived in Ireland a 'gentleman of the king's privy chamber' with a grant of the manor of Clontarf.

When Vernon arrived in Ireland he found Clontarf, formerly the chief seat of the King family, in the possession of Captain John Vernon, probably Edward's cousin, the former quarter-master-general of the Commonwealth army in Ireland, who had purchased the estate from John Blackwell, the Cromwellian grantee.[52] Unfortunately for Edward, the Act of Settlement exempted from confirmation all claims of title to Clontarf through the estate of Blackwell, who, as treasurer-at-war, had been responsible for defraying the cost of constructing the scaffold upon which Charles I had been executed.[53] The origin of the clause to protect Vernon can be traced to the discussions on the bill of settlement in the English privy council in late 1661, when note was taken that 'care [was] to be had of Colonel Edward Vernon in the general saving of rights to exclude John Blackwell as to any pretence to anything granted to the said Colonel Vernon'.[54]

Several other claimants to Dublin land appear conspicuously in the Act of Settlement. One was Sir John King, Lord Kingston, one of the most prominent New English figures in the country, who with his father (Sir Robert, who died before the Restoration), had purchased large numbers of transplanters' certificates and debentures from soldiers and adventurers, including most of John Blackwell's estate. This was acknowledged in Kingston's proviso, where it was stipulated that if any of these lands were restored to their former owners Kingston was to be reprised with *custodiam* (temporary) grants of equal value in Dublin, Cork, and Kildare.[55]

Another conspicuous name was Major (now Sir) George Rawdon, an Ulster planter who had been an officer in Ireland before the rebellion. Rawdon had been a member for Belfast in the 1639 parliament, while also private secretary to the second Lord Conway, whose daughter he later married. He became an intimate friend of Monck, under whom he served in Ulster in 1642. He retired from military service after the execution of Charles I but, like most of his New English contemporaries, accommodated himself to the new order after 1649, acting as commissioner of revenue in Belfast. Rawdon, however, was active in promoting Charles's restoration after Cromwell's death, and in 1659 made a trip to Scotland to consult with Monck.

The services which Rawdon rendered on Charles's behalf were recognized at an early stage and he was named as one of the thirty-six commissioners charged with the execution of the Declaration of 30 November 1660. By this time Rawdon was acting in an official capacity for Monck (now duke of Albemarle), who in 1661 sought Ormond's support for him, 'an old friend of mine and one I am much obliged for the care of my estate in . . . [Ireland], and therefore I desire your lordship if any difficulty arise concerning him that you be pleased to have a care of him.' The measure of Rawdon's influence in court may be gauged by the contents of his provisoes in the Act of Settlement, one of them for the satisfaction of arrears of a debt incurred in the royalist cause, worth over £2,300, to be realised out of a grant of 1,249 acres of forfeited land in Balrothery in Dublin.[56]

The proviso concerning the estate of Sir Charles Coote, earl of Mountrath, who died while the Act of Settlement was under discussion, reveals that a dispute had arisen between Mountrath's widow and her step-son, the second earl, over interpretation of the first earl's will. Pending settlement of the dispute it was declared that the estate was to be vested in the crown; meanwhile the lord lieutenant and council were to examine the will and attempt to resolve the problem.[57]

The only clause in the Act of Settlement dealing with a name of Old Irish origin, and relating to land in Dublin, concerned the heirs of Colonel Owen O'Connolly, a Protestant officer in Sir John Clotworthy's northern army who had acted as an informer in warning the lords justices in October 1642 of the plot to surprise Dublin Castle.[58] Three days after the rebellion erupted the lords justices and council recommended to the lord lieutenant that O'Connolly was 'worthy of very great consideration to recompense that faith and loyalty which he has . . . expressed in this business . . .'. A week later a proposal, probably inspired by Cromwell, was raised in the English parliament to reward O'Connolly with an immediate gift of £500 and to confer on him an annual pension of £200, 'until provision be made of inheritance of a greater value'. Provision of inheritance was slow in forthcoming, however, as was the pension. The payments seem to have fallen in arrears from the start; in April 1649 a Commons order for payment of the pension referred to the 'arrears thereof'.

O'Connolly was killed the following November in a skirmish in Ulster, the pension passing to his two orphaned children, who also found difficulty in collecting the money from the parliament. However, in 1658 the Commonwealth finally provided an 'inheritance' by granting the orphans land debentures in Ireland 'for a debt of £1,572. 6s', presumably the arrears due from the pension.[59] The O'Connolly proviso in the Act of Settlement passed forfeited land in Dublin worth £200 a year to his children, thus confirming the original pension scheme of 1641. It was then directed which forfeited estates might be used for the purpose, including, *inter alia*, the old Hollywood family seat at Artaine in Coolock and the former Finglas family seat at Westpalstown in Balrothery.[60]

Because of its affect on the land settlement generally, it can be argued that the most important proviso in the Act of Settlement dealing with an individual was the duke of York's, which vested in him most of the land that had been held during the Interregnum by the regicides. In 1661 Sir Maurice Eustace stated that confiscated regicides' estates in Dublin realised 36,000 acres, a figure which should be accepted with some caution.[61] But there is no doubt that in Dublin, given the size of the county in relation to the amount of land held by the regicides, it is clear that the need to provide York with an estate exerted a malign influence. Sixty-nine regicides are named in the act, five of whom—John Hewson, Miles Corbet, Edmund Ludlow, Hardress Waller, and John Jones—held estates in the county. The difficulty in providing York with an estate was compounded by the requirement, as stipulated in the act, that lands of equal value were to be set out to him if sufficient regicides' land was not available.[62]

The Act of Settlement restored all church land, including all forfeited land that had been held by lease from the church. These estates were vested in the crown and were then to revert immediately to the episcopal sees, or other church bodies, from which the lease derived, excepting only those lands which lay within the areas assigned to the '49 officers. A proportion of the forfeited land that had been held in fee-farm (permanent lease) from any episcopal see, or other church body, was to be set out for the augmentation of eight of the Irish sees (along with the provost of Trinity College). The see of Dublin was to receive sufficient land of this kind to provide an archepiscopal income of £2,000 a year.[63]

IV

In contrast to the thirty-six commissioners who had been appointed to execute the Declaration of 30 November 1660, only seven commissioners, all English-born, were entrusted to implement the terms of the Act of Settlement. Clarendon, who had a hand in their selection, described them in the standard rhetorical style of the day. They were, he said, 'gentlemen of very good extractions, excellent understandings, and above all suspicion for their integrity, and generally reputed to be superior to any base temptation'.[64] One of the seven was Winston Churchill, father of Marlborough, a successful Restoration court politician and founder of the family fortune. Churchill owed his official appointment to Sir Henry Bennett, who in December 1662 had replaced the ailing Sir Edward Nicholas as secretary of state. The genesis of the appointment, however, can be more accurately traced to the duke of York, who had taken Churchill's daughter, Arabella, as a mistress.[65]

York's influence probably also accounts for the appointment of Henry

Coventry of Droitwich in Worcestershire as one of the Commissioners. He was a brother of Sir William Coventry, the duke's secretary for many years and, like his brother, had impeccable creditionals; a lawyer, diplomat, a dedicated royalist during the war, a member of the exiled court, a close friend of Clarendon and a gentleman of the bedchamber in 1662. There is, therefore, no great mystery surrounding his selection. The appointment, however, only lasted eleven months. Coventry was recalled in February 1663 and spent the next nine years in diplomatic service, becoming secretary of state in 1672.[66]

Coventry was replaced, in May, by Sir Alan Broderick of Wandsworth in Surrey, a royalist officer and brother of St. John Broderick. His selection can be traced to Clarendon, with whom he had formed a close relationship while acting as a royalist agent in England during the final years of the Protectorate. 'Sir Alan has been loyal and has helped much towards our restoration', Charles said in acknowledging these activities in 1661. Broderick remained on friendly terms with Clarendon after the chancellor's fall from power in 1667; indeed, a short time after the event Clarendon described Broderick's presence in England at the time as being of great use to him. Broderick was appointed surveyor-general of Ireland in 1660; his surrender of the office in 1668 can probably be linked to Clarendon's downfall.[67]

Edward Cooke of Highnam in Gloucestershire had been a colonel in the parliamentary army. In 1648, however, while acting as one of the king's attendants on the Isle of Wight, he became involved in a scheme for Charles I's escape. Ten years later he is found attempting to win support for Charles II's restoration among the more moderate Presbyterians. Several months before the Restoration Charles was given assurances that Cooke was prepared to 'stand and fall' with him. He later earned the friendship of Ormond, with whom he maintained an extensive correspondence for many years. He was given to field sports and country affairs and has been described as Ormond's 'principal purveyor of hawks and hounds'.[68]

Sir Edward Dering was head of an eminent and versatile landed family that had for centuries been established at Surrenden in Kent. Unlike his famous father of the same name, Edward took no part in national politics during the Interregnum, living, as an authority on the family has noted, 'within his family rather than in political or literary circles, although it is noticeable that his family connections were of substantial political significance.' These connections stemmed chiefly from Dering's wife, Mary, daughter of Daniel Harvey, a prominent Turkey merchant and a brother of Sir William Harvey. Mary's elder sister had in 1646 married Heneage Finch, son of the speaker of the House of Commons. Heneage the younger, later attorney-general, lord chancellor, and first earl of Nottingham, provided Dering with a connection of vital importance, and there is little doubt that his emergence into public life after 1660, including his appointment as a commissioner of the Irish land settlement, can be traced to the patronage of the Finch family. Dering, who was highly regarded by Ormond, was appointed to the Irish privy council in 1667.[69]

The remaining three commissioners were lawyers who later became judges. The most obscure of the three was Sir Thomas Beverley, one of the king's remembrancers, appointed master of requests in 1662.[70] Sir Edward Smith sprang from an old landed family from Essex. His appointment can also be traced to Clarendon, with whom he maintained a close relationship. He also earned the approval of Ormond, who referred to him in 1663 as 'very honest and well natured. His capacity in business is well known'. Smith had the distinction of being the only member of the English bar to be raised to the Irish bench in the reign of Charles II, becoming chief justice of the common pleas in 1665. He was appointed to the Irish privy council the same year.[71] Sir Richard Rainsford, from Daventry in Northamptonshire, had been elected a member for Northampton in the Convention Parliament and sat for the same borough in the parliament of 1661. Shortly after completing his duties as commissioner in Ireland he was appointed a judge in England, eventually rising (in 1678) to chief justice of the king's bench in succession to Sir Matthew Hale.[72]

The commissioners, along with Ormond, who had succeeded Albemarle as lord lieutenant in early 1662, arrived in Ireland in July. Although they assumed office on 20 September (the date on which they published their commission),[73] they did not start their hearings until January 1663. The delay was due, in part, to the slowness in the printing of the Act of Settlement, which in turn caused them to be delayed in their study of its complex provisions. They were also involved at this time in arranging court procedure. This entailed the publication of the names of the claimants and the land they claimed. Since cases were to be treated as suits between the claimants and the Cromwellian occupants, it was also necessary to allow sufficient time for the attorneys of the Cromwellians to be given notice.[74]

Meanwhile, the arrival of the commissioners had stimulated fears among the Protestants that the land settlement would be radically altered. Reports reached Clarendon that many of them were despondent and preparing to sell their estates and return to England. By late autumn some of the commissioners, no doubt discouraged by the scope and complexities of the proposed re-settlement, or perhaps harrassed by private pleas of the prospective claimants, or intimidated by public rumours of corruption and favouritism within the court, were so weary of their work that it was felt necessary to increase their salaries as an inducement to stay on the job. The House of Commons, one of the commissioners remarked, was worried lest any replacements on the court might include Catholics. Only the steadfast support of Ormond and Clarendon, it would seem, prevented several of the commissioners from resigning.[75] Such were the unpropitious circumstances in which the commissioners prepared to begin their hearings.

CHAPTER III

The First Court of Claims

The court of claims, as it was known, opened its hearings at the King's Inns, Dublin, on 13 January 1663. Although most of the cases heard by the commissioners were claims of innocence, some claimed restoration by other provisions in the act, i.e., as ensignmen, nominees, or provisomen. Thus, not all successful claimants were restored by virtue of decrees of innocence, nor were all decrees of innocence equally efficacious. Most innocents were restored in fee, or in remainder, but a good number of decrees were awarded for a life interest only (mainly widows claiming jointures or children their portions) or to protect a mortgage interest, etc. (an encumbrance). By 21 August 1663, the final day of the hearings, the commissioners had handed down 829 decisions. Of this total at least 130 claims were dismissed on the grounds that the claimants were 'nocent', or not innocent.[1]

Clearly the commissioners were under considerable pressure to increase the rate of their adjudication as the final day of the hearings approached. This pressure is reflected in the steep rise in the number of decisions handed down after 30 May. Whereas only 292 had been issued by that date, 537 were awarded subsequently, including 69 in the final four days. The total of 829 is, however, somewhat misleading. Many of the decrees contained separate decisions awarded to different members of the same family; ten separate decisions, for example, were embodied in one decree given to the Hore family of Kilsallaghan.[2] Judged on this basis it is likely that the commissioners made decisions concerning the guilt or innocence of over a thousand claimants.

Approximately a quarter of all the decisions issued by the commissioners were awarded to individuals claiming land in Dublin or property in the city. This high proportion can be attributed to various factors, including the obvious one that the city was by far the largest in Ireland. Equally important was the fact, already alluded to, that for various social or political reasons the city had traditionally attracted to its environs many prominent families whose principal estates lay outside of Dublin, and whose influence was in general more potent than any other group of proprietors from a single county. Consequently, Dublin, small though it was, contained more individual estates than any other county. Sir William Petty, while mapping for the Down Survey in 1654, referred to Dublin as 'most troublesome and almost endless', with various lands lying in many 'small straggling parcels' of less than 40 acres each.[3] This had an important effect on the number of decrees issued to Dublin claimants because the order of procedure in the hearing of the claims was based, at the start of the hearings, on geographical considerations.[4] There was, finally, the factor, also alluded to earlier, and to which Ormond drew attention in a letter to Clarendon shortly after the court began its hearing, that more people from Dublin than from any other area of the country could claim as innocents because, having lived near the city, 'where the government and greatest force resided to awe and protect them then in all the rest of the kingdom', the claimants would find it easier to prove their innocence.[5]

Because all land confiscated since 1641 was vested in the king and could only be divested by decree of the court of claims, Protestants whose estates had been sequestered were also required to apply for decrees of innocence. With the major exception of the Ormond estate, however, little Protestant land had been confiscated. Nonetheless, at least 150 decrees of innocence were awarded to Protestants, some twenty of whom claimed estates in Dublin or the city. This provides telling evidence of the value placed on the decree of innocence.[6] Some Protestants probably viewed it as an added form of insurance, a hedge against an uncertain future.

In most of these cases the hearings were only a formality and the decrees were issued perfunctorily by the commissioners. Thus, John Exham, a Dublin lawyer and court official who claimed a modest estate in Dublin, was 'admitted of all hands an innocent Protestant'.[7] It was only when a question arose concerning the validity of a claim to Protestantism that a hearing might be prolonged. This was not an uncommon occurrence, and it usually involved a claimant, whose immediate ancestors were Catholics, attempting to claim as a Protestant. Walter Eustace, for example, a claimant to a substantial estate in Dublin, claimed from Alexander, his Catholic father, as a Protestant.[8] Richard Jacob, a Catholic who held a small estate in Dublin, died in 1641 leaving as sole heir a daughter, Bridget, a minor. During the Interregnum Bridget was dispossessed of her estate, but she later married Thomas Holiday 'according to the canons of the Church of England'. In the court of claims both parties were declared innocent Protestants.[9]

John Brice, a Catholic alderman of Dublin city in 1641 and sheriff in 1644, had, according to one of his sons, loaned several thousand pounds to Ormond for the royalist cause. He had also commanded a company of trained bands in the defence of the city and, in 1649, had been the 'only man' who kept Ormond informed of the activities of Michael Jones, the parliamentary commander, before the battle of Rathmines. After the battle Brice was imprisoned, where he died, and his estate was expropriated in 1652 for revealing to Ormond that Robert Ussher (also a Catholic) had been informing Jones of transactions in the royalist camp. John Brice's son, Richard, was restored as an innocent Protestant.[10]

A number of Protestants claimed decrees of innocence in order to recover encumbrances on an estate (usually a mortgage), or to establish title to land they had purchased from Catholics after 1641. One of these was John Borr, son of Christian, a naturalized Dutchman who had arrived in Ireland in the early part of the century and accumulated a large fortune as a merchant. The estate, Balally in Rathdown (over 500 acres), the chief seat of a branch of the Walsh family, was purchased by Borr after the rebellion had started.[11]

Court procedure called for the claimant to submit, prior to the hearing, a petition setting out his qualifications for seeking the decree, accompanied by a schedule, or claim, of the lands and other properties involved. To assist in their proceedings the commissioners used a variety of records, including the depositions of 1642–54 in which the Protestants had registered their complaints of loss of life and property during the rebellion. They also used the Civil Survey of 1654–6, and the so-called Books of Discrimination, notoriously known (among the Catholics) as the 'Black Books of Athlone', comprising records of the Catholic Confederates. Found by a Cromwellian officer in 1654, they were catalogued and indexed by the Commonwealth authorities and were used by the commissioners at Athlone to 'discriminate' the conduct of the transplanters during the rebellion. Also used by the commissioners were the Books of Distribution, records of the land allotted to the Cromwellian officers and adventurers, reference to which appears in the Act of Settlement.[12]

Extracts from these records, entered by officials of the court, often appear on the claims submitted to the commissioners. It was entered on Lord Netervill's claim, for example, that he had been a member of the supreme council of the Confederates 'and did sit and act amongst them, subscribed several oaths, signed several orders conceived by the supreme council, with many other things of like nature'.[13] All the documents were deposited in the 'Discrimination Office' in the King's Inns, where interested parties could search for 'letters, examinations, orders, petitions, muster rolls, and other material papers', which might be used in evidence in the court.[14]

Gorges Howard, a distinguished eighteenth century Irish jurist, maintained that the duties of the commissioners of the court of claims had been confined to the determination of the guilt or innocence of the claimants, and that they were not empowered to enquire into the validity of land titles. This interpretation of their powers, which was echoed in the nineteenth century by Sir William Betham is, however, manifestly too simplistic. As Howard observes, if both the plaintiff and the defendant agreed that the land in question had been held in 1641 by the plaintiff or his ancestors, the only question remaining was determination of the guilt or innocence of the plaintiff; if he was found innocent he was restored. But this was doubtless a rare occurrence, and in most cases the defendant challenged not only the plaintiff's claim to innocence but also his land titles. It was Howard's contention, however, that once having been declared innocent the plaintiff was declared 'innocent at large', and the determination of the validity of his land titles was 'left to law' (or 'dismissed to law'), that is, to the regular law courts. Howard thus infers that a defendant held the right to force a plaintiff to establish the validity of all his land titles in the regular law courts.[15]

It is the contention of the present study that the decrees of innocency at large were only issued when the innocent plaintiff was unable to establish proof of the validity to some, or all, of his land titles, and that the commissioners were indeed involved in determining this proof. When, for example, Luke Horstol, and Mary and Anne Shield were declared innocent they were given several weeks to examine records 'for proof of part of their claim, which if not proved is to be left to law'. Richard Brice's decree of innocence carried a provision to the effect that the land to which he had made 'no sufficient proof to this court thereunto, the claimant is left to take such remedy for recovery in law'. Similarly, Mary Bermingham and Maximilian Dempsey and his wife were adjudged innocent, to be restored 'to what they proved', as was Archbold Steward, who was to be restored to 'what he proved in his claim, and as to what he could not prove, to the dismissed'.[16] It can thus be demonstrated that the powers of the commissioners in this regard were not as circumscribed as Howard implies.

Even after awarding a decree of innocence the commissioners sometimes allowed time for a defendant to show cause why the innocent claimant should not be restored. After declaring Nicholas White innocent, for example, the court allotted 'three weeks time . . . to show cause why he should not be restored'.[17] The evidence does not suggest that this was a standard procedure; it may have been the result of some particular difficulty involving the White estate, part of which was in Dublin.

After obtaining his decree of innocence the claimant then received a certificate containing, *inter alia*, a schedule of lands to which he had established title. He was not obliged to take out letters patent for these lands, since he was not claiming new title but was restored to his former one by the power of the vesting clause in the Act of Settlement. If, however, the claimant had not been the proprietor on 22 October 1641, nor his heir or assigns, the land granted to him by the court would have to pass through the process of obtaining a patent. In such cases the commissioners issued a fiant, or warrant, to the court of chancery requiring letters patent to be made out under the great seal. Meanwhile, an injunction was dispatched to the sheriffs of the relevant counties ordering the innocent to be put in possession.[18]

It could not have been long after the court began its hearings that the commissioners became aware that some of the claimants were attempting to circumvent the intents of the Act of Settlement by the use of various questionable legal stratagems. One such gambit found the prospective claimant buying a small portion of his former estate from the Cromwellian planter, then submitting a claim for only the purchased part. Claims were also submitted for small parcels of land that had never been occupied by a Cromwellian planter. In both cases the plaintiff was automatically restored as innocent since no opposition to the claim was forthcoming, following which he could attempt to recover the remainder of his estate in the regular law courts. This procedure lessened the risk of being declared nocent and was also less expensive. In response to these ploys the commissioners began to issue decrees of innocence *quoad hoc*, entitling the innocent claimant only to those lands contained in his claim.[19]

One claimant attempted to exploit a decision of the court in a most imaginative manner. Anthony Delahide submitted his claim to an estate in Dublin, but because of his 'want of means' was unable to prosecute the case on the day appointed for a hearing. Some months after the rising of the court he pleaded, in a petition to Ormond, for a *custodiam* grant of some land in the county on the grounds that he had been found 'an innocent person in an other man's cause', which, he added, would appear in the records of the court.[20] A few claimants were declared innocent on the grounds that they were mad. The commissioners noted that it was 'endeavoured to prove . . . Charles Malloy a lunatic', and that David Howlin was 'distracted and cannot speak a word. . . . He is an idiot; has been so 7 years before the war, and so continually to this day. He runs away sometimes weeks together and eats grass'. Both were declared innocent.[21]

Although the commissioners probably heard over 900 cases, various procedural and legal difficulties often slowed their work. In 22 January, for example, much of the day was spent 'only in motions, and the 23 and 24 likewise produced nothing else'.[22] Patrick Bruton was declared innocent yet dismissed because, having lost his deed, he could not prove that he had purchased 7 acres in Tallaght parish before 1641; Stephen Reilly was also declared innocent, 'yet dismissed for that he could not prove a sequestration' of his property in Dublin city. Henry Cooley was 'dismissed as to his claim in innocency, but retained as to articles', that is, the articles of the peace of 1646 or of 1649. The hearing of the claim of Angel and Francis Plunket was postponed a week until a case could be drawn up and argued 'whether a tenant in tail could forfeit'. This brief memorandum entered on the court record appears to refer to an important legal question which first arose at this time. The Act of Settlement stipulated that no Catholic should be restored as innocent who derived their titles to their estates from any who died guilty of having been in rebellion. However, as both Prendergast and Butler have observed, the framers of the act had overlooked the legal principle that in cases where a father or grandfather was tenant for life, holding an estate that was entailed to his children, the law held that the heir did not claim through his father but through the original grantor, or 'donor'. Thus it sometimes occurred that an estate of a nocent tenant for life was restored to an innocent heir.[23]

Most decisions to postpone hearings can be traced to the order or precedency in the restoration of successful claimants as established in the Act of settlement, whereby the first to be restored were to be innocents who had not sued for decrees as transplanters. Those innocents who had sued for such decrees were to be restored next, followed by the ensignmen and articlemen.[24] As a result of this procedure, the hearings of the transplanters were often postponed (on the dubious principle that the acceptance of such land was the transplanters' own act), which was usually tantamount to permanent dispossession because the court rose for good before the commissioners had a chance to consider most of these cases. It was not even necessary for a claimant to have had lands actually allotted to him as a transplanter. Henry Plunket's hearing was postponed because he had sued for a decree as a transplanter even though he had never been assigned such land.[25]

The commissioners adopted a rather arbitrary policy in this regard, however. John Purcell and Thomas Aylmer, both claimants to land in Dublin, had heir hearings postponed on the grounds that they had been transplanted, yet both were eventually restored as innocents. So was Richard Nugent, who had also been transplanted; it was even noted on Nugent's claim that he 'Had a decree for lands in Connacht, yet restored as innocent'.[26] There is evidence that some claimants, after being restored to part of their estates, were postponed from claiming the remainder on the grounds that they had been transplanted.[27]

One of the more conspicuous Catholic landlords of the Pale who had been transplanted was Christopher Cruise of the Naul in Dublin and of Cruicetown in Meath. Cruise died in 1658 and by his will divided his estate between his two sons. To Christopher, his eldest son, he bequeathed his Dublin lands, and to Lawrence, his younger son by a second marriage, he left the Meath estate. Lawrence's claim was heard on 21 May 1663, some details of which can be extracted from Sir Edward Dering's minutes of the case. The defendant, Major [Robert?] Ormsby, charged that Lawrence had a decree for lands as a transplanter and that therefore his hearing should be postponed. Lawrence was able to prove, however, that he had in fact leased the land from his father and was not, therefore, the transplanted party. Ormsby also charged that Lawrence had sold to him the land to which his father had been transplanted, but this charge was also deflected when Lawrence proved that it had been his father who had sold the land to Ormsby. It was therefore adjudged by the commissioners that Lawrence's hearing should not be postponed because, as Dering noted, 'he had no interest in the land set out at Athlone, because they were set out to the heirs of Christopher, who the plaintiff is not; the eldest son by the first venter having left issue.' Lawrence was therefore awarded a decree of innocence and restored to his inheritance in Meath. There is no record, however, of Christopher having submitted a claim. In 1668 he was still, according to Dering, 'not restored to anything', a probable consequence of the fact that he was heir of a transplanter's first marriage.[28]

Delays sometimes occurred when individuals, having submitted claims to the abortive commission of 1661–2, failed to enter fresh claims to the new court. Others entered claims to both courts but neglected to provide 'retraxts' of the former claim, leaving the commissioners uncertain as to which claim to consider. The confusion thus generated led the commissioners to issue an order in January requiring all claimants to indicate, within thirty days, which claim they wanted heard.[29] This did not, however, deter John Hollywood from submitting what in effect amounted to three separate claims. He entered his first claim on 8 July and a second on 4 August, but with an amendment which almost duplicated what he had said in the second claim. Note of this was taken by the commissioners, who complained that 'the claimant . . . has exhibited 3 several claims but the 2 latter differ little or nothing in substance nor but here and there a word in circumstance'.[30] On 31 March Christopher Crump, a Dublin merchant, submitted what appears to have been two claims, the second of which the commissioners found to be 'so drawn as not to be understood'. This probably explains why the case was dismissed. But Crump managed to obtain a second hearing, and on 2 May was declared innocent.[31]

The proceedings of the court seem to have been conducted on occasion in a very public manner. In one session, apparently, a throng of 500 people was in attendance, which may have hastened the demise of John Bramhall, archbishop of Armagh, who, while attending court in a case involving a dispute with the cantankerous speaker of the House of Commons, Sir Audley Mervin, collapsed and died a short time later.[32]

The commissioners were hampered in their work following the recall, in February, of Henry Coventry, one of their members. Coventry's recall created the possibility, which indeed began to occur almost immediately, of causing an equal division of votes. In April one of the commissioners stated that the equilibrium of votes had almost brought the proceedings of the court to a halt. 'We do not like to hear important cases', he said, 'as, if we are evenly divided, we put the possessor in for ever by leaving the matter as it was before the hearing. Thus Lord Fingall's case remains, like Mohomet's tomb, between heaven and earth, in *equilibrio*. We are afraid to deal with it lest we ruin him by giving no sentence'.[33] Another victim of the equal division was Christopher Fagan, claimant to a large Dublin estate, whose case was heard on 13 March. But the court could come to no decision, being 'equally divided in their judgement of nocency or innocency, and so no judgment was given concerning him'. A week later, however, Christopher was declared innocent.[34]

It was said that the division of votes usually followed along predictable lines, with Smith, Dering, and Cooke voting for the 'English interest' (the Protestants) and Beverly, Rainsford, and Churchill 'for the king' (the Catholics). Broderick, after joining the court in May, was described by one observer as being 'for himself', but he later attracted the enmity of one of the courts', many critics, who denounced the decisions being handed down by the 'friends of Teig, McRainsford, O'Beverely, McChurchill, and O'Broderick'. Rainsford had a good reputation among the Catholics, one of whom described him as 'a most just and upright man'.[35]

The claims submitted during he first few months of the hearings tended to be simpler and more condensed in form than those entered subsequently. Thus, Mathew Meagh's claim, entered in February, contained only eighty-three words; Richard Donnell's, submitted a short time later, consisted of twenty-eight. After about 20 March, however, they started to become longer and more complex, with detailed schedules of land held in freehold, for life, or in fee-farm, together with portions or jointures due, often accompanied by complex statements of proof of inheritance, in some cases providing long genealogical histories. The longest claim (over 3,000 words) was entered in late July by the earl of Westmeath. This was rather late, in view of the importance of the claim, but it is likely that the task of preparing the claim, which contained the names of some 350 townlands, accounts for the delay.[36]

Several decrees relating to land in Dublin, one of which involved the estate of John Walsh of Shanganagh, were awarded under the name of a second party. John's grandfather had married a daughter of Robert Kennedy, a prominent Old Irish Protestant who had been connected with some highly questionable land transactions in Wicklow earlier in the century. In the court of claims Robert acted as guardian to his grandson, a minor whose father was dead, and presented the claim to the court. The decree was issued in Kennedy's name with John declared an innocent Protestant.[37]

The Act of Settlement required all claims to be submitted within thirty days from a date to be chosen by the commissioners, which proved to be 6 October 1662. Thereafter no claim might be submitted without royal permission, and only 'upon accidents or emergencies where justice shall require the same'.[38] Such permission, however, was routinely granted. Ormond stated that requests for permission to submit, or resubmit, claims after the expiration of the thirty days had 'not been refused to any that have sought for them, and the commissioners . . . have given way to the retracting of old and putting in new claims upon letters so directing, though thereby some do believe they violate the intention of the act. . . .'[39]

Roger Boyle, second earl of Cork, one of the greatest proprietors in the country, neglected to enter a claim, for what reason is not clear; given his eminence it may have been a simple case of arrogant complacency. But whatever the reason, six months after the court started its hearings he stated that he had 'got an alarm that I having not entered a claim for my whole estate . . . there may be some of trouble arise, and I may not be admitted to enter a claim unless I have the king's letter for it. For the procuring of this I have writ to my sister [Catherine, wife of Viscount] Ranelagh. . . . Letters of this kind are daily got . . . .' Several weeks later a royal letter arrived allowing Cork to submit a claim.[40]

The manner in which these letters were obtained often followed the normal pattern of corrupt court procedure which characterized the land settlement generally. One of the minor court officials involved in this business was Robert Leigh (O'Lee), descendant of an Old Irish family of hereditary physicians from Connacht, who had been a royalist exile during the Interregnum, and was to obtain generous grants of land in Wexford and Kildare after the Restoration. Leigh was in Dublin in 1663–4 as agent for a variety of English court figures, including the earl of St. Albans and Sir Henry Bennett, the English secretary of state. While the court was in session Leigh forwarded to Bennett's undersecretary, Joseph Williamson, a petition from a Christopher Cusack requesting a letter from the king to enable Cusack to amend his claim. 'I will desire Mr. William Godolphin to deliver you £8,' said Leigh, 'viz., Mr. Secretary

[Bennett] £5, £2 for yourself, and £1 for the signet'. This may have represented the standard legal fees charged for such services. Leigh added, however, in the same letter, that 'the sum sent is what I intend all shall pay who have letters sent from thence by my way'.[41]

In one of these instances permission was given to resubmit a claim because of the death of counsel a short time before the case was due to be heard. In another case, John and Patrick Fleming were permitted to enter a second claim on the grounds that on the first occasion they attempted to derive proof of title through the wrong person, although a claimant named Andrew Cod had his case dismissed for the same reason.[42]

Having failed to submit their claim within the prescribed time, members of the family of Philip Hore of Kilsallaghan were granted permission to 'amend ... or put in new claims'. A royal letter explained that the material evidence needed in the case had not been available when the claim was originally set to be heard.[43] Sir George Lane, to whom letters patent had been issued for the Hore estate in 1661 and 1663, viewed the royal letter with alarm. Lane was well aware of the quality of patronage at the command of Philip Hore. In a letter to Sir Henry Bennett he expressed chagrin that Hore, having been unsuccessful in obtaining such a letter 'in your office, he succeeded with the other secretary [Sir William Morice] in obtaining a letter which will be a very great prejudice if I be not relieved by the king's favour'.[44]

Two claims were eventually submitted by the Hore family, the first by the four sisters and a younger brother of Philip, the claim being based on the provisions (mainly for portions for the sisters) of a deed of feoffment executed in 1636 by their father, now deceased. The second claim was entered by Philip and his two sons, George and Mathew (both minors), which was also based on the deed of 1636.[45]

Meanwhile, in letters to both Clarendon and Bennett, Lane asserted that the deed was a forgery. He asked Clarendon to recommend his case to commissioner Rainsford, and referred to letters which had been dispatched in Philip Hore's behalf by the king, the queen-mother, and various courtiers.[46]

Once the case came to a hearing Philip Hore appears to have immediately withdrawn his name from the claim in favour of his sons. Hore had been a transplanter and he obviously foresaw the danger that, as such, his hearing would be postponed. He is reported as 'not claiming as having land in Connacht'; Lane told Bennett that Hore 'wisely postponed himself'.[47]

Ormond's position in this contest is hard to assess. Given Lane's long-standing official relationship with the lord lieutenant it would be natural to assume that his grip on the estate was assured, and Ormond may indeed have provided some kind of unofficial protection. But there is no evidence that this occurred; indeed some months earlier Ormond had reported favourably on a petition to the king from Hore, pleading to be restored. 'Hore should be restored', he said. 'You will find other ways to satisfy Sir George Lane.'[48] The most plausible explanation is that, in order to cultivate a posture of impartiality, he prudently chose to remain aloof from the struggle. There may, however, be another, more mundane explanation for Ormond's behaviour. It was Sir Robert Southwell's opinion that Lane's credit with Ormond rested 'not for any great parts', but on his efficiency as a secretary, his 'fidelity, and a kind of superstitious care in keeping all papers in order'.[49] At any rate, Lane's pleas for protection proved unavailing and on 20 August Philip Hore's two sons were declared innocent and ordered restored after the death of their father.[50]

Lane later said that commissioner Broderick had told him that Hore's claim was scheduled to be heard only as a formality, 'being 21st on the list of the last day', thus giving the impression that it would never come to a hearing. Lane felt that he had been deceived, particularly on hearing that it had been Broderick himself who was responsible for putting back the hearing by two days, although Broderick denied the charge and pointed a finger at Smith. Lane concluded that his difficulties in the case stemmed from certain misunderstandings with secretary of state Morice, with whom he exchanged several rather acerbic letters following the rising of the court.[51]

Some fifteen nocent decisions were awarded against individuals claiming land in Dublin, some of them people of considerable eminence, including the earl of Tyrconnell and Lords Dunsany and Nettervill, along with James and Christopher Plunket, James Eustace, and Patrick Sarsfield. The fact that a claimant obtained such a decree, however, did not always result in the loss of his estate. It has already been observed, as in the case of the Hore's, that the commissioners often handed down separate decisions to different members of the same family. The son or grandson of a nocent claimant was sometimes restored as innocent 'in remainder', i.e., following the death of the nocent claimant. William Sarsfield of Lucan, for example, was ordered restored as innocent following the death of his nocent father, Patrick.[52]

Nocent decisions were often awarded posthumously, usually against a father or grandfather, while the son was restored as innocent. There was a slight variation in this procedure, however, in the case of the Eustace's of Confey. Nicholas Eustace, deceased, the grandfather, was with his son, James, declared nocent, but his grandson, Thomas, was declared innocent, to be restored after the deaths of his father, mother and grandmother.[53]

Although he was named as one of the fifty-six nominees in the Act of Settlement, Nicholas, third Viscount Nettervill, was declared nocent on 23 March, largely on the testimony of 'sundry witnesses that he was in arms amongst some party of the rebels', even though, as the commissioners later acknowledged, he was only '12 or 14' years old in 1641. Nettevill's grandfather and father, the first and second viscounts, were at the same time also declared nocent posthumously, both having been active in the rebellion.[54]

After the decisions had been awarded, however, Nettervill succeeded in obtaining a royal letter directing Ormond to extend the time within which his younger brother and sisters might submit a claim. Some weeks later another royal letter to the commissioners explained that the legal documents relevant to the case were in Nettervill's possession, and that as a result his brothers and sisters had been unable to submit a claim. They had no doubt of Nettervill's innocence, they said, but now found it necessary to submit a separate claim because of the 'foul practice of perjury' which had convicted their brother. The case, Ormond said, was regarded by the king as an 'emergency', and in June directions were given to the commissioners to allow a fresh claim to be entered 'at any time'. In July the younger brothers and sisters were duly found innocent, to be restored to the estate until their respective portions and remainders had been satisfied, following which it would revert to the Cromwellian claimants, Edward Smith and Sir Courtney Poole, providing however that Nettervill had male issue, of which he was deficient in 1663. If he had no male issue the estate would remain in the possession of his brothers and sisters, in the proper legal order of the family descent.[55]

Nettervill's deceased uncle, Luke of Corballis, who had died in the rebellion, was also declared nocent. The claim was submitted by his widow Margaret, the daughter of Sir Patrick Barnewall, under the name of her deceased second husband, Sir Richard Bolton, the former lord chancellor. But the commissioners were obviously not impressed by this ploy and the claim of 'Dame Mary [*sic*] Bolton' was dismissed.[56]

Although Christopher Plunket, second earl of Fingall, had died a prisoner in Dublin Castle in 1649, he was subject to a posthumous nocent decision. His son Luke, however, the third earl, was declared innocent. The question of Christopher's activities in the rebellion proved decisive. Particularly damaging were the depositions made against him by no less than thirteen witnesses, many of them the Catholic gentry of the Pale, including Patrick Barnewall of Kilbrew and John Talbot of Robertstown, both of whom testified that Christopher had played an active role in the rebellion. It was noted on Luke's claim that his father had been '7 times indicted and outlawed'.[57] The hearing of the claim was postponed several times, to be finally heard on 23 February, when a question was put to the court whether the claimant, 'being specially provided for [as a nominee] in the . . . [Act of Settlement], might be admitted to claim otherwise than by the said proviso . . .', that is, whether Luke could claim as an innocent rather than as a nominee. After protracted debate the hearing was again postponed for two days, when the court ruled in Luke's favour, and the following day he was declared innocent, not being 'personally criminated' in the rebellion. Further argument, however, was to be heard regarding legal title to this land.[58] Fingall's successful plea to be permitted to claim restoration as an innocent rather than as a nominee provides further evidence of the value claimants placed on the decree of innocence.

Fingall's uncle, Edward, also submitted a claim. He explained that after the death of his father, Luke, the first earl, in 1637, he had been sent 'in foreign parts' for his education but upon returning to Ireland in about 1647 was taken at sea by the Turks and spent some five years in 'miserable imprisonment'. During the Interregnum he was released, however, and eventually made his way to England, where, after petitioning the council of state, was 'put in a way of restitution in regard he had no hand in the late rebellion'. But this plea had no effect and he was declared nocent, the reason for which remains unclear.[59]

Although the Fingall estate in Dublin was a small one, Dunsany, whose case was the first to be heard by the commissioners, claimed several hundred acres, but of course thousands in other regions of the country. After the decision was handed down, Dunsany's son, Edward, explained that he failed to put in a claim because he was confident of his father's innocence. Edward was allowed to submit a second claim and on 21 August, the final day of the hearings, and after a lengthy debate, was declared innocent and ordered restored on his father's death. It was entered on Edward's claim that he had been permitted to submit a claim as a result of a royal letter, the dispatch of which can probably be traced to the influence of his uncle, the marquis of Antrim.[60]

One of the more fascinating episodes in the whole history of the Restoration land settlement surrounded the case of Oliver, Viscount Fitzwilliam of Merrion, created earl of Tyrconnell in 1661. Tyrconnell had fought under Ormond, later repairing to France where he became involved in the exiled Henrietta-Maria's efforts to exert pressure on Ormond and the Catholic Confederates to reconcile their differences in hope of raising Irish troops for the king's service. With this in mind Tyrconnell crossed to England, where he arrived in time to join the battle of Naseby in June 1645. Two weeks later he was in Ireland, carrying with him a letter to Ormond from the king containing a reference to the battle (the 'late misfortune') and a recommendation that he be employed in the royal service. He was then involved with Glamorgan, Digby, and others, all independently negotiating with the Confederates. In 1646 he was campaigning in Connacht with Thomas Preston, but later that year he was back in France. He subsequently returned to Ireland, but during Cromwell's campaign went to England and, after another brief exile in France, returned once again to England and succeeded in insinuating himself into Cromwell's good graces. As a result, he was able to avoid the sequestration of at least a part—if not all—of his Irish estate.

When Tyrconnell submitted his claim to innocence someone produced a letter in evidence, written from Paris by Tyrconnell in 1647 to the supreme council of the Confederates, in which he pleaded for a vigorous prosecution of the war and emphasizing the special need to take Dublin city.[61] Unfortunately for Tyrconnell, the Act of Settlement prohibited the restoration as innocent anyone who had 'held correspondency with, or gave intelligence to such as were then in opposition' to the crown. On 6 March, therefore, Tyrconnell was declared nocent 'upon the attempt of a seditious and rebellious letter sent by him in anno 1646 [-7] to the supreme council'.[62] Tyrconnell, however, could enlist the help of powerful patrons, and eventually he was able to turn aside the effect of the dismissal of his claim.

Even after obtaining a decree of innocence the successful claimant sometimes found it difficult to gain actual possession of his old estate. In April 1663, in letters to Clarendon and Bennett, Ormond reported that the commissioners had complained to him that the sheriffs of Dublin were refusing to execute orders for restoration because they had not received injunctions from the courts of chancery or exchequer. The commissioners suspected that the sheriffs had privately conspired to obstruct the work of the court, and Ormond regarded it as 'inconvenient' that the army should be in arrears of pay at a time when he feared that there was danger of 'war' if the innocents were not put in possession. The question of whether the decree of innocence emanating from the court of claims obliged the courts of chancery or exchequer to issue injunctions ordering the restoration of the innocents must be resolved, Ormond added, unless the powers of the commissioners were to be limited only to the establishment of proof of ownership and not the actual repossession by the innocents.[63] This question was raised in the Irish privy council on the very day Ormond stated the problem in these letters, and several weeks later an order from council directed the commissioners to order the sheriffs to execute the decrees of the court.[64]

One of the successful claimants who had to face problems of this nature was James Wolverton, who was declared innocent on 28 March and ordered to put in possession of his estate, based on Stillorgan in Rathdown, on 15 May. But Stillorgan was one of a number of forfeited estates in the barony that had been granted in 1662 to Lord Chancellor Sir Maurice Eustace,[65] and when Wolverton arrived to take possession he found that Eustace had leased the manor to Major Henry Jones.[66]

On the day Wolverton was ordered to take possession Jones saw Eustace, pleading that he had no alternative residence and no other land on which to graze his cattle. Jones also claimed that he had expended some £300 on improvements to the estate. In response, Eustace ordered Wolverton to permit Jones to remain in possession for a year, paying the prescribed rent. But it would appear that Jones did, in fact, have a house, elsewhere, and moreover, Wolverton offered to let him have another 'stone built house' in Stillorgan as a substitute, and agreed to permit him to pasture his cattle at Stillorgan temporarily, providing Jones agreed to an immediate surrender of the estate. This Jones refused to do, following which he obtained an injunction from chancery putting him in possession, presumably for a year.

Ormond received a report on the case on 23 May and referred it to the commissioners, who rebuked Jones for 'this proceeding in chancery [which] entrenches upon [the power with] which we are entrusted. . . .' They also pointed out, however, that they had publicly declared it their wish that tenants on land restored to innocent claimants should not be dispossessed 'until they had reaped their corn . . . and have had convenient time to provide for themselves'.[67] It was probably the Wolverton episode which inspired an order in council on 15 May against the 'violent' removal of tenants by the restored innocents. This was followed on 1 July by another order, reminding the judges of the need to provide reprisals 'forthwith' for the adventurers and soldiers who were removed to accommodate the innocents.[68]

Meanwhile, Jones had been imprisoned for suspected complicity in an armed conspiracy aimed against the government, led by the notorious Colonel Thomas Blood. While he was in jail Wolverton had him summoned to appear before the court of claims, where, as his wife feared, he was 'like to have advantage taken against him by reason of his present restraint'. Her fears proved, indeed to have been justified, for by the time her husband was released, in August, Wolverton was back in possession of Stillorgan. Jones, now impoverished, requested permission to emigrate.[69]

If the commissioners resented the encroachment on their powers by proceedings in chancery, it is equally certain they resented orders from the privy council to award decrees of innocence to certain claimants. No evidence has emerged which connects this practice with Dublin claimants, and it does not appear to have occurred very often; indeed, in one such case the council stated that it was not their intention to interfere in the future, which did not, in the event, prove to be true.[70] However, it would seem that in most of these instances the council was acting on orders from the king, the most notorious example of which involved royal interference in the case of the decree of innocence awarded to the marquis of Antrim.[71]

James Wolverton was not only restored to his chief seat at Stillorgan, but also to his secondary holdings in the same barony, Leopardstown and Little Newtown, both of which had been included in the letters patent issued to Lord Chancellor Eustace in 1662. Eustace in fact lost nearly all of the property contained in his grant to restored innocents, despite having obtained a private act of parliament securing him in his estate.[72] The major exception was Kilmashogue, also in Rathdown, which had been sequestered from the Harold family. John Harold had died about 1661, leaving as heir Nicholas, a minor. Harold's widow, Clara, submitted a claim to the estate, but only for 'her thirds', that is, her jointure. Nicholas, being 'wholly ignorant' of the proceedings, never entered a claim. It is difficult to understand why his mother failed to do so, especially since her husband had been named as ensignman in the Act of Settlement. It may have been due to lack of funds. Later, however, Nicholas applied to 'his kinsman' Eustace, who promised to deliver Kilmashogue to the Harolds once he had recovered his expenses from the rents and profits. But the promise, if in fact it was ever offered, was never honoured. Eustace died in 1665 and his nephew and heir, Sir Maurice Eustace, was able to retain a rather tenuous hold on the estate by skilfully fending off various challenges to his title.[73]

One of the more contentious legal issues surrounding the operation of the court of claims centred on the question of the time limit within which the commissioners were empowered to conduct the hearings of claims to innocence. When it became apparent that the start of hearings would be delayed, an Act for the Enlargement of Time in the hearing of claims was passed in the autumn of 1662 granting discretionary powers to the lord lieutenant and council to extend the period of the hearings up to twelve months from the first day of sitting.[74] Since the act did not specify calendar months, this was later taken by law to mean lunar months, with the result that the court held that its powers to hear claims to innocency extended to 21 August 1663, i.e., twelve lunar months from the first day of its sitting on 20 September 1662. The court's interpretation was challenged, however, on the grounds that the Act for the Enlargement of Time had stipulated that the periods of time could only be extended, in total, to twelve months from 1 August 1662, as fixed in the Act of Settlement. Enforcement of this principle would have resulted in the closing of the hearings twelve lunar months from that date, or 2 July 1663

Although the hearings to claims of innocency did, in the event, close on 21 August, the debate on the issue continued for several years and various difficulties arose in enforcing decrees of the court issued after 2 July. A compromise solution, initiated by Orrery, finally resolved the problem, the terms of which were incorporated into the Act of Explanation of 1665.[75] Even though the hearings to claims of innocence closed on 21 August, and not 2 July, thousands of claims remained unheard, which became a major source of Catholic discontent for the remainder of the reign.[76]

It was the intention of the commissioners to conduct their hearings in an ordered manner. To this end, in October 1662 they issued a list of rules governing the order in the hearing of claims, whereby claimants from Leinster were to be heard first, followed by those from Munster (except Clare), then Ulster and finally Connacht. Within these broad geographical categories the order was further refined. Claimants from Dublin city and county were to be heard first, followed by those from Wicklow, then Carlow and Kildare. Next were to come claims form the town of Drogheda, followed by those from Louth and Meath. The midland counties of Leinster were to be considered next, followed by those of Munster, then Ulster, and finally Connacht, with Clare and Leitrim scheduled last.[77]

The whole procedure seems to have been designed so that the hearings would be conducted on a pattern of concentric half-circles, progressing outward from the capital to Connacht. This might be attributed to the relative political influence of the Catholic gentry of the Pale, but it is more likely the explanation was more prosaic, i.e., that the schedule was a simple administrative expedient designed, as the commissioners explained, 'to prevent the unnecessary attendance of claimants and defendants' at court.[78] Moreover, one of the commissioners' rules was clearly intended to modify the entire procedure in the interest of those claimants whose principal holdings lay outside Leinster. Here it was provided that those intending to claim land in more than one county or province were to be heard 'in that county and province wherein they shall first come to be heard'.[79] It is for this reason that when, on 16 December 1662, the commissioners issued a further order governing the hearing of the claims from Dublin city and county, the names of some claimants whose principal estates lay outside the county are to be found.[80] Thus, one of the first cases scheduled to be heard was the earl of Fingall's, who claimed one house in the city and 35 acres in the county, but thousands of acres in Meath and Cavan.[81]

In the event, Fingall's claim was not heard until February, by which time it was already clear that the procedure was proving unworkable. As a result, on 15 February the commissioners suspended the rules and began to hear the claims at random. Henceforth claimants were instructed to indicate to the chief clerk of the court, in writing, the date on which they wanted their hearing to take place. The written request was then to be posted publicly on the 'outward door', following which, no cause being shown within two days why the claim should not proceed to a hearing, the commissioners would assign a day for the case to be heard.[82]

Even before its publication, however, news of the suspension of the rules was abroad, leading Sir Audley Mervin to refer to it in a speech delivered to Ormond, in the name of the House of Commons, on 13 February. Ormond was asked to instruct the commissioners to proceed in the trial of the innocents according to the original schedule. Mervin then proposed that, in effect, clause five of the rules be circumscribed by requiring any person claiming land in several counties 'be not heard, till the last county come to be adjudged . . . wherein . . . he is concerned'. In justification of this request he argued:[83]

> for example, if a man have but three acres in the county of Dublin, and a thousand pounds per annum in the county of B, as much more in the county of C . . . and postponing of trial to the last county is established and published, all the defendants are secure until the trial of the last county comes; and then the several three counties make an united defence; whereas otherwise, if he slip into his trial for the three acres in . . . Dublin, and by a faint defence . . . be adjudged innocent, it is likely . . . [he will] recover the remainder of his estate in the other counties, that never had notice of his trial. . .

Shortly after publication of the suspension the Commons returned to the attack. In a petition to Ormond on 25 February they pointed out that the new order of procedure, by admitting claims at random, was inconsistent with the provisions of the Act of Settlement, which gave precedence to those claiming as innocents. They argued that by limiting to two days the time during which cause had to be shown why a claim should not come to a hearing, people in the more remote regions of the country would not have time to prepare. Furthermore, the new order of hearings would prove expensive, since some defendants, having already brought witnesses to town, might now have to maintain them for months without knowing exactly when their claim would be heard. Finally, the petition alleged that the new procedure would lead to a 'great confluence' of people descending on the court, causing confusion and disruption.

Ormond's response to the petition gave little satisfaction to the Commons.

He and the council would do as they saw fit in the matter, he said, and meanwhile no further answer could be expected presently, nor did he know if any could be expected in the future.[84] It became clear therefore, that the commissioners' order of 16 February was to stand.

Despite the suspension of the order in the hearing of claims it is notable that in the first three months of the hearings approximately half of all the decrees were awarded to people claiming land in Dublin or property in the city. The advantage of living in close proximity to the city was an obvious factor in this, and of course many of the Dublin claimants had already been given a hearing before the commissioners suspended the rules of procedure; the claims of others must have been in-train when the suspension occurred.

The court, its membership reduced to four with the recall to London of commissioners Rainsford, Broderick and Beverley, continued to sit after 21 August for various administrative purposes, including the 'rectifying of mistakes in decrees'.[85] In September 1663 a Henry Burke was allowed to take out his decree upon a sworn copy of his claim, which had been lost. For reasons which are not explained, the decree of innocence awarded to James Haly on 17 August was revoked shortly thereafter. On 24 September, therefore, the commissioners heard his plea to be declared innocent 'as he had been on 17 August'. But the commissioners ruled that their powers of adjudication in this regard had expired and they could 'not now judge any'.

The commissioners were also continuing to hear complaints of the refusal to acknowledge the efficacy of the decrees of the court. On 29 October they heard such a complaint from Nicholas White of Leixlip, whose estate straddled the Dublin-Kildare border, that 'soldiers' of Sir Theophilus Jones had turned him out of some land to which he had been restored. In response, they could only repeat what they had previously declared: that they had executed their powers as judges and could do 'no more than reiterate the injunction to the sheriff' to implement the orders of the court.[86] In the summer of 1664 the court heard a plea from a Gibbon Fitzmorris Gibbon to be relieved of arrears of quit rent on land in Clare to which he had been transplanted.[87]

There was some uncertainty, however, regarding the precise scope of the court's authority after 21 August. A statement from the commissioners was read in the English privy council in November 1663 providing reasons wh, they 'conceived it not for them' to proceed in the execution of the Act of Settlement beyond 21 August until 'obstruction' had been removed by further legislation. The following month they pointed to certain particulars in the act which needed 'explanation', for example how to proceed in cases where an innocent was restored to land that had already been allotted as a reprisal, since they were not empowered under the act to provide second reprisals.[88]

The legal uncertainties surrounding the question of the court's authority after 21 August probably had some connection with the origin of a memorandum, undated and anonymous, entitled 'Heads of things the commissioners may do after 22 August'. Here it was proposed that the commissioners carry out a general examination of the Cromwellian land settlement, together with an estimate of the reprisals due to the adventurers and soldiers who had been displaced by the restored innocents, the purpose being to gain a fuller knowledge of the stock of reprisal land available.[89] There is no evidence, however, that the commissioners ever undertook such an ambitious study. Moreover, their presence was required in England to assist in the final stages of the land settlement.

CHAPTER IV

Claims and Counter-claims

It was probably inevitable that the Protestants should soon begin to express dissatisfaction with what they regarded as the excessively generous policy being shown by the commissioners to the Catholic claimants. The dissatisfaction was stimulated by the growing realization that sufficient land was not available to compensate them for the loss of their estates to the restored innocents. The verbal attacks on the commissioners became so vitriolic that Ormond felt compelled to defend them, and in letters to Clarendon and the king in early 1663 he referred to their 'diligence, discretion and justice' and to their decisions as 'just and impartial'.[1]

In the House of Commons, however, there was talk of impeachment proceedings and rumours of Protestant plots and conspiracies were already abroad when, on 21 January, one of the commissioners stated that the Commons had become so alarmed at the restoration of a few Catholics ('an act of justice, and therefore an unheard-of crime in this land') that they were planning to submit an official complaint to the government.[2] Such was the heightened sense of tension in the Commons that on 10 February it adopted a series of resolutions designed to restrict the powers of the commissioners in the adjudication to claims of innocence. The resolutions were presented in more elaborate form when, on 13 February, the whole House of Commons proceeded to Dublin Castle and heard the speaker, Sir Audley Mervin, who was himself being threatened with the loss of his Dublin estate, deliver a speech to Ormond in which he referred to the Act of Settlement as the 'magna carta Hiberniae' and the 'apple of the eye'. Although the Commons did not question the integrity of the commissioners, Mervin said, their decisions in restoring the Catholics were threatening to undermine the established religion. He then asked Ormond and the council to prescribe rules for the court of claims in accordance with the series of resolutions drawn up by the Commons on 10 February in which it was suggested that a more rigorous construction should be put on the term 'innocency'.

Among the twenty proposals designed for this purpose it was suggested, for example, that all written evidence concerning the rebellion be admitted as good evidence in barring claims to innocence. If adopted this would have admitted as valid evidence the depositions of 1642–54 in which the Protestants had registered their complaints of loss of life and property. It was also proposed that all proclamations and acts of state published by the lords justices before the cessation of 1643 declaring any person a rebel, and all orders of the Commons since 23 October 1641 for expelling any 'rotten member', might also be admitted as good evidence in the trial of innocents, meaning principally those Catholic members of parliament who had been expelled in 1641–2. Another proposal revived an earlier suggestion of barring innocency on the basis of residence in rebel quarters during the rebellion. It was demanded that the widest interpretation be applied to the term 'rebels' quarters', and that any witnesses called to prove the innocency of a claimant must have consistently lived in 'English quarters'.[3]

The address, which was published on orders of the Commons, prompted a furious reaction from the king, who assured the commissioners of his support and satisfaction with their work. Clarendon, who said he had never seen the king so angry, rebuked Mervin, telling him that Charles was 'pleased neither with his speech nor with the propositions of the House, much less the printing of them'. Special care, he added, was taken in the Act of Settlement to prevent the Commons from prescribing rules for the commissioners because many of the members had a personal interest in maintaining the existing land settlement. Ormond accused the Commons of encouraging Protestant fears and of spreading undue alarm. Meanwhile, however, largely through the diplomatic efforts of Orrery, the Commons were eventually persuaded, in March, to withdraw their February resolutions from their journals and agreed to allow the commissioners to serve out their legal term of office.[4] But in May 1663 Colonel Thomas Blood's armed conspiracy, which was inspired chiefly by Protestant opposition to the proceedings of the court of claims, although abortive, had the effect of forcing the government to hurry its consideration of a new bill of settlement that would be more palatable to the Protestants.[5] Accordingly, the draft of such a bill, drawn up by the Irish privy council, was dispatched to England on 9 September, but the king deferred consideration of it until commissioners Rainsford, Broderick, and Beverly were free to come to London in order to join in the discussions. They arrived several months later, and on 16 November the English privy council began its hearings on the new bill. The discussions proved to be long and acrimonious, however, and were not concluded until 14 August 1665.[6] Meanwhile, agents representing the various landed interests in Ireland once again flocked to England, among them Richard Talbot and Sir Nicholas Plunket, principal agents for the Catholics.

Talbot carried with him, according to Carte, £18,000 in securities for 'procuring distressed gentlemen their estates'.[7] If we can accept as reliable a contemporary report concerning the cost of procuring a proviso in the Act of Settlement, even this figure would seem to represent only a relatively small proportion of the spoils in a cynical business in Irish land traffic which flourished at this time. We are told that Sir James Shaen, chief registrar to the court of claims, was approached by two Catholic claimants who wanted him to speak to the earl of Anglesey with a view to obtaining provisos. Shaen is said to have replied that his price for persuading Anglesey to do so would be £2,000, a large sum in Restoration Ireland.[8]

It would be futile to attempt to ascribe purely altruistic motives to Talbot's activities in this crass business in Irish land, especially since, largely as a result of his participation in it, he had by the end of the reign accumulated a substantial estate. If he harboured an abstract desire to see justice done for his dispossessed co-religionists, that desire coincided with an aggressive and cynical policy of exploiting the very people whose restoration he sought. Ormond remarked that 'Colonel Talbot and his brothers . . . have not in their endeavours omitted to consider themselves even to the prejudice of the generality of the [Catholic] party. . . .' Even Gramont, who was favourably disposed toward Talbot, said that while his zeal for his countrymen was 'very commendable in itself', it was 'not altogether free from self interest', and that from all the estates that he had 'procured the restoration of to their primitive owners, he had always obtained some small compensation for himself. . . .' Talbot, he added, had an income of £40,000 a year from his estates .[9] Talbot's altruism, then, was severely circumscribed, but it is essential to add that he was only one—albeit the most enterprising—of a considerable number of courtiers, including some of the commissioners of the court of claims, who were closely involved in the Irish land trade.

The centre of influence for the Catholic lobby rested mainly in a group of courtiers in the English court, many of whom had formed a part of the duke of York's exiled household. The queen-mother, Henrietta-Maria, appears to have played a vital role. On various occasions her influence can be discerned in attempts to obtain the restoration of the dispossessed Catholics. At one point she recommended Sir Nicholas Plunket to Ormond, who referred the recommendation to Orrery with the remark that he had told the queen that Plunket was 'looked on as a person more obnoxious than others in his condition'. The queen-mother was also exerting herself on behalf of Sir Luke Bath, Patrick Sarsfield, Christopher Archbold, Christopher Russell, and John Arthur, all of whom were claiming substantial estates in Dublin.[10]

Henrietta-Maria's concern for the fate of the Catholic claimants can often be traced to the patronage of her favourite courtier (and secretary) Henry Jermyn, earl of St. Albans, the old *roué* who, later in the reign, was described by John Evelyn as a 'prudent old courtier, much enriched since his majesty's return.[11] St. Albans was one of the prime land-brokers of the period, and he usually acted for his clients in the name of the queen-mother, with whom he had long maintained a close relationship; indeed, one eminent historian has suggested that they may even have been husband and wife.[12]

While the court of claims was in session St. Albans sent a memorandum to Joseph Williamson concerning 'the interest of some Irish gentlemen for whom the queen-[mother] has entreated the king's justice and favour. I shall be personally obliged if you will confer with him on what is to be done for them'.

The memorandum contained a request for the king's letters of recommendation for five clients, including Bath, Sarsfield, and Archbold. 'The king as well as the queen-mother herself is satisfied of Sarsfield's innocence', Ormond was told in March 1663.[13]

It was probably St. Albans who blocked Bath's estate, which included the manor of Balgriffin, from falling into the hands of Bennett. Michael Jones, to whom the estate had been granted during the Interregnum, had died in 1649. In 1663 it was being claimed by Jones's brother (in the name of Michael Jones's son), Henry, bishop of Meath, who maintained that he bad been in possession on 7 May 1659. In March 1663 Winston Churchill told Bennett, for whom he was acting as agent in an attempt to secure an Irish estate for the secretary, that the commissioners were of the opinion that Henry Jones had never been in actual possession of Balgriffin and that the estate was ripe for the plucking. Several weeks later, however, Churchill discovered that Bath was being protected by St. Albans and he advised Bennett to drop the case. He added in a subsequent letter that he doubted if Ormond would have approved of Balgriffin being passed to Bennett.[14]

One of the more conspicuous courtiers whose influence had a profound effect on Restoration Ireland was Daniel O'Neill, the Protestant nephew of Owen Roe O'Neill. Daniel had been energetic in his services in the Stuart cause during the war and royal exile, when he became associated with Richard Talbot.[15] At the Restoration he was groom of the bedchamber, captain of the King's Own Regiment of Horse, a member of Gray's Inn and of parliament. He had great influence with the king, often acting for Charles on family and private business matters. He was instrumental in the rise to power of his friend Sir Henry Bennett.

O'Neill was also a close friend of Ormond,and seems to have played an important role in obtaining the appointment of Sir William Domville as Irish attorney-general. In 1662 he married Catherine [Stanhope], countess of Chesterfield, who had been governess to the princess Mary of Orange, daughter of Charles I, and who became lady-in-waiting to Queen Catherine. There seems little doubt, therefore, that O'Neill was in a position to exert considerable influence on the course of events in Restoration Ireland, even to the extent of helping his nephews and nieces, one of whom married Viscount Netterville in 1661. O'Neill's cousin was the marquis of Antrim, in whose favour the king personally intervened in the first court of claims.[16] On the day O'Neill died in 1664 Samuel Pepys recorded the event in his diary: 'This day the great O'Neill died; I believe, to the content of all the Protestant pretenders in Ireland.'[17]

Another, albeit more obscure, source of Catholic patronage at court can be traced to Richard Bellings, whose father (of the same name) had played a prominent role in the Catholic Confederacy, acting as secretary to the supreme council. In 1650, following the victory of parliament, he had joined the exiled Stuart court, where he became a trusted adherent of the royal family and, for a time, secretary to Ormond. At the Restoration he was named in the Declaration of 30 November 1660 as one of the twenty-six nominees especially meriting the king's favour.[18]

Richard the younger became a rather shadowy but not unimportant figure in the Restoration court, where he acted in a confidential capacity for both the king and Clarendon. In the summer of 1662 Bellings was in Paris negotiating for the sale of Dunkirk; a short time later he was in Rome on a mission to the Pope. After Charles' marriage to Catherine he became secretary and master of requests to the queen. In 1670 he completed the first draft of the treaty of Dover, and in fact was one of its signatories. He was knighted in 1666. As early as 1660 Bellings was described as being in a position to 'aid our afflicted country of Ireland', and although the evidence is fragmentary there seems little doubt that he was able to exert a modicum of influence on behalf of the Catholic gentry.[19]

Over exalted patrons also seem to have been working through the queen-mother in the interest of the dispossessed Catholics of Ireland. In 1664 Eleanor Eustace, the widow of Nicholas Eustace of Confey, testified that she had offered Sir George Lane £200 if he would procure Ormond's support for a petition to restore her son, Thomas, to his estate, a considerable part of which was situated in Dublin. After Lane had 'utterly rejected' the offer, Mrs. Eustace turned to her nephew, Francis Taaffe, son of the first earl of Carlingford. Taaffe, who did not share Lane's scruples, was able to 'get the job done' for £300, and a letter was obtained from Ormond on Eustace's behalf directed to Sir Henry Bennett. Taaffe refused to divulge the name of the person who had procured Ormond's recommendation for Thomas Eustace, although Lane was probably correct when he claimed that it had been Carlingford, an old Catholic royalist who had played an important role in the exiled court and was highly regarded by both Charles and the queen-mother. He became the adoptive father of Mary, the daughter of Lucy Walter and the king.

Nevertheless, Lane was accused of obtaining Ormond's recommendation, much to the chagrin of the lord lieutenant, who asked the king to suspend judgment in the case until he had got to the bottom of the matter. But the tone of Ormond's letter to the king is guarded and conveys the impression that the Eustace recommendation may have been extracted from him under false pretences. His disenchantment with Lane is apparent. He suggests that Lane may have been the guilty party and he (Ormond) innocent, yet 'the contrary may be suspected' which, he added, would be hard to disprove. Eleanor Eustace's brother later testified that it had, indeed, been Francis Taaffe who had obtained Ormond's letter.[20] Nevertheless, Ormond's reaction to the incident provides added evidence of the rather distant relationship which existed between the lord lieutenant and his secretary.

If the recommendation on Thomas Eustace's behalf was obtained from Ormond under questionable circumstances, such was not the case in regard to many similar letters which he provided for a considerable number of the dispossessed Catholic proprietors of Dublin and elsewhere. It is not always possible to ascertain the precise motives which inspired these letters, although many of them were written on behalf of those who had consistently served the royalist cause during the war. It is necessary to reiterate, however, that there is no doubt that Ormond sought the restoration, as far as possible, of the old proprietary order as represented by the Old English Catholic gentry. Indeed, Ormond's patronage of many of them was already acknowledged in 1661 by Richard Bellings, who reminded him that it would not prove beneficial to his family if the land of Ireland was possessed by a 'generation of mechanic bagmen who are strangers to all principles of religion and loyalty'.[21]

A typical letter of recommendation by Ormond can be cited in the case of Sir Nicholas White of Leixlip. White died before the Restoration, but his son and heir, Nicholas, was provided by Ormond with a certificate of recommendation in which the elder White's royalist activities during the rebellion were enumerated: 'he often went forth with us well mounted and armed when we marched against the rebels. We also certify that . . . we did give him . . . leave to go to Leixlip and other quarters under pretence of recovering some goods . . . which at his return he gave us a faithful and serviceable account.'[22] Many similar examples might be cited, including those provided by Ormond between 1660 and 1663 for Christopher Fagan, the earl of Westmeath, Edward Plunket, Lord Timleston, Sir Richard Barnewall, and the earl of Tyrconnell.[23]

The official records of the period also contain numerous references to the influence of Sir Maurice Eustace, the lord chancellor, on behalf of the Catholic gentry. Indeed, in 1661 Ormond felt compelled to rebuke Eustace for his excessive leniency toward the Catholics, pointing out that he had put two of them on the commission of peace and had permitted Catholic lawyers, including several who had been active Confederates, to practice in court.[24]

Several illuminating reports in the Carte manuscripts cast considerable light on the inner workings of the Irish land trade.[25] The reports, dated 1664, were submitted to Ormond by Patrick Moore, who was acting as a kind of political informant for the lord lieutenant during his absences from Dublin.[26] They provide us with useful detail concerning the arrangements worked out between the patrons and their clients. It is clear that the usual procedure was to enter into a bond, or some equivalent form of security, in return for successful restoration of the client. Occasionally the patron received a portion of the restored estate or an income from it for a specified time.

The name of the earl of St. Albans figures prominently in the reports. He is alleged to have accepted bonds of £1,000 each from Philip Hore, Sir Luke Bath, Patrick Sarsfield, and Christopher Archbold in return for restoration, with Richard Talbot's brother, Thomas, acting as agent for Bath and Hore in their dealings with St. Alban's. Bath agreed to pay £400 immediately, but could only raise £300. This he obtained from a London merchant named Daniel Arthur, for which Bath agreed to pay Arthur £60 a year for the life of his daughter, a minor.[27] Bath my have found his finances rather strained, since it also appears that he, along with Sarsfield and Archbold, also offered bonds of £500 to the duke of Albermarle.

The same report asserts that Sir William Domville, the Irish attorney-general, concluded an agreement with Robert Preston and Marcus Fitzsimons, both claimants to large Dublin estates, with Domville 'getting one half of the estate for recovering the other half'. Substance is lent to the accuracy of this report by a reference to an order, issued late in 1663, for a grant to Domville of two parcels of land in Dublin that had been restored to Preston and Fitzsimons.[28]

Fitzsimons enjoyed the patronage of the queen. Although the evidence relates to a period shortly after the rising of the court of claims, it may nevertheless be of some significance that Catherine expressed to Ormond her concern for Fitzsimons, pointing out that his son, Richard, was in the service of the Portuguese ambassador. Shortly later the ambassador expressed similar sentiments to Ormond. The 'service' performed by Richard refers to his assistance rendered to the ambassador in England during the marriage negotiations between Charles and Catherine.[29]

Another name which appears prominently in Moore's reports is the earl of Fingall, who entered bonds of £1,500 to two army officers named Herne and Stopford. Moore alleged that the two actually carried £100 into the court for use in the interests of their clients, and that Herne, who claimed to enjoy the patronage of commissioners Rainsford and Beverley, would deal with 'none but Pale men, and none under 3 or 400 pounds a year, accounting under that not worth his labour'.

Moore's second report maintained that Sir Maurice Berkeley was responsible for procuring Thomas Luttrell's proviso in the Act of Settlement. Sir Maurice, a member of the Irish privy council from early 1663, was a brother of Sir Charles Berkeley, first Viscount Fitzharding, afterwards (1664) earl of Falmouth, and a nephew of John Lord Berkeley of Stratton, president of Connacht between 1662 and 1665, later (in 1670) lord lieutenant in succession to Ormond. Both Berkeleys figured prominently in the exiled Stuart court of the duke of York, John as governor to the duke in Paris and Charles as groom of the bedchamber in Flanders. Despite attempts by the king to undermine the influence being exerted by the Berkeleys on York, the close relationship survived the Restoration; indeed, the king finally succumbed to Charles Berkeley, who in 1662 was depicted by Pepys as a 'vicious person', but one who (along with Sir Henry Bennett) 'had the king's ear'.[30] Charles, who died at sea in action against the Dutch in 1665, became a close friend of Richard Talbot. The two had collaborated in 1662 in blocking an attempt by the earl of Mount Alexander to secure a grant of St. Wolstan's (Alen's Court) in Kildare, which was being claimed by James Alen, part of the demesne of which extended into Newcastle in Dublin.

A fiant had been issued in late 1661 for a grant of St. Wolstan's to Mount Alexander. But Talbot and Berkeley had purchased an interest in the estate and were anxious to protect their investment.[31] Talbot was able to elicit a letter from Bennett ordering Lord Chancellor Eustace to put a stop to the patent before it reached the great seal. Eustace pointed out, however, that the day after he had received Bennett's letter, Ormond had received an order from the other principal secretary of state, Sir William Morice, directing Mount Alexander's patent to proceed to the great seal. 'What to do in the strait I know not,' said Eustace, 'being between Scylla and Charyblis'.[32]

Talbot's success in obstructing Mount Alexander's grant can therefore be traced to Bennett, who was himself engaged in 'predatory designs' on Lord Clanmaliere's great estate in King's and Queen's counties, in which design he was being assisted by Talbot and Sir William Domville, Sir John Temple, the solicitor-general, along with Sir Audley Mervin, and at least three of the commissioners of the court of claims, Churchill, Coventry, and Broderick.[33]

Meanwhile, Mount Alexander had obtained a private proviso in the Act of Settlement for the Alen estate to be 'delivered' to him if it was found to be forfeited.[34] The case was heard in the court of claims on 3 February. The following day Talbot held out little hope for Alen. Though he was 'as innocent a person as could be', Talbot said, 'yet the horrid practices of my Lord Mount Alexander suborning witnesses against him will I fear prove him nocent'. If, as Talbot expected, this proved to be the case, he advised Bennett to secure a royal letter ordering the estate to be used to reprise the adventurers and soldiers who were removed from the Clanmaliere estate when it was granted to Bennett.

It must therefore have come as a happy surprise to Talbot when James Alen was declared innocent. Now it was Mount Alexander's turn to register surprise. He complained bitterly that the decree was awarded despite the fact that fourteen witnesses had testified to Alen's 'eminent acts of rebellion'. Four of the witnesses, he said, each identifying Alen independently in a large crowd, swore that he had lived in rebel quarters. On this basis, he added, '100 to 1 was offered on my side, yet . . . the court adjudged him innocent. . . . One of my council said . . . "Sirs, if you judge this man innocent, we must believe the English cut one another's throats and that there was no Irish rebellion or rebels."'[35]

The court's decision in the Alen case seems to have been regarded by the Protestants as especially significant. The 'English now conclude themselves utterly lost', Ormond said, and the general belief that the decree of innocence was issued on a 'private direction' from the king was given credence because it was known that Talbot and Berkeley had a financial stake in the estate.[36]

It may have been the shock of losing against such favourable odds which hastened Mount Alexander's death later the same year. His son, however, took up the cause, and in a letter to the duchess of Ormond in 1665 maintained that by a 'seasonable interception' of one of Richard Talbot's letters he could prove that Alen had procured his decree of innocence by fraud. He begged the duchess to urge the king to order a re-hearing of the case.[37]

II

The decrees of innocence awarded to the children of Philip Hore precipitated a prolonged struggle between Hore and Sir George Lane that was not resolved until 1665. Even before Hore's claim came to a hearing Lane said that he had been approached by Richard Talbot's brother, Sir Robert, with an offer that would have given Lane part of Hore's estate if Lane would agree not to challenge Hore's claim to innocence.[38] Lane refused the offer, probably because he had been given to understand that Hore's claim would not even come to a hearing. A week after the decrees had been awarded Lane told Bennett that he had refrained from asking 'my lord's favour, as I did not think he should support me in a matter of this kind'.[39] If, as seems likely, Lane was referring to Ormond, his reluctance to approach the duke probably stemmed from the foreknowledge that such a request would not be received with much enthusiasm. This was soon made manifest when Lane enlisted the support of Sir Thomas Clarges, one of the members of the committee within the Irish privy council charged with drafting the new bill of settlement. Clarges (who was Albermarle's brother-in-law) wrote to Ormond pointing out that Lane's case looked 'very hard' and that relief for him would be difficult unless some way could be found to mitigate the effect of the Hore decrees of innocence. He then asked permission to use Ormond's name as a means of obtaining relief for Lane. Ormond's reply was lukewarm. If it was found, he said, that similar provisions were being made in the new bill of settlement for other persons who were 'in the same case with . . . Lane' (i.e., Hore), he would have no objection to his name being used; but he was opposed to private provisos 'till they are admitted in the case of others'.[40] At the same time Lane maintained a constant flow of letters to various eminent figures, but especially Clarendon, to whom he begged for assistance and complained of his ill luck, which he attributed to the fact that the Hore deed was a forgery.[41]

Lane was later advised that even if the deed was genuine its provisions were void due to the attainder of its author, and that, since Hore was a transplanter, Lane was at the very least entitled to the estate for life.[42] But in April 1664 Hore obtained an order in the English privy council for a proviso in the new bill of settlement restoring him for life. Lane, in response, petitioned the council and succeeded in getting a hearing of the case.[43]

The hearing in the English privy council emerged as a *cause célèbre* in court circles, even inspiring an entry in the diary of Samuel Pepys, who was in attendance at one session which he described as the 'great and famous cause between . . . Lane and Mr. Phill. Whore . . . [concerning] Lane's endeavouring to reverse a decree of the late commissioners of Ireland in a rebel's case for his land, which the king had given as forfeited to . . . Lane, for whom the solicitor[-general, Sir Heneage Finch] did argue most angel-like, and one of the commissioners . . . for himself and his brethren who had decreed it'.[44]

The struggle between Lane and Hore raged on for another seven months until a compromise solution, negotiated by Richard Talbot and drawn up by Sir Nicholas Plunket, was concluded. The agreement, which was signed in June 1665 by all the concerned parties, was incorporated as a private clause in the new bill of settlement, discussions concerning which were then drawing to a close.[45]

* * *

Another great and famous cause emerged as a result of the decrees of innocence awarded to the heirs of Patrick Sarsfield of Lucan. Sir Theophilus Jones, occupant during the Commonwealth, was a man of considerable influence in Ireland. He was the eldest son of Lewis Jones, bishop of Killaloe, and a brother of Colonel Michael Jones, the victor over Ormond in the battle of Rathmines, and of Henry Jones, bishop of Meath. He played a key roll in wresting control of the government from the hands of the Commonwealth commissioners in early 1659 and served as one of the agents of the General Convention in London shortly before Charles's return. Moreover, in May 1663 he was responsible for disclosing to Ormond the news of Blood's impending conspiracy.[46]

However, although Jones occupied a conspicuous place in Restoration Ireland, note has already been taken of the claim which Patrick Sarsfield had on the patronage of the earl of St. Albans, whose influence reached to the throne. In 1663 Robert Leigh wrote to Joseph Williamson soliciting favour for Sarsfield; 'On behalf of Mr. Sarsfield,' he wrote, 'for whom Lord St. Alban's so much interceded, I ask that if Sir Theophilus Jones pass anything to Sarsfield's prejudice, you first be pleased to acquaint Lord St. Alban's. . . .'[47] Jones asserted, in a letter to Sir George Lane the following year, that Patrick Sarsfield was unworthy of royal favour, having 'lurked at home and never served his majesty abroad but received lands in Connacht'. Jones added that Sarsfield already possessed an estate of greater value than Lucan which, he said, 'may be thought enough for one that has so little merited as Patrick Sarsfield'. Then, in a suggestion which illuminates the siege mentality of a seventeenth century planter, Jones urged consideration of the strategic implications which would attend Sarsfield's restoration:

> It may further be considered that the Irish are all restored to their estates on the west side of Dublin, viz., Mr. Luttrell, Mr. White, Mr. Eustace, Mr. Alen, Mr. Nottingham, Mr. Foster, and score others, Lucan estate is only yet preserved, and in point of policy I offer how necessary it may be that a scoutmaster may be kept in the heart of them. . . .

Moreover, Jones concluded, in the whole region 'there is not a place for a Protestant to resort to divine service but unto Lucan,' which he added, 'may not be least worthy of consideration of debate of the whole matter'.[48] The debate, in fact, was to continue for a number of years.

* * *

Although Lord Nettervill had himself been adjudged nocent, we have seen that his estate was restored to his younger brothers and sisters. However, the family hold on the land was tenuous because the commissioners had ruled that if Nettervill died with male issue it would revert to the Cromwellian planters, Edward Smith and Sir Courtney Poole, after the portions and remainders of his brothers and sisters had been satisfied.

This arrangement Nettervill obviously found unsatisfactory. Therefore, toward the end of 1663 he went to England and appealed directly to the king for redress. His plea was supported by commissioners Rainsford, Beverley, and Churchill, who acknowledged that some of the witnesses in Nettervill's trial had been perjurers, and they recommended that he be restored by proviso in the new bill of settlement. In April 1665 the English privy council ordered this to be done.[49] We are justified in assuming that Daniel O'Neill, husband of Nettervill's niece, had a hand in this decision.

* * *

The Act of Settlement empowered the commissioners of the court of claims to set aside an estate in Dublin worth £200 a year to the orphans of Colonel Owen O'Connolly, the informer who in 1641 had warned the lords justices of the impending attempt to seize Dublin Castle. The £200 was to be realized, if possible, from certain forfeited estates earmarked by name in the act. These consisted primarily of the former estate of John Finglas of Westpallstown in Balrothery, but also included was Artaine, seat of the Hollywood family in Coolock.[50] John Finglas had been killed in the sack of Drogheda in 1649, and although Elizabeth Finglas, widow of Richard (presumably John's son, who had died before 1641), had been declared innocent, the decree applied only to her jointure lands, and only for her lifetime. No claim was heard for the bulk of the estate, most of which was eventually granted to the O'Connolly children.[51]

Nicholas Hollywood's son and heir, John, was also declared innocent. Meanwhile, however, Sir Nicholas Armorer, a garrulous north-countryman who had been equerry to Charles II and a most active and adventurous royalist conspirator during the Interregnum,[52] had discovered that the land allotted to the O'Connolly's would yield an annual income far in excess of £200. On these grounds Armorer was able to obtain a letter from the king, in April 1663, directing Ormond to grant him Artaine and as much of the other land intended for the O'Connolly's as exceeded that figure. Shortly later a warrant was issued for an inquisition to determine the value of the land in question. When the inquisition was taken, in May, the jurors found Armorer's contention correct, concluding that the land intended for the O'Connolly's would in fact realize £470 a year. This having been established, Armorer was awarded a lease of Artaine for thirty-one years from 1663.[53] The lease must have proved a bitter pill not only to John Hollywood but also to the earl of Cavan, whose father had obtained a *custodian* grant of the estate in 1647, following the attainder of Nicholas Hollywood. Although John Hollywood (or his heir) was eventually restored to Artaine, Armorer's lease provides a useful, albeit unusual, example of how an important segment of an estate temporarily alluded the grasp of an innocent claimant.[54]

* * *

The contest for possession of the forfeited manor of Clontarf in Coolock, granted to Colonel Edward Vernon in 1660, can be cited as a representative sample of the complex set of interests which often accompanied the struggle for the land of Ireland under the Restoration settlement. A report on the disposition of Clontarf, submitted to the king in 1661 by Lord Chancellor Eustace, deserves extensive quotation, serving as it does to illustrate the nature of these conflicting interests:[55]

> I have seen a report . . . dated 17 November 1660, certifying that George King . . . submitted and adhered to the peace . . . in 1649. [Ormond] appointed him excise master of Waterford, where he was besieged by Cromwell, and died during the siege.
>
> If these were all the facts, there would be a case for restoring [the daughter]; but upon a petition of . . . Vernon I reported . . . that George King had been indicted and outlawed . . . and that it was in your power to dispose of the lands; and they have been granted to Colonel Vernon. On the other hand the articles of peace made between your majesty and the . . . [Confederate Catholics] contains an agreement that all indictments, attainders, outlawries, etc., and all patents, grants, leases, bonds, etc., depending thereon . . . since 7 August 1641, in prejudice of the said Catholics, shall be vacated. The indictment and outlawry in question were within that time.
>
> The earl of Mountrath is also a suitor to the king that he may have . . . Clontarf in reprisal for some land which he supposes he shall lose by . . . [the Act of Settlement]. And whether your majesty will settle the said lands on the said daughter, whose right is bound up by nothing but by the . . . articles of the peace . . . or . . . [on] Vernon, who has already proceeded so far as the great seal . . . or upon . . . Mountrath . . . this is a matter for your royal consideration.

The claim of the King family rested on a deed of feoffment drawn up before 1641 by George King the grandfather, entailing the estate as a marriage settlement not to his son, John, but to his grandson George. The deed also stipulated, however, that if George the younger died without male issue the estate should revert to the daughters of John, who had no sons at the time the deed was drawn up.

In the event George the younger, as we have seen, died in the siege of Waterford in 1650, leaving only one child, Jane, the wife of James Aylmer. John King had three daughters, only one of whom, Katherine (unmarried), was alive in 1663; he also left a grandson, aged about twenty-four. It was therefore through Katherine and her nephew that the family attempted to recover Clontarf.

The claim was based, in part, on the assertion that George King the younger, although outlawed in 1642, had submitted and adhered to the articles of peace of 1649. On this claim James Aylmer and his wife succeeded, in late 1661, on obtaining permission to begin legal proceedings to reverse King's outlawry. The claim was also based on the plea that John King, who had also been outlawed, had never been the proprietor of Clontarf, but only held an annuity in the estate; rather that George King the younger had been the proprietor during the life of his father. Vernon's grant, they maintained, had been based on misinformation.[56]

Vernon responded in a letter to Joseph Williamson, by referring to the claims of the King family as a 'cheat' that looked 'five descents backward. . . . [They] can do nothing against me but by some forged deeds. . . . I am on my defense and rely on your help and that of Mr. secretary [Sir Henry Bennett]. . . .'[57]

Although there are references to various members of the King family submitting claims to Clontarf, the case never came to a hearing.[58] The Kings were being sponsored by the earl of Carlingford, a cousin of George King the younger.[59] But Vernon's patronage was stronger; he was able to obtain a letter from the king ordering Ormond to prohibit any claims to the estate from being submitted 'without first finding that they were well founded'. Several months later, after Vernon had played a vital role in keeping Ormond informed of the impending threat of Blood's conspiracy, another royal letter directed the commissioners of the court of claims to desist from considering any claims to Clontarf until they had 'examined the grounds' of the claim.[60] Despite this proviso the commissioners obviously got the point: no claim to Clontarf was to be heard. The hand of Ormond can be discerned here, for in May 1663 he wrote to Bennett stating that in the discovery of Blood's plot he was 'principally beholding to the industry and villigence of . . . Vernon', notice of which, he added, should be brought to the king's attention 'for his advantage'.[61] One of the 'advantages', it is clear, was the obstruction of all attempts by the Kings to obtain a hearing of their claim to Clontarf.

* * *

The struggle between Lord Gormanston and the heirs of Sir Charles Coote, who died in December 1661, three months after being created earl of Mountrath, was complicated by two concurrent disputes, one involving the still unsettled quarrel between the countess-dowager and her step-son, the second earl, over the interpretation of the first earl's will. The point of the dispute centred on the question of how Mountrath had intended to dispose of the estate he had acquired during the Interregnum. Since the dispute was still unresolved in 1662, provision was made in the Act of Settlement to vest the estate in the crown until such time as the lord lieutenant and the council should examine the case and arbitrate on the will. Their decision, made in October 1663, appears to have been that the second earl was entitled to the estate as it existed in 1641 and the countess-dowager and her other children that portion acquired during the Interregnum, excepting the land that had been restored to innocents, for which they were to be immediately reprised.[62]

The principal prize in the contest was, of course, the manor of Gormanstown, already occupied by Lord Gormanston, who had meanwhile been awarded a decree of innocence. Moreover, the countess-dowager and her new husband, Robert Reading, had received no succour from the court of claims, where, on 10 March, they were told that the court could not relieve them and the case was dismissed.[63]

The second dispute involved claims made by Anne, the widow of Sir Thomas Lucas, to whom Gormanstown had been granted in 1644 (following a custodiam grant in 1642) following the attainder of Gormanston's father Nicholas, the sixth viscount, as compensation (as it was claimed) for having expended £10,000 in the royalist cause. Lucas died in 1648 and several years later Coote was in possession of the manor. Lucas's widow and her current husband, Sir Edward Sutton, had however been allowed by Coote to remain on the estate as tenants. Lady Sutton was also seeking compensation for the loss of Gormanston's wardship, granted by Charles I to Lucas but voided (as Gormanston claimed) by the attainder of his father after his death in 1643. After the Restoration Gormanston succeeded in getting the attainder removed, but Ormond held the view that it had been Charles I's intention to recompense Lucas for his service in the royalist cause and that therefore some compensation should be made to Lady Lucas out of the estate. It was finally proposed, and confirmed by the king, that Gormanston should pay Lady Sutton £1,500, at the rate of £300 a year, following which she would relinquish all claims on the estate.[64]

* * *

The nocent decision handed down to the earl of Tyrconnell, based on a letter he had written from Paris in 1647 to the supreme council of the Confederate Catholics, was issued, said Clarendon, 'without considering how long since it was writ or the reason of writing it, that they had served the king, and never in the least degree against him. . . . They without any pause declared him nocent . . . . ' It would appear, however, that Tyrconnell's failure in court rested to a considerable extent on other factors, principally his personal character, and that the commissioners were in fact eager to seize upon any legal pretext to justify what they regarded as condign punishment.

Tyrconnell had many enemies whose malevolence was stimulated by an element of jealousy inspired by his success in avoiding the sequestration of his estate during the Interregnum, and even Clarendon's panegyric fails to conceal what must have been a less than endearing personality. 'The man was . . . elate and proud,' Clarendon says, with 'a greater value of himself than other men had, and a less of other men than they deserved, whereby he got himself not beloved. . . . They who thought the judgment very unjust, laughed at the ill luck of a man whom they did not love; and all men were well enough pleased with the sentence, who were displeased with the person.'[65] Tyrconnell, however, could call upon powerful patronage, one of whom was Henrietta-Maria. She was, Anglesey told Ormond, 'very earnest' for Tyrconnell.[66]

Several weeks after the nocent decision was awarded Ormond suggested to Bennett that Tyrconnell's former service to the crown might 'outweigh the oversights in that letter which was the cause of his being declared nocent'. But later the same year, in a letter to the earl of Clare, he made it clear that it was in fact Tyrconnell's connection with the Holles family, and not a regard for the man, that had inspired his concern.[67]

It is probable that it was also the connection with the Hollesses that accounts for Albermarle's interest in the case. Shortly after the court of claims rose he expressed to Ormond his concern that the '49 officers, who were claiming the estate, not be allowed to succeed.[68] Tyrconnell's fate also attracted the sympathy of Richard Talbot. In a letter to Bennett he referred to the possible ruin of 'so ancient and noble a family', and called attention to Tyrconnell's history of eminent service to the crown.[69] It is tempting to speculate whether Talbot's concern for Tyrconnell may have owed something to the recognition that they both possessed common traits of character which attracted to them similar degrees of enmity. In any event, as a result of the eminence of his patrons Tyrconnell was granted a royal pardon in June 1664, and it was then arranged that the dismissal of his claim be made null and void by proviso in the new bill of settlement.

CHAPTER V

The Act of Explanation

I

Ormond returned to England in June 1664 to seek to break the deadlock in the discussions on the new bill of settlement which had been in progress, intermittently, for seven months. The need for such legislation had been anticipated by many. Ormond was reported to have held the view, before it became law, that the Act of Settlement was so long and complex that it might be subject to some 'explanations', and in May 1662 Orrery referred to the need for an 'explanatory' bill that would clarify certain clauses in the Act of Settlement which were 'diametrically opposed'. Later, while the court of claims was in session and the difficulties in executing its provisions had become manifest, Sir Alan Broderick expressed the view, which may be taken as representing the general sentiments of the commissioners, that further legislation would be necessary because of the 'almost irreparable errors' in the Act of Settlement.[1] Moreover, the Act of Settlement had had only two readings when, in May 1662, the Commons began discussing a 'bill of explanation'. Shortly later the House of Lords followed suit.[2]

The motives behind this initiative by the Irish parliament can be traced to the general fear among the members that the execution of the Act of Settlement would lead to a radical alteration in the existing land settlement. As a result, the heads of proposals for an 'explanatory bill', which was drafted by a committee of the Commons and submitted to the government in November 1662, was judged by Ormond and a majority of the council as 'very unreasonable'.[3] 'It is nicknamed an explanatory bill,' said commissioner Cooke, 'but the drift of it is, not to explain doubtful places [in the Act of Settlement] but to alter plain ones'. According to Cooke, one of the proposals would have rendered all entails made by Catholics forfeited on the 'suspicion' that some of them were forgeries. Cooke added that it was only the prudence and moderation of Ormond and the commissioners which prevented the Cromwellian interest from attempting, like wolves, to 'ravenously devour' the land of Ireland.[4]

The government was at the same time drawing up its own version of a new bill of settlement (which Clarendon found 'very hard to understand'), but by the time it was introduced to the Commons, in February 1663, the proceedings of the court of claims had so enraged the members that the bill was rejected on the first reading.[5] Sir Audley Mervin's speech to Ormond a week later, already alluded to, must be seen in light of this highly charged atmosphere, as does Blood's conspiracy the following May. Although an abysmal failure, the plot was a dramatic reflection of the deeply held conviction which existed among the Protestants that the commissioners of the court if claims were intent on dismantling the entire settlement and that this process must be reversed and the Act of Settlement amended in order to protect the existing proprietors.

Although the suppression of the conspiracy had temporarily strengthened the government's hand, it was nevertheless judged prudent, especially in view of the unreliability of the army (which was in arrears of pay), to make additional concessions to the Protestants, thus further compromising the form of settlement as originally conceived by Ormond.

Ormond undoubtly regarded the generality of the adventurers and soldiers as little more than crude interlopers into the ancient social fabric of the country, and 'had a mind', as Carte puts it, 'to serve the old and great families of English race. . . .' The 'old and great families' included many of the dispossessed Old English Catholic gentry for whom, Ormond remarked in 1660, he was 'sorry'.[6]

Ormond, as we have seen, had never been persuaded that his concept of a desirable settlement could be achieved through the execution of the Act of Settlement'. The proceedings of the court of claims had only corroborated these sentiments. In June 1663 he told Clarendon, whose opinions in this regard generally coincided with his own, that he was becoming 'daily and more confirmed' in his belief that the settlement which was emerging from the operation of the court of claims would never produce the desired results. He expressed similar views to Sir Henry Bennett, adding that all the 'best and soberest persons concerned, English and Irish', shared his opinion.[7]

Ormond's objections to the Act of Settlement stemmed not only from the inherent contradictions contained in some of its provisions, or from the difficulties which attended its execution, but also from the broader principle that the rigidity of its provisions for the qualification of innocence had frustrated his general designs for an acceptable settlement by obstructing the restoration of many 'eminently deserving' claimants.

Although events of 1663 had imposed further compromises on his designs, Ormond continued to press for new legislation that would salvage as much as possible of his original concept of a desirable settlement. 'The course that you are upon by this new act . . .' he was told in the summer of 1663, 'is all that is possible for your grace to do to mitigate the vigour of the . . . [Act of Settlement] and to preserve some of the ancientist families and best estates. . . .'[8] The 'course' refers, in part, to Ormond's proposal, which formed an essential component of the new bill of settlement, providing for the restoration by royal favour of a select group of prominent Old English Catholic proprietors who would otherwise remain dispossessed after the court of claims ended its hearings to claims of innocence. He was 'still persuaded', Ormond told Anglesey shortly after the bill was dispatched to England, 'that the readiest and most equitable way of settlement is, or may be, by nomination, and not by trial of qualifications and innocency. . . .'[9]

Another key proposal contained in the new bill called for the surrender (or 'retrenchment') by most of the adventurers and soldiers of a proportion of their holdings in order to create a stock of land that could be used, first, as reprisals for the Protestants who were to be removed from their land in order to accommodate the restored innocents and, second, for the restoration of the royal 'nominees'.

Although Ormond lent his support to these proposals, it was the assiduous Irish attorney-general, Sir William Domville, who provided the legal and moral justification for their inclusion in the new bill. Domville, whose grasp of the legal technicalities of the land settlement was unrivalled among his contemporaries, set out his arguments in a series of briefs, in one of which he defended the scheme to restore some of the Catholic gentry by royal nomination on the grounds that they were more fit to be restored than that 'tinkers and cobblers should possess their lands'. It is unremarkable that here we have an echo of Ormond's attitude, and it might be observed that in 1663 Domville was still promoting the traditional English argument for the salutary benefits of the plantation approach. His argument, however, contained an interesting twist on the traditional theme in the Irish context, for he suggests that the shift in land ownership that would result as a consequence of the enactment of the two proposals would not only have a civilizing effect on 'the Irish of great septs' by settling them in English quarters, but that the adventurers and soldiers would be 'reformed' by planting them in 'Irish territory'.[10] A similar attitude can also be discerned in a proposal which was drawn up by John Walsh, Ormond's family lawyer, who suggested that the claims of the adventurers and soldiers be satisfied in money rather than land, for if they were settled in Ireland they would become the 'most considerable party' and would 'carry all before them'. If, however, they were to be satisfied with money they would 'turn to their former trades, all of them being mechanics, and will repair to . . . [England] where they are sure to make better use of their trade'. The adventurers and soldiers, Walsh added, 'in their hearts are still against kingly government. They are all sectaries, and every one of them absolutely against episcopacy'.[11]

In the discussions on the new bill of settlement various fresh solutions were being proffered. The Catholic agents proposed that the English land acts of 1641–2 relating to Ireland, together with all attainders since 23 October 1641, be repealed, and that all decrees of the court of claims be confirmed. They then proposed that all land belonging to the Catholics in 1641 be vested in the crown, from which 1,600,000 profitable acres would be assigned to the adventurers and soldiers. The rest would be allotted to the '49 officers, the restored innocents, and those claiming payment of debts incurred in the royalist cause before the cessation of arms of 1643, along with the nominees who had not yet been restored. It was also suggested that the king reserve in his hands 200,000 acres until after the redistribution had been completed, following which half would be given to the Protestants who were most injured by the alteration, the other half to the Catholics for the same purpose. Each half was to be taken respectively out of the lands that had been assigned to the Protestants and Catholics under the terms of the Act of Settlement, each party providing what was to be allotted to those who had been injured of their own religion.

The soldiers proposed that the Catholics be restored to two-fifths of the land they had held in 1641, and that the other three-fifths be distributed among the various Protestant interests. The adventurers complained that they had already lost over 200,000 acres by decrees of the court of claims; they only wanted to be confirmed in what remained to them.

These suggestions were in turn rejected by the Catholic agents, whereupon a joint proposal by all the Protestant interests was made, viz., that the restored Catholics be confirmed in their holdings, that 400,000 acres be set aside for the nominees, but that all the rest of the land vested in the crown be distributed to the various Protestant interests. This proposal was also rejected by the Catholics because no mention was made where the 400,000 acres were to be set out, and because it fell far short of meeting the needs of thousands of people whose claims had never been heard as well as the nominees and the transplanters.[12]

Thus, a stalemate was again reached, and it was to be another year before a solution was found, by which time, according to Clarendon, the various factions had come to the conclusion that 'any settlement would be better than none; and that more profit would arise from a smaller proportion of land quietly possessed . . . than from a much greater proportion under a doubtful title'.[13] With all the parties now amenable to some form of a settlement, a compromise was finally reached in the summer of 1665, whereby the adventurers and soldiers agreed to surrender a third of their holdings, thus creating a stock of land that could be used for reprisals and for the restoration of individuals nominated by the king.[14]

The scheme of retrenchment was not a sudden inspiration; indeed, it is likely that the idea had been germinating since the Restoration. The evidence suggests, however, that the plan was first seriously considered during the discussions on the Act of Settlement. In a petition drawn up in July 1661, sponsored by a group of peers, including Aungier, Montgomery, Ranelagh, and Drogheda, who claimed to represent a majority in the House of Lords, it was proposed to ask the king to consider the possibility of undertaking a 'proportionable defalcation out of every reprisable and restorable interest, for the just accommodation of the whole'. The proposal was prompted by an attempt to reconcile a difference of opinion in the Lords, but a minority, according to Aungier, being 'steered' by Orrery, rejected the idea and insisted (along with a majority in the Commons) that the Declaration of 30 November 1660 be 'inviolably maintained'.[15] Carte maintains that the scheme was debated in the English privy council when the Act of Settlement was under discussion but that it was never moved by the Catholic agents.[16] There is no indication that the sponsors of the proposal had in mind a precise definition of what constituted a 'proportional defalcation'. As early as September 1663, however, a suggestion for a retrenchment of a sixth of the holdings of the adventurers and soldiers was advanced. Shortly later a retrenchment of a fourth was being considered, followed the same year by a proposal for one of a third.[17]

The scheme was justified, in part, on the grounds that the adventurers, under the terms of the Adventurer's Act of 1642, were to be allotted lands based on the English acreage measure,[18] whereas in the event they had been given lands based on the Irish measure. While it was true the Act of Satisfaction of 1653 had stipulated that both the adventurers and soldiers were to be satisfied with land based on the Irish measure,[19] that act had been passed by an usurped parliament and was thus null and void after 1660.

The adventurers were able to claim that a general retrenchment violated the terms of the Act of Settlement, by which they were to be confirmed in their holdings as of 7 May 1659 'with allowance or correction of the respective acts of parliament of xvii and xviii Caroli I, as to English or plantation measure, except as is hereafter excepted. . . .'[20] The first citation refers to the Adventurers' Act of 1642, the second to a series of acts passed shortly thereafter in order to stimulate lagging investment in the scheme, in particular that of 16 Car. I, *c*. 37,whereby investors were offered land in Ireland 'measured out and enjoyed according to the plantation measure', if, having paid in at least a quarter of their original subscription, they now paid in the residue by 20 July 1642.[21]

But few of the adventurers, according to Sir William Domville, could prove they subscribed fully under the terms of the Adventurers' Act, let alone the subsequent acts.[22] Domville's scepticism regarding the adventurers' claims was only one aspect of his general attitude toward the whole question of the readjustment of the Irish land settlement. He had concluded that about £220,000 was subscribed under the Adventurers' Act and the acts of 16 Car. I, *c*. 34, 35, and 37. A further £53,000, or about a quarter of the original subscription, had been invested under the terms of the 'doubling ordinances' of 1643 and 1647. Although the doubling ordinances were disallowed by the Act of Settlement, it was stipulated that any money actually paid in under the provisions of the two ordinances was to be satisfied under the terms of 16 Car. I, *c*. 37, that is, in Irish rather than English acreage measure.[23] Such land, Domville said, should be deducted from the holdings of the adventurers, who ought to retain 'only satisfaction for such moneys they did really and *bona fide* pay' according to the Adventurers' Act and those of 16 Car. I, *c*. 34, 35 and 37.

Domville also maintained that the adventurers, by fraud and deception, were in possession of far more land than they were entitled to, which if proved would result in the vesting of such land in the crown as provided for by the Act of Settlement.[24] Moreover, much of the land the adventurers and soldiers were claiming as unprofitable (nearly a million acres) was in fact profitable, in which case (fraud being proved) this land would also be liable to seizure by the crown.[25] Finally, Domville concluded, both the adventurers and soldiers should be made aware of the of king's 'many great advantages by laws to void their whole pretentions. Therefore, if they shall agree to subdivide that proportion which they still have amongst themselves by the English acre it will be a reasonable satisfaction . . . [and] his majesty will have above five hundred thousand Irish acres to restore the Irish. . . .'[26]

Domville's briefs are valuable not only as a useful synthesis of the legal case for a retrenchment of a third, but also because they provide us with a convenient distillation of the approximate views of a number of spokesmen representing a variety of Irish proprietary interests. Many of the legal points raised by Domville had been anticipated by others, including Aungier, Sir Nicholas Plunket, Lord Chancellor Eustace, and some of the commissioners of the court of claims.[27] While it is difficult to trace the circuitous course which the discussions on retrenchment followed during these years, it may be conjectured—given the thoroughness of his briefs, together with the respect with which he was held by Ormond—that it was Domville's advocacy, along with a sense of weariness, which ultimately proved decisive in inducing the agents of both adventurers and soldiers to agree to a retrenchment much larger in scope than they had hitherto been willing to accept.[28] Once the principle of a retrenchment of a third had been accepted, the bill was pressed into final form in July, at Hampton Court, by Ormond, Orrery, Anglesey, Arlington, Morice, and Finch. The scheme was then incorporated in the Act of Explanation which finally passed the Irish parliament, largely through the skilful advocacy of Ormond and Orrery, under dramatic circumstances in December 1665.[29]

It is regrettable that the sources do not yield much information regarding the actual administrative machinery by which the retrenchment was carried out. The problem is a formidable one that has been evaded by every historian of the period except W.H. Hardinge, who has warned us not to conclude that when the retrenchments were made, and new titles taken out, that there was a new vesting of land into the hands of the crown and a fresh distribution. No such process took place. The operation, says Hardinge,[30]

> was one on paper, which calculated and exhibited the exact portion of the lands previously assigned to each soldier and adventurer that should be retrenched by each possessor, and placed at the disposal of the commissioners . . . for the benefit of the new participating interests. . . . When a paper retrenchment was thus effected, the commissioners confirmed the respective parties in the residue of their land by certificates. . . .

Hardinge's explanation is satisfactory as far as it goes, but it still leaves unanswered the question of how the land thus released was eventually distributed. The question is an intriguing one, especially since the Act of Explanation gave the adventurer and soldier the right to select the two-thirds portion of his estate he chose to retain, providing the retrenched land remained contiguous.[31] This must have led, *per force*, to the creation of many curious and serpentine boundary lines as the proprietor strove to preserve the most profitable parts of his estate. We only get an occasional glimpse of the process in operation when, for example, in 1667 Major Samuel Bull, Lord Wharton's attorney, wrote to John Adams, an adventurer holding an estate adjacent to Whartons in Westmeath. Adams replied:[32]

> The several parcels of Lord Wharton's lot are Tuitestown, Stockstown, Ballina, Corstown, and Glinstown. Of all the whole lot Tuitestown is the best . . . so that if it be for retrenching, you need not much care to cut of any of the rest, that being secured. But, as I remember, the act [of Explanation] says it must be contiguous, and then the worst of the lot . . . is Glinstown, Ballina, and Corstown, which be contiguous, and then Stockstown lies next to Ballina, a good part of which . . . must be [cut] off to make up your third, considering the overmeasure which is made by Down Survey; so that I think your third will near reach 700 a[cres]. . . .

The realignment must have left some areas of the country speckled with small islands of isolated portions of land set adrift from many estates. It is true, of course, that great numbers of adventurers' and soldiers' debentures had been purchased in large blocks by speculators, thus, by the creation of large contiguous estates, facilitating the process of retrenchment. Nevertheless, the problem resists description, although it is most likely that much of the land that was released was eventually absorbed by the local proprietors.

No sooner had the Act of Explanation been passed than various subterfuges began to be used to evade the worst effects of retrenchment. Petty refers to the practice, in Kerry, by which those seeking to protect their more valuable land would purchase half the amount of poor land they held in profitable land elsewhere, then 'compound both into one claim, to cut off the Kerry acres for their thirds', a procedure that we are justified in assuming took place throughout the country.[33] Another means of evading the loss of good land by retrenchment was by the purchase of unsatisfied adventurers' of soldiers' debentures on poor land. The land represented by these 'deficiencies' was then applied toward the one-third retrenchment. A London newspaper reported in 1666 that 'most persons . . . [were] active for buying deficiencies to make up the thirds, which are cut off from soldiers and adventurers by the act'.[34] Although the commissioners had by this time already drawn attention to this procedure as being destructive of the whole intent of the Act of Explanation, they permitted the practice to continue, and indeed accepted its legality in their adjudications. 'I had a very favourable dispatch [of my claim]', said Sir George Rawdon in 1666, 'and had the deficiencies I purchased allowed for my third part'.[35]

The general subject of retrenchment is somewhat tangential to the present study, Dublin not having been allocated, under the Cromwellian settlement, for the satisfaction of the adventurers or soldiers, although the scheme did of course affect those Dublin proprietors who were claiming land in areas in the country where retrenchment applied. But even in Dublin there was one individual who held land in the country as an adventurer. This was John Blackwell, who by special favour of Cromwell had been permitted to choose his estate where he pleased.[36] As such, that portion of his estate that was not restored to innocents was subject to retrenchment, including Clontarf. But Colonel Edward Vernon, who was now in possession, was able to avert this threat by obtaining an exemption from the need to retrench by proviso in the Act of Explanation.

II

The Act of Explanation, like the Act of Settlement, vested in the crown all land in Ireland that had been forfeited as a consequence of the rebellion of 1641, with the exception of the land held by Trinity College and the church. Also excepted from the power of the vesting clause were the lands of those who had been declared innocent in the court of claims, together with a handful of individuals who had been similarly protected in the Act of Settlement. Those who had been awarded decrees of innocence but were as yet unrestored, or partly so, were left to the regular law courts to recover their estates, the Cromwellian occupants of which were given the option of submitting to a court trial (within thirty days) or relinquishing the land in the hope of obtaining a reprisal of two-thirds. Twenty-two individuals were declared exempt from the obligation to retrench a third of their estates, among them the duke of York, Lords Kingston and Mountrath, along with Sir Theophilus Jones, Sir George Rawdon, the children of Colonel Owen O'Connolly, and, as we have seen, Colonel Edward Vernon, all of whom held estates in Dublin.[37]

Fifty-four individuals, including six peers and twenty-seven others of the fifty-six nominees who had been named in the Act of settlement, were singled out to be restored to their principal seats and 2,000 adjacent acres, but only after reprisals had first been allotted to those who were dispossessed for the purpose. Among the fifty-four appear the names of five claimants to Dublin land, Lords Westmeath and Trimleston, Sir Richard Barnewall, Sir Luke Dillon and John Walsh. Similar provision was made for those, not already provided for in the act, who were in possession of any land on 22 August 1663 solely by force of royal letters (the 'letterees').[38]

A number of other prominent Catholic claimants were also provided for in the new act. Lords Dunsany and Netttervill and the earl of Tyrconnell, all of whom had been declared nocent, were given individual provisos for their restoration. Dunsany was to be restored immediately, without previous reprisals, to his chief seat and a third of his former holdings, and, with 'all convenient speed', to the remainder following the reprisal of the Cromwellian occupants.[39] Nettervill, whose plight attracted the sympathy of a number of eminent people, obtained a clause for his full restoration 'as he ought to have had . . . [if] he had been adjudged innocent', but only after lands equal in size to two-thirds of his estate had been set out to the Cromwellian claimants, Edward Smith and Sir

Courtney Poole.[40] Tyrconnell, who had been granted a royal pardon in 1664, was given a proviso which declared his nocency to be null and void 'as if the same had never been had or made'.[41]

Also ordered restored by private proviso were Sir Richard Bellings (unconditionally), John Talbot of Malahide (after prior reprisals to some of the Cromwellian occupants), Sir Luke Bath (after prior reprisals to the duke of York), and John Arthur (partly *in specie*).[42]

Two provisos dealing with Lord Gormanston's estate did little to disentangle an already confusing situation. By the first Gormanston was restored, but only after the heirs of the earl of Mountrath had been reprised with lands of equal size and quality. Moreover, until the heirs had been allotted their reprisals Gormanston was required to pay them the profits he had earned from the estate since he had taken forcible possession in April 1662. The second proviso confirmed Mountrath's heirs in the land he held on 7 May 1659, 'except such as had been decreed away, or shall be by this act, or restored unto the Irish proprietor, for which he or they shall [be reprised]. . . .' It also called for a division (unspecified) of the first earl's estate to be made between the second earl and his family pursuant to the decision concerning the first earl's will taken by Ormond and the council in October 1663.[43]

The private settlement of the dispute between Sir George Lane and Philip Hore, negotiated in 1665, was embodied in two provisos in the new act. Comprising more than three pages of the act, the first proviso presents a brief historical summary of the events which led to the compromise: that after Lane had obtained letters patent for Hore's estate in 1661 and 1663 the court of claims had issued 'two several decrees . . . to the prejudice of the said grants'; that Lane had then petitioned the king and succeeded in obtaining a hearing of the case in the English privy council, where he was given liberty to 'impugne the said decrees by any matter in fact or law', whereupon Hore and Lane then 'did mutually agree for avoiding of all future differences touching that matter, that the said estate . . . should be divided, and a share thereof settled on . . . Lane . . . for quitting his whole pretence and right to the estate, and the remain[der] thereof settled on . . . Hore . . .' The proviso then declared that the decrees of innocence that had been awarded to the Hores were null and void 'as if there had never been any such', following which the lands earmarked for Lane in the city and county of Dublin were enumerated in exact denominations: 'two stables, one piece of waste ground . . . three messuages covered with straw . . . one shop or room in High street. . . .' Lane's allotment came to over 800 acres of Hore's estate in Dublin, including the chief prize, Kilsallaghan in Castleknock, along with about the same amount of land in Meath. Hore was by the second proviso restored to nearly 900 acres in Dublin and some 3,000 in Wexford.[44]

All the prominent Protestants who claimed estates in Dublin were also amply provided for in the Act of Explanation. Under the terms of the Act of Settlement Ormond was entitled to claim large amounts of forfeited land in the country. In 1662 an official investigation had revealed that the crown was indebted to him, 'on all grounds', for over £71,000, most of which (£50,000) was incurred in the form of a mortgage he had taken on his vast estates to raise money for the royalist cause before 1649.[45] Moreover, Ormond was also entitled, by the terms of the Act of Settlement, to claim arrears as a '49 officer.[46]

It became apparent, however, that any attempt by Ormond to press these claims to the full would have deleterious affects on the entire land settlement. For this reason he was persuaded to accept a payment of £50,000 in lieu of claiming his arrears out of forfeited land, provision for which was made in the Act of Explanation.[47] Ormond, according to Carte, 'could not bear the reflection that the settlement of a whole kingdom should be delayed for his particular benefit or interest; especially in a time when the jealously, envy and emulation, faction and self interest . . . were so rife . . . this reason determined him to . . . accept a sum of money in lieu thereof'.[48]

Lord Kingston, who had acquired a considerable estate in Dublin during the Interregnum, was by the act of Explanation confirmed in the lands ratified to him in the Act of Settlement, with, however, certain important reservations: the lands decreed away from him by the court of claims and those granted to the earl of Falmouth, who had died shortly before the passing of the act.[49] Falmouth's father and heir, Charles, second Viscount Fitzharding, was confirmed in the letters patent his son had obtained.[50]

Sir Theophilus Jones's name appears scattered throughout the Act of Explanation, as it had in the Act of Settlement. The most important of his provisos confirmed the decision of the court of claims by putting him in possession of the Sarsfield estate, including the manor of Lucan, for the life of Patrick Sarsfield, who had been declared nocent. Jones was to be reprised for Lucan and the rest of the estate when he finally surrendered it to William Sarsfield, Patrick's son and heir.[51]

Ormond's great plan to create a royal park near Dublin city that could also serve as a suitable site for a viceregal residence was substantially realized by a clause in the Act of Explanation which confirmed the purchase by the crown of 440 acres in Chapelizod, a few miles to the west of the city on the Liffey river, form Lord Chancellor Eustace. Eustace had agreed to the sale in 1663, but only a portion of the purchase price of £10,000 had been paid to him at the time of his death in 1665. Therefore, a clause in the new act stipulated that the payment of the balance be paid to Eustace's heir.[52]

Whereas the Act of Settlement had vested in the duke of York most of the land in Ireland that had been held during the Interregnum by the regicides, this provision was considerably modified in the Act of Explanation. Excluded from the vesting clause in the new act were various categories of land, including the estates that had been decreed away by the court of claims; the land that had been purchased from the regicides, provided the buyer paid the purchase price to York; and regicides' land that had been granted since 1660 to a select group of people, including Ormond, the archbishop of Dublin, and Sir George Lane.

But in all these cases York was to be reprised, if possible in Dublin, Louth, Kildare, or Cork, with equivalent land.[53]

A special clause—almost an afterthought it would seem—was inserted in the new act to protect twenty-five prominent individuals, including nine who claimed Dublin estates, who, along with 'all others particularly provided for in the said former act [of Settlement] and not particularly mentioned in this present act', were to enjoy the estates settled on them if they had not been decreed away by the court of claims.[54]

The passing of the Act of Explanation represented a compromise solution to a complex and highly volatile situation, arrived at as much through weariness as reason. The act may have had the virtue, as Ormond put it, of not pleasing 'the more violent of English or Irish', yet it was patently a compromise which favoured the Protestants.[55] Although a pool of land was created which could be used for reprisals and to restore a few prominent royal nominees, the act proved ruinous for the Catholic proprietors generally because no provision was made for a resumption of the hearings to claims of innocence. No one who had not already been adjudged innocent was to be so judged in future in order to claim land; they were indeed barred from all such claims not particularly allowed in the act, that is, unless they were entitled to claim under other provisions (as letterees, articlemen, etc.) of the act.[56] As Sir William Petty put it, it was agreed 'among the grandees of both parties' that those 'not adjudged innocent should pass for nocent.' The vast majority of the Catholics who had failed to obtain decrees of innocence were, therefore, permanently disinherited; in their view the Act of Explanation was indeed the 'Black Bill'.[57] But at least the log-jam was broken and the commissioners appointed to execute the act—Sir Edward Dering, Sir Edward Smith, Sir Alan Broderick, Sir Winston Churchill and Colonel Edward Cooke—were back in Dublin toward the end of 1665 prepared to start hearings in the second court of claims.[58]

CHAPTER VI

The Second Court of Claims

I

When the second court of claims began its hearings in the King's Inns, Dublin, on 4 January 1666 the first court of claims was abolished. The hearings were not to conclude until 2 January 1669, although there were various recesses, including one period of five months in 1667 during which the sub-commissioners did the preliminary work prior to the distribution of reprisal land.[1]

A list of thirty-eight rules governing the procedure of the court, most of them based on provisions in the Act of Explanation, was published on 5 January 1666, some of the more salient of which may be summarized: all adventurers, soldiers, and Protestant purchasers of transplanters' certificates were to submit their claims, containing the precise denominations of land, both profitable and unprofitable, they held on 7 May 1659, within thirty days from the date of the publication of the rules. They were then required to indicate what lands they had been removed from since 7 May 1659, and the legal means by which this occurred (i.e., by decree of the first court of claims of otherwise), along with the names of the people to whom the land had been restored or granted, and the kind of titles obtained (i.e., for life, in fee-farm, etc.). Any adventurer or soldier holding an estate whose former proprietor had been adjudged innocent but had been left to law to recover his land was to decide within three months (if he 'conveniently' could) whether to stand trial at law or to surrender the estate and take his chances at obtaining a reprisal of two-thirds. The Irish bishops whose sees were to be augmented (there were eight) were to submit a list of the lands they already possessed, and their yearly value, so that any deficiency could be made up and any 'overplus' (surplus) retrenched. The fifty-four nominees were to submit the acreage and denominations of the principal seats to which they elected to be restored, indicating the person then in possession. Those who had been restored by virtue of royal letters alone were to enter a list of the lands they held. If they possessed more than 2,000 acres they were to elect that portion, not above 2,000, that they chose to retain, providing they held as much in 1641. Finally, anyone who claimed an estate by 'any particular proviso in either of the acts [of Settlement or Explanation], or by virtue of any grant or patent mentioned therein or confirmed thereby', were to submit a schedule expressing the date of their patent or grant with the denominations of the lands they claimed and the names of the persons then in possession.[2]

Some of the rules provide information regarding the administrative procedures of the court. After the claims or petitions had been entered and marked by the registrar, they were then transmitted to the sub-commissioners, who were to examine them and indicate (by comparison with the decrees of the first court of claims) which lands had been decreed away. They were then to be returned to the registrar with the results of the examination and a statement of the quit rents due to the crown, following which the commissioners would appoint a time for a final hearing of the case. The registrar was also required to keep an alphabetical table, to be posted in the court for 'speedy reference', containing a list of all the claimants and petitioners, with the date of the delivery of their claims and the names of the attorneys who signed them. No claim or petition was to be heard without prior public notice of fourteen days; no claimant was to change attorneys except in open court. If there were several claimants to the same land the first was to give adequate notice to the attorneys of the other claimants. Proof of possession of land on 7 May 1659 or 22 October 1641 was to be given verbally in open court, as was the testimony of witnesses, unless the commissioners ruled otherwise.[3]

These rules, together with some of the entries in the Book of Orders of the commissioners, a record of the court's proceedings between January and May 1666, suggest that the jurisdiction of the court was somewhat wider than was implied by J. P. Prendergast, who described it as 'a court for English and Protestants only, or for such Irish [Catholics] as had provisoes in the Act of Explanation ordering them restoration without the incumbrance of previous reprisals'.[4]

The entries in the Book of Orders make it clear, for one thing, that the court acted on occasion as a kind of court of appeals to which claimants who had appeared in the first court of claims reverted. Some of these cases involved Catholics pleading to be restored, by virtue of their decrees of innocence, to land still occupied by Cromwellian planters. Several entries confirm the fact, previously alluded to, that some of the sheriffs had refused to execute the injunctions of the first court.[5] On occasion the former Cromwellian planter appears as plaintiff, pleading to be restored to land from which he had been dispossessed by decree of the first court of claims. In a few cases both the plaintiff and defendant were Catholics, in one instance involving land in Dublin. On 27 March 1666 the earl of Anglesey appeared as plaintiff, alleging that he had been dispossessed by Thomas Luttrell of the townland of Loughtown (alias Bellaghan) in Newcastle. The hearing of the case, on 2 April, reveals that Anglesey's plea was based on the claim that the two townlands were separate entities, and that Luttrell was in illegal possession of one of them. But the commissioners ruled that the two parcels were, indeed, 'one and the same land' and ordered it to be excepted out of the certificate for Anglesey's patent.[6]

The evidence in the Book of Orders suggests that a considerable number of

Catholics appeared in the court in an attempt to avoid being dispossessed from land in Connacht or Clare to which they had been transplanted under the Cromwellian settlement, nineteen of them from Lord Mayo's estate alone.[7]

II

The claim of the beleaguered Lord Gormanston was heard on 10 April 1666, with the countess-dowager of Mountrath and her second son, Richard Coote, together with her husband, Robert Reading, appearing as defendants. After establishing that the first earl of Mountrath was in possession of Gormanstown on 7 May 1659, the court ruled that Lord Gormanston's title would be confirmed only if reprisals were first allotted to the defendants, as provided for in the Acts of Settlement and Explanation. Since, however, Gormanston was in actual possession of the manor and had already earned a decree of innocence, it was ruled that he was to remain in possession until further orders of the court.[8] It was also ruled that Gormanston was to pay the defendants £944 from the profits of the manor which had accrued over the course of the previous four years (i.e., from April 1662, when Gormanston took forcible possession) and £236 a year thereafter, pending allotment of the reprisals to the defendants.

In a petition to the king the following year, Gormanston pleaded that he had been forced, to avoid losing Gormanstown, to sell some of his estate and that the income which remained to him was insufficient to satisfy the £472 due to the Cootes in 1668. Gormanston's plight earned the sympathy of Ormond, who blamed his difficulties on the incompetence of his lawyers in allowing a proviso to be incorporated into the Act of Explanation requiring the Cootes to be reprised before Gormanston's title could be confirmed.

In the summer of 1668 Gormanston was still not legally restored even though, as he claimed, he had paid some £1,300 to the Cootes yet was still £400 in arrears. He complained bitterly that all of the king's good intentions toward him proved fruitless; that over the previous eight years he had spent most of his fortune of £10,000, together with his wife's portion of £4,000, in prosecuting the case both in England and Ireland. He was now, he said, £1,500 in debt, yet all he got from the court of claims was a threat that if he defaulted on his payments from the manor he would be turned out. The commissioners had not restored him to 'a foot' of his estate.[9]

By now Gormanston was convinced that the Cootes were refusing to accept all offers of reprisals, hoping to delay proceedings until the court of claims rose for good, when they could claim the estate on the grounds that the terms of the Acts of Settlement and Explanation had not been carried out.[10] In December 1668, however, Gormanston and Robert Reading made another appearance in the court, when the commissioners, after ordering Gormanston to pay all the arrears due to the Cootes, declared it their intention to 'lay out as good a reprise as they could for Mr. Reading and confirm my Lord [Gormanston] in his estate'.[11] Seven months later Gormanston was issued letters patent for his former estate, including the manor of Gormanstown with its 600 adjacent acres in Dublin.[12]

* * *

Although the estates of the regicides were earmarked for the duke of York, Clarendon maintained that the duke had not been inclined to prosecute the grants on the understanding that most of the land in question would be used to satisfy the claims of the dispossessed Catholics. It was not until the duke heard of 'great quantities of land every day granted away by his majesty to his servants and others . . . [that] he resolved to be no longer a loser . . . and so proceeded in getting that grant from the king to himself of those lands designed to him'.[13] Many of the entries in the Book of Orders of the commissioners are related to York's claims, and there is ample evidence that the need to provide him with an Irish estate exerted a disruptive influence on the whole land settlement.

The problem was compounded, first, by York's exemption from the need to retrench a third of his holdings, and, second, by the character and background of some of his land agents. As early as 1662 Ormond had warned Clarendon that the formation of Irish estate for York would lead to the ruin of many people, and he asked Clarendon to use his influence to urge restraint on the duke.[14] Unfortunately, some of the agents seem to have been impervious to restraint; indeed, in view of the previous histories of several of them, and the subsequent careers of a few others, York's choice of agents seems almost inexplicable.

From about 1665 his principal Irish land agent was Dr Robert Gorges, who had arrived in Ireland ten years earlier as Henry Cromwell's secretary, later becoming clerk to the council.[15] The genesis of Gorges's appointment can be traced in part to his uncle, Orrery, but more precisely to his cousin, Clarendon, who, while acknowledging that Gorges had been 'corruptly educated', nevertheless recommended him to Ormond as a man who had 'discerned his error'.[16] Gorges's appointment is to some extent, therefore, understandable. Less explicable were the appointments of some of the sub-agents.

Robert Shapcote, a lawyer from Devon, had a remarkably elastic political career even by the standards of the day. He had sat in the Long Parliament but was secluded in Pride's Purge. In 1654 he was alleged to have 'royalist leanings' yet we find him the same year in Cromwell's parliament. His speech in 1656 in opposition to the proposal for a hereditary Protectorate, having been printed, led to warrants being issued for his arrest, yet in 1658 he was appointed solicitor-general for Ireland. He was returned for Richard Cromwell's parliament in 1659 but his claim to a seat was successfully challenged. He is next found in the Convention Parliament of 1660, and the following year he sat in the restored Irish parliament.[17] Imprisoned by May 1663 for complicity in Blood's conspiracy, he was nevertheless pardoned in August (despite the king's 'absolute' refusal to do so nine months earlier) but was expelled from the Commons the following year for his activities in the plot.[18] Despite this chequered career, Shapcote was by this time already acting as one of York's agents; it is small wonder Ormond referred to him as a 'bold seditious spirit', or that a contemporary newspaper should describe him as 'one that's half a soldier, half a lawyer'.[19]

The irascible Sir Jerome Alexander (who was related by marriage to Robert Gorges), appointed second justice of the common pleas in 1660, had some years earlier been disbarred in England.[20] Robert Thornhill, a Cromwellian officer, had spent some time as a prisoner in Dublin Castle for opposing the Stuart restoration. Moreover, in 1655 he had been convicted of a felony for the spoilation and sacrilege of a church in Tipperary. Nevertheless, in 1667 he was appointed to 'aid and assist . . . Gorges in the management of the affairs in Ireland of . . . [York]'.[21]

Given these circumstances, Ormond's attitude toward the agents is understandable. Gorges, he said in 1668, was attempting to manage York's Irish affairs with 'the worst under-instruments he could well light on. . . . I mean Judge Alexander and Mr. Shapcote . . . Thornhill, Townly, Dunbavin, and others; fellows of notorious infamy'. Robert Leigh shared these sentiments; he called the agents 'trash', and their employment in York's service as a 'shame'.[22]

It is hardly surprising, therefore, that a feeling of mutual enmity between the agents and the commissioners of the court emerged soon after the hearings started. The antagonism finally led Gorges, in late 1667, to make an appeal to the king in parliament against the commissioners, charging them with illegal and unjust proceedings in the handling of York's claims. The commissioners in turn accused Gorges of submitting claims which contained far more land than York was entitled to and thousands of acres which could not be used for reprisals, at a time when the duke's claim was nearly satisfied. The scope of York's claim, and the appeal which was launched in connection with it, caused a one month delay in the court's proceedings, leading many soldiers and adventurers to complain that Gorges had initiated the appeal without York's approval. The king, however, disallowed the appeal and early the following year the commissioners resumed their hearings.[23]

The animosity between York's agents and the commissioners continued, however. Edward Cooke told Ormond in May 1668 that Alexander had made an appearance in court, 'pressing so immodestly for unreasonable things that he put the court in some heat, and himself broke forth into some flames of passion'. Cooke complained on numerous occasions about the delays caused by the agents' activities. In one session, he said, the court had devoted an entire day to York's business, adding that such time consuming procedures were proving ruinous to other claimants. It would seem that the delays were not always the result of the agents' special devotion to York's interests. Cooke asserted that they were obtaining fees by leasing the land York held in *custodiam*, for a year at a time, 'for filthy lucre's sake'. It was obviously not in the agents' best interests to conclude York's business as rapidly as possible. Sir Winston Churchill accused them of being 'a pack of knaves and cheats', and when Thornhill tried to force a retraction from Churchill he narrowly avoided being kicked down the stairs of Churchill's lodgings. Churchill later found it difficult to explain his position to York, who, he complained, was being told (by the duchess) that he was the duke's greatest enemy among the commissioners.[24]

One of the vital areas of contention between the agents and the commissioners centred on the question of ascertaining the precise amount of regicides' land, or its equivalent, which was due to York. In this connection one fact can be stated with confidence, viz., that the agents attempted to apply the widest possible interpretation to the provisions of the Acts of Settlement and Explanation to support their contention that the duke could justly claim an Irish estate of some 100,000 profitable acres. The agents, said Robert Leigh in 1668, had 'stretched the last string as long as the act could possibly bear it to do him service'.[25]

The decision to proceed in this manner seems to have been taken in 1666, as an abstract of York's claim found among the Clarendon papers demonstrates. The document contains no particulars as to denominations of land, but appended to it is a series of critical memoranda, probably written by Gorges, which make the following points: that the abstract took no account of the deficiencies due to the regicides for 'money lent and advanced for the service of Ireland'; that no account had been taken of the estates of the individuals who were exempt from pardon under the terms of the act of oblivion of 1661, 'whose estates are likewise by the explanatory act passed and settled in his royal highness'; and that York was justified in claiming the land which the regicides had sold or otherwise disposed of before 7 May 1659. 'I conjecture', the author concludes, 'we shall be able to make out at least one hundred thousand acres of profitable land to be his highnesses by virtue of the two acts.'

The abstract does in fact put York's claim at 97,619 profitable acres, of which 52,064 had already been decreed away in the first court of claims. Of the remaining 45,553 acres 'undecreed', York was in possession of only 16,677, leaving 28,856 (*sic*) acres which were being 'injuriously withheld' from him, and for which his agents were now seeking a *custodiam* grant. The abstract enters the holdings of the five regicides in Dublin—John Hewson, Miles Corbet, John Jones, Sir Hardress Waller, and Edmund Ludlow—as having amounted to 20,424 acres, of which York was then in possession of only 680.[26]

Further evidence that York's agents adopted this procedure can be deduced from another abstract of his claims to be found in the same collection. Here we find the agents contending that Ludlow, having been granted lands to the value of £5,065, was to be satisfied, at the same rate as the adventurers, with 8,442 acres of land in Dublin. Since the evidence is fairly conclusive that Ludlow's estate in the county as composed on 7 May 1659 was probably less than half this size, it is evident that the agents were basing their claim on the amount of land that had been due to Ludlow rather than the amount he was actually allotted. The fact that the commissioners had only 'allowed' the claim to 5,500 acres suggests this to have been the case; the remainder of the lands claimed, or 2,942 acres, were 'controverted'.

Another entry in this abstract was based on the claim that John Jones, in a survey undertaken by himself, had put the size of his estate in Dublin at 3,000 acres, whereas the Down Survey put it at 5,193. The commissioners, however, while allowing the claim to the 3,000, did not allow the remaining 2,193 acres, which had been restored to innocents. The entry opposite Corbet's name makes the point that York should be reprised for the loss of Malahide, which had been restored to John Talbot. The entry against Waller's name appears only in the 'controverted' column, and only for 398 acres. Against the name of Hewson only a single figure—6,400 acres—is entered, which was 'allowed' by the commissioners.[27]

A considerable amount of the acrimony surrounding York's settlement involved the attempt by his agents to claim land already restored to innocents. Indeed, the Book of Orders of the commissioners contains numerous references to his claims to the land of restored Catholics, including some Dublin proprietors: Marcus Fitzsimons, Robert Finglas, Peter Nottingham, James Humprey, James Barnewall, John Talbot of Belgard, Dr Richard Murphy, Lord Gormanston, and William Sarsfield. The hearings revealed that the agents had already dispossessed both Murphy and Barnewall, although York did not succeed in acquiring these estates.[28]

Other innocent claimants were not so lucky, including Sir Luke Bath of Balgriffin. In 1667 a royal letter, directed to the commissioners, ordered Bath's restoration. The estate, it pointed out, had not been possessed by a regicide and was only being claimed by the duke as a 'cautionary reprisal' until a permanent reprisal could be found. 'You shall forthwith reprise the duke for the land so adjudged from him', the letter read, 'and restore Sir Luke to his estate before any other person save the duke of York, and the adventurers and soldiers who are settled on his estate.'[29] But of course by this date lands of equal value to Balgriffin could seldom be found. The provision in the Act of Explanation to restore Bath only after York's reprisal placed him in a desperate situation; in fact he was never able to recover Balgriffin.

An interesting gambit was used to frustrate York's agents in their efforts to secure the old Harold family seat at Kilmashogue, held by Sir Maurice Eustace, nephew and heir of the former lord chancellor of the same name, who died in 1665. In June 1668 the agents submitted a claim to the estate as a reprisal for York, but Eustace and the dean of Christ Church, apparently by prior agreement, appeared in court and alleged that the estate was church land, having been let in fee-farm to the Harold's in 1592. The commissioners thereupon rejected York's claim, but after the court rose for good in 1669 Eustace denied the church claim and produced the patent his uncle obtained in 1662. But its validity was soon challenged and the struggle for Kilmashogue was to continue for many years.[30] At any rate, these were the kind of ploys which led to complaints that York was being deprived of lands that were rightfully his, and the king found it necessary to reiterate that his brother was to stand 'absolutely first' among persons to be reprised.[31]

* * *

The activities of Michael Boyle, archbishop of Dublin (from 1663), lord chancellor (from 1666), and a cousin of the earl of Cork, also absorbed much of the court's attention. The Act of Settlement stipulated that forfeited land which had been held in fee-farm from episcopal sees (or other church bodies) was to be vested in the crown and a proportion of it allocated for the purpose of augmenting eight sees, including Dublin, whose incumbents should receive a sufficient amount to bring their yearly income up to £2,000. Each bishop's proportion was, if possible, to be set out within his own see, but if this did not prove possible any deficiencies should be made up out of similar lands in other bishoprics 'most contiguous and convenient'.[32] It was for this reason that Boyle's final settlement contained various forfeited townlands that had once been leased in fee-farm from other episcopal sees. The printed calander of letters patent enrolled under the Restoration settlement makes the point that certain forfeited lands in Cork, worth £313 a year, had been formerly held in fee-farm from the bishoprics of Cloyne and Ross, but that these two sees, not having been provided for in the Acts of Settlement and Explanation, the lands were 'declared and adjudged to be the most convenient lands that the commissioners could find . . . to supply the defect which is in the forfeited fee-farms held of the . . . [see of Dublin], to make up the augmentation by the said acts, designed for the see of Dublin; . . . .'[33]

To ascertain the amount of additional land needed for the augmentation of their sees, the rules of procedure issued by the commissioners required the bishops to submit a list of the lands they then held, either in *custodiam* or by patent, or otherwise, and their yearly value, so that any deficiency could be made up and any surplus retrenched.[34]

Boyle submitted a list of lands to the court which contained claims on some 15,000 acres, about half of which lay in Dublin. His schedule of lands carried with it the information that his yearly income in 1663 was £1,034. 11s. 2d. Inquisitions were taken shortly later which showed that Boyle was entitled to a further £430 a year arising out of forfeited land which had been leased from the church in fee-farm. Some of this was passed to him in 1664. At the same time he was holding a considerable amount of land in *custodiam*, from which he hoped to have enough set out to him to realize the £535. 8s. 10d needed to complete the augmentation of his see. In the court of claims Boyle pleaded for confirmation of the lands already passed to him in 1664, together with a sufficient added income to complete his augmentation, to be derived from additional grants either from among the lands he held in *custodiam* or from other lands which might prove to be alienated church land.[35]

Boyle's attempts to recover alienated church land led to a series of protracted legal struggles, described in 1670 as a 'tedious prosecution against several persons who had possessed ... them'.[36] One of the victims of the 'tedious prosecution' was Thomas Conran, whose principal holdings lay in the barony of Nethercross. By late 1666 Boyle had established in court that Conran's estate was in fact alienated church land, by which time he was already making leases of the estate (nearly 500 acres), described as 'formerly the reputed property of Thomas Conran, and now the archbishop's'. Another victim was Walter Eustace, part of whose estate in Uppercross was also described in 1665 as archepiscopal land 'formerly the reputed property' of Eustace.[37]

Boyle was also successful in establishing title to over 250 acres in Coolock held in 1641 by the Chamberlain family. Boyle managed to gain possession of a few acres of the estate, but Robert Chamberlain refused to surrender the bulk of it, including the townland of Kilreesk, 'pretending to be an innocent Protestant',[38] as Boyle's agent asserted in court, yet Chamberlain had been outlawed in 1642 and adjudged innocent in the first court of claims.[39] Nevertheless, he still held Kilreesk on 14 May 1666 when he appeared as defendant in the second court of claims, begging the court not to issue Boyle a certificate for the estate. But Chamberlain had no hope of success and the court ordered Boyle to be confirmed in possession, with the recommendation, however, that he take cognizance of Chamberlain's plight and 'afford him such relief as his grace shall think fit'. Yet on 15 August Thomas Chamberlain, Robert's son, appeared in the court to plead for a 'saving of his interest in the lands of Kilreesk'. In response the commissioners noted that the case had been fully considered on 14 May and that no further arguments were contemplated. Boyle's title was then re-confirmed, but the commissioners, who appear to have taken a particular interest in the case, declared that they did not think it appropriate to issue an injunction ordering Chamberlain's removal.[40] Boyle may have privately agreed to allow him to remain as tenant.

Among the estates also claimed by Boyle as having been held in fee-farm from the church was the townland of Ballough in Nethercross, held in 1641 by James Bermingham. Bermingham died before 1663 but his widow, Eleanor, was awarded a decree of innocence and an income from the estate, as her jointure, of £30 a year for life. The efficacy of her decree seems to have been limited to her jointure only; indeed, Boyle's claim noted that the 'widow Bermingham who had her jointure decreed is departed'.[41]

In the hearing of the case, which took place on 13 November 1667, the defendants are seen to be the '49 officers. The legal basis for their claim rested on their right to acquire land, in satisfaction for their arrears, by the redemption of mortgages of forfeited estates. In 1639 Ballough was mortgaged for £300 by James Bermingham to a Captain Henry Smith, who in turn sold it to Dr John Stearne, founder of the medical faculty of Trinity College. Stearne then gave Colonel Alexander Piggot, one of the trustees for the '49 officers, £590 with which to redeem the mortgage, and in May 1668 a patent for the estate was issued to Piggot in trust for Stearne. A month later Piggot assigned Ballough to Stearne.[42] Boyle, however, succeeded in establishing his right to the chief rent, and the commissioners ordered that a savings clause be inserted in the certificate of the court, reserving to the archbishop and his successors the sum of two shillings in the pound 'at the improved value' of the estate.[43]

* * *

A considerable number of these savings clauses were appended to the letters patent which Boyle, and others, obtained under the Restoration settlement. They reserved to individuals, or their heirs, various rights in estates, sometimes (as in the case of Eleanor Bermingham) in the form of income by way of jointures, mortgages, or annuities. In some cases they reserved the right to eventual restoration.[44]

The force of the savings clauses is, however, open to question. The land records are nearly devoid of reference to them after 1669, and there is no indication that there was any significant shift of land ownership during the 1670s and 1680s as a result of them coming into operation. The few extent references are inconclusive. Nevertheless, it may prove illuminating to investigate the origin and content of one such savings clause, if only to illustrate some of the procedures of the second court of claims.

We may cite for this purpose the patent which Archbishop Boyle received for the townland of Jordanstown in Newcastle barony, held in 1641 by James Aylmer. Aylmer was dead by 1663, but his widowed mother, Eleanor, submitted a claim to the first court which was grounded on an agreement, concluded in 1636, between herself and James following the death (in 1634) of her husband, Richard. By the terms of the agreement Eleanor became entitled, for life, in lieu of her dowry, to a third of the estate, of which Jordanstown was a part. In 1663 she was declared innocent and ordered restored. Jennett Aylmer, James's widow, was also declared innocent, but the efficacy of her decree was limited to a life annuity, as her jointure, of £50 a year following Eleanor's death. Eleanor died shortly after obtaining her decree of innocence, but it is unlikely she was ever able to regain actual possession of her estate because following her death the Cromwellian occupants refused to pay Jennett's annuity. Their justification seems to have arisen from a dispute among them (there were seven) over allocation of the annuity charges on each portion of the estate.

To assert her claim to the annuity Jennett Aylmer appeared in the second court of claims on 20 January 1666, when the case was ordered to be heard on 31 January. At the hearing on that day the case was referred to the sub-commissioners, who reported on 27 February. They had been charged with apportioning the annuity charges according to the number of acres in each denomination of land comprising the estate. On 27 February the commissioners ordered the defendants to appear on 12 March to show cause why the report should not be accepted. The final hearing occurred not on 12 March, however, but on 2 April, when, the defendants having failed to show cause, Jennett Aylmer was empowered to submit her case to the regular law courts in order to recover her annuity. For this reason a savings clause in Archbishop Boyle's patent reserved to Jennett Aylmer her 'right by decree to Jordanstown', i.e., her right to proceed in law to recover her annuity.[45]

* * *

The general evidence suggests that there was a considerable amount of mortgaged land in Ireland in 1641, most of it held by Protestants from Catholic mortgagees. As a result, the commissioners devoted much of their time in resolving the disposition of these estates. Two examples will serve to illustrate some of the problems this involved.

Note has already been taken of the mortgaged Fitzwilliam estate in Dublin. Most of them had been redeemed by 1662, but several townlands, including Kiltiernan and Ballybetagh in Rathdown, had not. These two townlands were mortgaged in 1639 to Sir Robert Dixon, a former mayor of the city (and father-in-law of Lord Chancellor Eustace), but were still unredeemed in 1666. In April that year the earl of Tyrconnell and Richard Dixon, Robert's grandson, appeared in the court of claims, Dixon pleading that they be omitted from the certificate to be issued to Tyrconnell for his letters patent. But the plea was futile because Tyrconnell was of course the ultimate landlord who had been secured in his estate under the terms of the Act of Explanation. The court ruled, however, that while Dixon's right and title to the two townlands, based on the mortgages, was confirmed, yet Tyrconnell was empowered to exercise his right of redemption. Tyrconnell was issued letters patent for both denominations only three months after his court appearance, although a savings clause protected Dixon's benefit of his mortgage. The mortgages on Kiltiernan and Ballybetagh were finally redeemed in 1678 by Thomas, fourth Viscount Fitzwilliam.[46]

Another example was Palmerstown in Newcastle, which had been mortgaged for £2,000 before 1641 by its proprietor, Mathew Allen, to Arthur White, a younger son of Sir Nicholas White of Leixlip. Following Arthur's death in 1648 the mortgage passed to Nicholas, Arthur's elder brother. Having established his right to the estate in the first court of claims, Nicholas sold the mortgage for £2,000 to the Irish solicitor-general, Sir John Temple, a son of the master of the rolls of the same name and a brother of Swift's mentor, Sir William Temple. In 1666 Temple entered a claim to Palmerstown in the second court of claims as the holder of an incumbrance on a forfeited estate, the benefit of the redemption of which was, under the Act of Settlement, settled on the '49 security. The commissioners, after valuing the estate at £240. 7s a year, set a price at ten years' purchase, or £2,403. 10s. From this they allowed Temple the £2,000 he had already paid for the mortgage, ordering him to pay the balance of £403. 10s to the '49 security. Upon payment of this sum Temple was to have a certificate for passing letters patent for the estate. In fact, the £403. 10s was paid, by warrant dated 12 May 1666, by the trustees of the '49 security to Temple, who was acting as counsel for the officers.[47]

CHAPTER VII

The Situation at the End of Ormond's First Viceroyalty

I

When the second court of claims finally rose for good at midnight on 2 January 1669 the work of settling legal title to the land of Ireland under the terms of the Acts of Settlement and Explanation had, with the major exception of the transplanters, been largely completed, although litigation involving certain estates was to continue for some years.

The rising of the court found ninety-seven Catholic landlords holding title to 46,967 acres in Dublin, although in a few cases they were not in actual possession of the land to which they were restored. This represented 35 per cent of the land of the county and 63 per cent of what they held in 1641. Sixty-five Catholics were fully restored, or approximately so. About three-fifths of the Catholic total was restored to only twenty-five claimants, foremost among them James Alen, John Arthur, Christopher and James Barnewall, Sir Richard Bellings, Walter Cheevers, Christopher Fagan, Thomas Luttrell, Nicholas Plunkett, John Talbot of Belgard, Sir Henry Talbot, James Wolverton, and Nicholas White, together with Lords Tirmleston, Barnewall of Turvey, Gormanston, and Tyrconnell.

Others like John Hollywood, John Talbot of Malahide, Patrick Sarsfield, and Bartholomew Russell, were restored in part, or in remainder, with expectations of obtaining full restoration at a later date, in most cases pending the operation of a proviso in the Acts of Settlement or Explanation, or of a savings clause in a patent, the expiration of a lease, or a decision in the regular law courts. Philip Hore was partially restored as a result of a prior agreement with Sir George Lane.

However, at least seventy Catholics were wholly unrestored. Such families as King, Cruise, Preston, Goodman, Delahide, Bath, Goulding, Travers, and many more, had not recovered an acre of land in the county; these names disappear as Dublin landlords, although some recovered land in other counties.

Nearly all the restored Catholics bore Old English names. Whereas in 1641 there were eighteen Old Irish Catholic proprietors, holding 3,271 acres in Dublin, the Restoration settlement found just seven holding only 1,191 acres. But the estates of two of these (John Connell and Mathew Meagh) had not been sequestered under the Cromwellian settlement, so that the amount of land in the county actually restored to the Old Irish Catholics was very small indeed, well under 1,000 acres.

The same year found ninety-three Protestant proprietors in possession of 50,550 acres, or 38 per cent of the land of Dublin, representing an increase of 17,222 acres over what sixty-one of them held in 1641. When to this is added the land held by the church and Trinity College, then the general Protestant interest in 1669 held 63,366 acres, or about 48 per cent of the land of Dublin, as opposed to 32 per cent in 1641. A further refinement of the figures show the Old English in possession of 59,538 acres, a loss of nearly 19,000 since 1641; the New English 32,065, a gain of nearly 10,000; the Old Irish 3,925, a loss of about 1,000.

* * *

Those claimants who had been singled out by name for restoration in the Acts of Settlement of Explanation fared only marginally better, on the whole, than those not so named. John Arthur and Thomas Luttrell, who obtained individual clauses in the Act of Explanation, were fully restored, as were two of the four ensignmen, Nicholas Plunket and John Talbot of Belgard. But John Harold and Christopher Russell, the other ensignmen, were wholly unrestored, although Russell's son, Bartholomew, was earmarked for restoration after his father's death. Six of the twelve nominees who claimed estates in the county were fully restored, viz., Sir Richard Bellings, John Walsh, and Lords Trimleston, Fingall, Gormanston, and the son of Dunsany. But Sir Richard Barnewall, John Talbot of Malahide, and Lord Nettervill were only partially restored, and Sir Luke Bath, Sir Luke Dillon, and the earl of Westmeath were wholly unrestored.

It needs to be reiterated, however, that some of these claimants had held very modest estates in Dublin but large ones in other counties. The 1641 Dublin estate of Nettervill, for example, consisted of only 72 acres. The fact that Nicholas, third Viscount Nettervill, succeeded in recovering only 35 acres in Dublin carries little significance when seen in the light of his success in regaining over 8,000 acres in other areas of the country.[1]

A few Dublin claimants obtained letters patent at the Restoration for land in Connacht to which they, or their immediate ancestors, had been transplanted under the Cromwellian settlement. Thus, in 1677 Robert Barnewall, ninth Baron Trimleston, received a patent for over 1,600 acres in Galway which had been assigned to his father, Mathias, as a transplanter. Mathias, who was fully restored to his estate in Dublin but failed to recover several thousand acres in Meath, died on his Galway estate in 1667.[2]

Given the structure of land ownership in Dublin in 1641, it is unremarkable to find that about a third of the restored estates contained less than 100 acres. In some cases they represented the sole holding of the restored proprietor, ranging in size from Ann Shield's 4 acres to John Foster's 88. It is often difficult to account for the success of some of these obscure claimants. Shield was awarded a decree of innocence; Foster was restored by royal letter obtained in 1661.[3] He was then, a letteree, but the source of his patronage remains a mystery. Less mysterious was the source of the patronage at the command of Patrick Moore, a pursuivant of Ormond's, who was restored to his 8 acres in Dublin. William Denn was restored to his 20 acres in the county probably on the successful plea that he was a Protestant.[4]

The letters patent issued under the Restoration settlement were rather slow in forthcoming, although the Leinster claimants generally obtained theirs earlier than those from the other provinces. Most of those dealing with Dublin were issued by about 1670, a few in the 1680s.[5] Various reasons may account for this slow process, the first being the delay caused by what must have been the large backlog of work facing the regular law courts in settling title to land referred to them by the two courts of claims. In 1673 Essex, the lord lieutenant, complained about the delay in the passing of patents on certificates from the courts of claims, the first having ceased its hearings four years earlier. 'I have ventured to pass four of these certificates,' Essex said, 'Mr. Robert Reading's, M. Chidley Coote's, Clement Spillman's and Henry Finch's, in regard that [they] have some suits at law they cannot so well go on with 'till their patents be passed. . . .' Essex made the point that another reason for the delay arose from an order in 1671 that put a stop of all grants of land in Ireland. The circumstances surrounding this order will be discussed presently, but despite his complaint about the delay in the passing of letters patent, Essex stated in 1673 that over 1,500 of them had passed the great seal and that no more than forty remained to be passed.[6]

Instruments of title to land under the Restoration settlement came in various forms, each of which is indicated by symbol for every proprietor in the Books of Survey and Distribution.[7] Many claimants were restored solely on the basis of their decrees of innocence'; others by certificate of the court of claims; still others by letters patent under the Acts of Settlement and Explanation. Some were restored under all three forms of title.

It has already been observed that innocent claimants were not obliged to take out new letters patent for land to which they had established proof of title. Even so, some restored claimants obtained them for their entire estates, one of whom, Sir Richard Bellings, was in 1666 restored to 1,500 acres in Dublin. Bellings, though, never submitted a claim as an innocent; he was restored as a nominee. Later in the reign some of his titles were challenged on the grounds that certain townlands (mainly in Wicklow) contained far more land than was indicated in his letters patent. As a result, in 1684 he obtained new letters patent with a more accurate rendering of the acreage figures.[8] It is not surprising, in view of the complexities and acrimony surrounding his contest with the heirs of the first earl of Mountrath, that we find Lord Gormanston taking out fresh letters patent for his entire estate in 1669.[9]

II

By 1669 the proceedings of the two courts of claims had resulted in the loss to the Catholic landlords of over 27,000 acres in the county, nearly two-thirds of which was acquired by only fifteen individual Protestants, one of whom was Old Irish, two Old English, two Restoration Protestant, and ten New English. Over half of the 27,000 acres was taken from the expropriated estate of only ten Catholic families: Alen, Harold, Hore, King, Nettervill, Preston, Sarsfield, Talbot, Travers, and Walsh.

Ormond, who among the fifteen was the only one who held a substantial estate in Dublin in 1641, received letters patent for over 2,300 acres, nearly all in the north of the county, and about half of which consisted of the forfeited estate of Luke Nettervill of Corballis. The remainder was composed of the expropriated estates of the four families of Blackney, Travers, Walsh, and Delahide.[10] When to this is added his 1641 estate, already recovered, the result was that he emerged at the Restoration as one of the greatest proprietors in the county, with over 3,300 acres.

John King, Lord Kingston, also emerged as one of the more substantial Dublin landlords under the Restoration settlement. His estate (over 1,500 acres) was composed almost wholly of the forfeited land of Richard Goulding, Walter Plunket, and Robert Preston.[11] Although Preston's son, Simon, was declared innocent, no acreage figures are entered against his name in the records of the first court of claims. Robert, who was still alive in 1663, was indicted and outlawed during the rebellion. After the Restoration Simon was charged (by Sir Paul Davies, who had his eye on the estate) with being active in the service of Owen Roe O'Neill. But this would not have been unusual in the 1640s and it does not provide a satisfactory explanation for the decision of the commissioners of the court of claims.

The claim for the estate was submitted by Simon while his father was still living. It would appear that he proved that the estate had been conveyed to him by his father before the rebellion, although the relevant entries in the Book of Survey and Distribution do not substantiate this. In the first court of claims Simon claimed 'by Margaret and Jane, his sisters', only 'the rectory of the parish of Ballymadun', the site of the chief seat of the family. Six months later, when it appeared that Ballymadun was about to be granted to Sir William Domville, Robert Preston petitioned the king for restoration to the estate not as a consequence of his son's decree of innocence, but by virtue of the Declaration of 30 November 1660 and the Act of Settlement. But the plea proved futile and Ballymadun was passed to Lord Kingston.[12]

If no acreage figures appear opposite Preston's name in the records of the first court of claims, neither do they appear against the name of Katherine, widow of Richard Goulding. Katherine was awarded a decree of innocence, but she claimed only a portion of the estate as her jointure. Most of the Goulding estate, including the chief seat at Kinsaley in Coolock, was also granted to

Kingston, as were the adjacent lands of Grange Portmarnock, the principal holding of Walter Plunket, who was declared nocent.[13]

Another large segment of the Preston estate (nearly 500 acres) was passed in 1668 to Charles Berkeley, second Viscount Fitzharding, father and heir of Lord Falmouth, who died in 1665. Aside from the Preston estate, Fitzharding's grant (over 2,000 acres) consisted largely of the forfeited land of the families of Cruise and Travers. No claim was entered for the Travers estate; nor had Christopher Cruise submitted a claim, the reasons for which remain obscure.[14]

Yet a third large block of the Preston estate (over 400 acres) was included in the patent awarded to Sir George Rawdon. Rawdon's patent (over 1,000 acres) also included the townland of Lispopple in Balrothery, held in 1641, according to the Book of Survey and Distribution, by Nicholas Barnewall, now Viscount Kingsland and Baron Turvey. But there is a rare contradiction here between the Book of Survey and Distribution and the Civil Survey, which shows Richard Barnewall as the 1641 proprietor. Richard, who died in Flanders about 1656, is, however, shown as paying Nicholas a yearly rent for a mill on the estate. Richard's widow, Jane, who claimed a life annuity was declared innocent in the first court of claims, but was left to establish proof of it by law. Since Nicholas was otherwise restored to his entire estate in Dublin, it would seem that Richard was indeed the legal proprietor of Lispopple in 1641, probably the consequence of a jointure negotiated at the time of his marriage to Jane before the rebellion.[15]

The children of the informer Colonel Owen O'Connolly were issued a patent for 657 acres in Balrothery, including Westpalstown, the Finglas family seat. Elizabeth, widow of Richard Finglas, the 1641 proprietor, was given a decree of innocence, but only for her life and for those lands held as her jointure in 1641. The lands her husband held were never recovered. Another smaller portion of the estate created for the O'Connolly children was taken from the forfeited land of the Begg family, no member of which obtained a decree of innocence.[16]

The attempts of the King family to obtain a hearing of their claim to innocence having been frustrated, a patent was finally issued in 1671 to Colonel Edward Vernon for the manor of Clontarf (593 acres) in Coolock.[17] In the event, the threat of the Kings to Vernon's grip on Clontarf was never serious, especially after the vital role Vernon played in the suppression of Blood's conspiracy in 1663.

The Irish attorney-general, Sir William Domville, whose erudition in connection with the various legal and statistical aspects of the land settlement, together with his prosecution of the conspirators in Blood's plot, had attracted Ormond's admiration, was granted Loughlinstown (460 acres) in Rathdown, the Goodman estate whose last proprietor had been executed for rebellion.[18]

The Irish solicitor-general, Sir John Temple, was awarded a patent in 1666 for the entire parish of Palmerstown (563 acres) in Newcastle, the mortgage on which he had purchased after the Restoration from Nicholas White of Leixlip.[19]

The private agreement arrived at between Philip Hore and Sir George Lane is reflected in Lane's patent for over 800 acres of Hore's estate in Dublin, including the manor of Kilsallaghan, the approximate working of the agreement being incorporated in the patent.[20]

Edward Brabazon, second earl of Meath, and Roger Jones shared in the spoils of the estate of a branch of the Walsh family in Rathdown, a substantial one of nearly 900 acres. Carrickmines, the chief seat, was granted to Meath and the contiguous property of Glenamuck went to Jones, no claims having been submitted by the heirs of the 1641 proprietor, Theobold Walsh.[21]

Many of the letters patent awarded under the Restoration settlement contained important qualifications, in some instances protecting the interests of innocent claimants to land granted to Protestants. The questionable value of these 'savings causes' has already been noted. An example may be cited in the case of the grant to Colonel Alexander Staples and Sir Audley Mervin for 1,900 acres, representing nearly the entire parish of Garristown in Balrothery, most of which was claimed by a nominee, John Talbot of Malahide, and his son, Richard.

Staples, of Lissan in Tyrone, son of the Ulster planter, Sir Thomas Staples, had obtained a ninety-nine lease of his land in Garristown in 1658 as a Cromwellian '49 officer. He was sheriff of Tyrone in 1661 and represented Strabane in the Irish parliament of that year. In 1665, however, he was expelled from the Commons for complicity in Blood's conspiracy even though he had been pardoned, largely on Ormond's recommendation, the previous year.[22] The savings clause in his patent protected John Talbot's right to restoration to Garristown and reserved to Richard Talbot his claim, following his father's death, to two-thirds of the same land by virtue of his decree of innocence. The savings clause in Mervin's patent reserved to Richard Talbot, and to his aunt Jane, their right to recover the rest of the Talbot estate in Balrothery, and to John Talbot the same right, but only after reprisals had first been found for Mervin.

John Talbot died in 1671, when he was described, by an inquisition taken in 1687, as being in possession of a third of the 'village and land of Garristown' i.e., part of the land that had been granted to Staples. The same inquisition shows Mervin holding land in Garristown at he time of his death in 1675. He was succeeded by his son, Henry, and it is most unlikely that adequate reprisals could have been found after 1675 to compensate him for surrendering his portion of Garristown to Richard Talbot.[23]

Although Sir Theophilus Jones obtained a patent for the former Sarsfield estate (1,390 acres), including Lucan manor, his hold on the land was precarious because by proviso in both the patent and the Act of Explanation his tenure was limited to the life of Patrick Sarsfield, at whose death the estate was to revert to Patrick's son, William. For his eventual loss of the estate, however, Jones was to be reprised with lands of equal value elsewhere.[24]

Sir Maurice Eustace had successfully contrived to retain possession of the old Harold family estate at Kilmashogue (703 acres) in Rathdown which his uncle, the late lord chancellor, had been granted in 1662, but the question of the validity of the patent continued to threaten Eustace's grip on the estate throughout the reign.[25] The challenge to his title rested on the dual claim that Kilmashogue was vested in the crown because John Harold never obtained a decree of innocence, and that the patent awarded to Eustace's uncle in 1662 had never been confirmed. In 1670 Eustace obtained a new patent, but due to a clerical omission a second one was ordered in 1673 which had still not been passed in 1678. Meanwhile, in 1676 Nicholas Harold obtained a hearing of his claim in the Irish privy council and several years later received an order for a patent, but only on condition that the estate was found to be forfeited and vested in the crown. The defects in Eustace's title had meanwhile attracted the attention of a variety of assiduous land speculators, including the duke of Grafton, the bishop of Kildare, and Sir William Talbot, a nephew of Richard, who was then acting as land agent for the duke of York. As late as 1684 title to the estate was still being contested.[26]

Taken together, the fifteen Protestant proprietors discussed above were granted nearly 15,000 acres in Dublin under the Restoration settlement, although the point has been made that some of them, notably Mervin, Staples, Jones, and Eustace, held their land under rather tenuous circumstances.

* * *

There were, of course, numerous grants to other Protestants for much smaller amounts of land. Samuel Hughes, for instance, was in 1668 granted 154 acres forfeited by the Finglas family. Samuel was the son of John Hughes, an attorney in the second court of claims who was murdered in 1666.[27] Richard Foster, heir of alderman Charles Foster, was granted Dardistown (43 acres) in Coolock, held in 1641 by Patrick Bermingham.[28] Anthony Piercy, the son of a trunk-maker, sheriff of Dublin city in 1689 and, as Sir Anthony, lord mayor ten years later, obtained a certificate from the second court of claims for 37 acres in Newcastle that had been forfeited by the Chilliam family.[29] Thomas Witched also obtained such a certificate for a tiny parcel of 8 acres in the same barony that John Talbot of Belgard failed to recover. Witched was a prominent barrister, later MP for Wicklow in the first Williamite parliament, father of William, chief justice of the common pleas from 1727.[30] Dr John Westly, a lawyer and auditor in the second court of claims, received a patent for 78 acres in Newcastle.[31]

These smaller grants amounted to perhaps another 1,000 acres which passed form Catholic to Protestant hands. To this must be added about another 1,000 acres restored to Protestants claiming as heirs of Catholics, names such as Brice, Holliday, Denn, and Walsh. This probably occurred more frequently than the official records would suggest, since the sources often present conflicting evidence as to the religious persuasion of some of the claimants.

* * *

Besides this approximately 17,000 acres thus transferred from Catholic to Protestant hands, the duke of York was granted 7,400 acres in the county, the bulk of which (over 4,000) was comprised of the forfeited estates of only five Catholic families: Bath, Cruise, Sherlock, Fitzsimons and Eustace.[32]

Note has already been taken of the obstacles placed in the way of Sir Luke Bath's restoration; he lost his entire estate in the county to York. Christopher Cruise, we saw, failed to submit a claim to innocence, nor is there any evidence that Patrick Sherlock or Thomas Fitzsimons, or their heirs, submitted claims. We have also seen, however, that Thomas Eustace had indeed been awarded a decree of innocence, although his father was declared nocent. For this reason York's patent for the estate contained a savings clause providing for Thomas's restoration following the deaths of his father, mother, and paternal grandmother. But it does not appear that Thomas was able to recover a great deal of his estate. York forfeited much of it under the Williamite confiscation.

Patrick Sarsfield, Philip Hore, and John Delahide, all innocents, also obtained savings clauses which reserved their rights to restoration to various denominations of land that had appeared in York's grant. But some of this land was also forfeited by York under the Williamite confiscation; it can be seen, therefore, that savings clauses were of dubious value.[33]

The remainder of York's estate in the county was composed of land held in 1641 by no less than twenty different Catholic proprietors. Many of these estates were under 200 acres and in some cases represented the sole holding of the forfeiting proprietor. As a result, such names as Freene, Mills, Malone Stoakes, and Penteny disappear as landlords in the county. No claims had been submitted for most of this land. Nicholas Freene submitted a claim but was declared nocent; James Malone was declared innocent but was described only as an 'inhabitant' of Dublin city. No acreage figures appear against his name in the records of the first court of claims, though he may have recovered property in the city.[34] There were, however, a few innocent claimants—some rather prominent—who lost small parcels of land to York, for example Sir Richard Barnewall and Lawrence Bellings, perhaps because they failed to prove title in the first court of claims or in the regular law courts.

Despite the provisions of the Acts of Settlement and Explanation, it does not appear that York's grant included a significant amount of Dublin land that had been held by the regicides during the Interregnum, although the sources will not warrant much certainty in this regard. The existing records suggest that the regicides had been granted some of the better estates in the county, many of whose owners in 1641 were prominent Old English Catholics who were restored at the Restoration. In the event, York's final settlement in Dublin seems to have consisted largely of the forfeited lands allotted to him in reprisal for the loss or regicides' estates now restored to innocents. At any rate, although he was granted 7,400 acres in the county there is ample evidence that his effective possession never extended much more than about 6,000.

* * *

The church was restored to over 12,000 acres in Dublin, about half of it archepiscopal land.[35] This amounted to over 3,000 acres above what it held in 1641. The increase represented mainly alienated church land to which Archbishop Michael Boyle succeeded in establishing title in the second court of claims. Other church bodies were also successful on a more modest scale. The cathedral and chapter of Christ Church, for example, was able to prove title to several hundred acres as a result of the vigorous advocacy of Dr William Lightburne, the proctor, who acted as agent for the cathedral.[36]

* * *

Ormond's scheme for the creation of a royal park near the city, which might also serve as a site for a vice-regal residence, was meanwhile being realized. The nucleus of the park was found in certain crown lands which had once formed a portion of the demesne of the priory of the Knights Hospitallers in Newcastle and which, prior to the Henrician dissolution, consisted of the entire parish of Kilmainham on both sides of the Liffey river.[37] In the half-century following the dissolution much of the land of the priory was sold or leased, so that by about 1610, with the sale of 400 acres north of the river, almost all of the parish had been alienated from the crown. This portion, however, was repurchased by the crown in 1618 from Sir Edward Fisher and the house which he had meanwhile built on the site, the Phoenix House, became the viceregal summer residence, and the land surrounding it the germ of the new park.[38]

Once the decision had been taken to proceed with the creation of the park the king directed Ormond, in late 1662, to ratify the purchase from Sir Maurice Eustace, which had already been negotiated, of some 400 acres near the Phoenix demsne, and forming a part of the manor of Chapelizod to the west of Kilmainham.[39] At about the same time negotiations were completed for the purchase of Newtown (about 100 acres), north of the Phoenix lands in Kilmainham. The proprietor was Christopher Fagan, recently restored as an innocent. But Fagan had leased the land, for sixty-one years, to Daniel Hutchinson, a Dublin merchant and alderman. In April 1663 Fagan and Hutchinson agreed to sell to the crown, the appraised price of £3,000 to be paid to Hutchinson for the lease.[40] There is no record of anything being paid to Fagan; he may perhaps have obtained a portion of the price from Hutchinson by private agreement, or there may have been an understanding with the crown prior to the awarding of Fagan's decree of innocence.

At this point the park took the size (about 1,000 acres) originally contemplated. This was soon found to be insufficient, however, for what was now conceived as a deer park, so in May 1663 another royal letter authorized Ormond to purchase from Eustace the entire manor of Chapelizod 'and several other lands which be most convenient to enclose for a park', the purchase price being fixed at a maximum of £10,000.[41] Acting on these instructions, smaller parcels of land were acquired from a variety of proprietors in Kilmainham, Castleknock, and Grangegorman parishes.

It was now evident, however, that the park was proving far more costly than originally anticipated, Chapelizod alone having absorbed the entire £10,000. In May 1665, therefore, the king authorized a further outlay of money, not to exceed another £10,000.[42] Over the next few years there were several more acquisitions, including a small parcel of 21 acres purchased form Philip Hore for some £1,000.[43] But the most sizable block (150 acres), was in Ashtown, situated on the northern fringe of the park, purchased by the crown in 1667 from John Connell, whose estate had not been sequestered during the Commonwealth.[44] As a result of these purchases, by 1669 the park extended to over 1,200 acres on both sides of the Liffey and had cost the crown over £31,000. But even this considerable sum did not prove to be sufficient; the total cost rose eventually to over £40,000, much of it expended on a stone wall around the park on both sides of the river.[45]

Another reason for the escalation of the cost of the park was the interest charges accruing to proprietors not fully compensated for their land at the time of the original sales. Up to the end of the reign, and beyond, these charges were still accumulating. At the time of the sale of Chapelizod in 1664, for example, only half (£5,000) of the purchase price was paid to Lord Chancellor Eustace. Despite provision in the Act of Explanation for payment of the balance,[46] Eustace's heir had still not been paid by 1670, when he was claiming £7,750 as principal and interest, a claim which the lord lieutenant, Berkeley, regarded as unreasonable because Eustace had purchased the estate shortly before the Restoration for only £4,000. Eustace's heir had still not been paid the balance in 1693, when the principal and interest had risen to £8,653.[47]

In 1670 Daniel Hutchinson complained that although he had obtained a warrant for payment of £3,000 for Newtown, he had received nothing. Moreover, although the land had not been officially conveyed to the crown, he was being kept out of possession and was unable to collect the profits from the estate. The interest due to Hutchinson on the purchase price, with the uncollected profits, amounted, on 25 March, to £1,950, of which he had received only £800. He was due £1,150.

A report on Hutchinson's case was heard in the English privy council in November, by which time the principal and interest had reached £4,300. At this point Hutchinson agreed to abate £500 of the interest in return for an immediate payment of part of the principal. Orders were then issued for an immediate payment of £900, leaving a balance of £2,910 (the £10 represented the interest on the balance), the balance itself to be paid in three equal instalments between 24 December 1670 and 24 December 1671. Upon any failure to meet these payments Hutchinson was to be paid 10 per cent interest on the unpaid balance. In fact he was never fully paid. He died about 1684 and the following year a warrant was issued to his executor for payment of the balance of the debt, which had now risen to over £3,000.[48]

The size of the park as it emerged about 1670 remained unchanged until 1679, when several hundred acres to the south of the Liffey river were assigned for the use of the new Royal Hospital, thus alienating this land form the body of the park.[49] Meanwhile, various smaller portions of land had been cut off from the park as a result of the straightening of the stone wall, so that by 1688 its size had been reduced to just over 1,000 acres, all north of the river. Thus the Phoenix Park assumed the shape it has substantially retained to the present day.[50]

CHAPTER VIII

The Settlement under Attack

I

While the second court of claims was in the process of carrying the land settlement to a conclusion, the dispossessed Catholic landlords of Ireland were turning to other methods in an attempt to recover their lost estates. It was not, however, a propitious time for such endeavours. The interest of the crown was focused on other, more pressing matters. The plague of 1665, followed by the Great Fire of London the following year, together with the second Dutch war of 1665–7, drew much of the government's attention.[1]

However, great political undercurrents, soon to affect Ireland, were at work in England. Clarendon, who had been steadily losing his influence at court, and who had been blamed for a series of misfortunes connected with the war, was finally driven from office in 1667 and impeached in the Commons by a combination of his enemies. Ormond's position in Ireland, which rested to a significant decree on Clarendon's power at court, was immediately threatened because the new administration, the Cabal, was as hostile to him as it had been to Clarendon. Buckingham, it appears, wanted the viceroyalty of Ireland for himself, or so Ormond was told.[2] Lady Castlemain, the king's mistress, also harboured a personal grievance against Ormond, who had earlier blocked an attempt to grant her the newly-formed Phoenix Park.

The attempt to bring down Ormond began in the autumn of 1667, shortly after Clarendon's removal from office, when a petition was read in the Commons concerning 'some wrongs and injuries done to . . .[the petitioners] touching lands in Ireland'.[3] In fact, the petition was the opening move in the attempt to prove a case of fraud against Ormond in his Irish land transactions, thus providing a telling charge in any future impeachment proceedings. The intention, Sir Alan Broderick told Ormond, was 'to unravel as much of the settlement as is possible. My Lady Ranelagh is still said to have many designs and indeed all the sectaries grow to a high degree of confidence and promise themselves an interest in government very speedily'.[4]

Orrery too was anxious to see Ormond brought down; there had long been a lingering antipathy between them. Sir John Nicholas, clerk of the privy council and son of the former secretary of state, reported to his father in 1668 that he had spent an entire day hearing a complaint against the commissioners of the court of claims, especially Rainsford, Beverley, and Broderick, who were accused of 'favouring the popish Irish too much'. The petition was submitted by the agents of the adventurers, but a 'second part' of it, Nicholas said, was designed as an attempt at 'setting aside the . . . Act of Explanation. It's believed this business is chiefly levelled at . . . Ormond, in order to the impeaching of him, and that it's principally promoted by . . . Orrery.'[5]

The intrigues of his enemies finally bore fruit and in February 1669 Ormond was removed and replaced by Lord Robartes. But Robartes remained in office less than a year and was in turn replaced by Lord Berkeley of Stratton, a nephew of the first Viscount Fitzharding. The Catholics of Ireland had some reason to expect a modicum of support from Berkeley. The Talbots had known him since the time of the Stuart exile, when he had been a prominent figure in the duke of York's household, and they believed that some significant alteration in the land settlement might be forthcoming. In the event Berkeley did not prove as useful an instrument in their plans as the Talbots had hoped. Nevertheless, by 1670 the time seemed ripe to revive Catholic claims, and it was therefore decided to make a direct appeal to the king. To this end, in November, a petition signed by fifty-two members of the Catholic nobility and gentry, at least fifteen of whom were Dublin landlords, was drawn up. Richard Talbot was empowered, as accredited agent of the signatories, to carry the petition to England.[6]

Talbot arrived in December and on 18 January the petition was read in the privy council. It described the 'ruination' of the petitioners, dispossessed for their loyalty to the crown. They had suffered great trials at home and abroad in the royalist cause, but 'for want of a full and just representation of their case', their estates, despite the declared intentions of the king, were possessed by others. They asked for an impartial tribunal to hear their grievances and, meanwhile, that all grants of undisposed land be stopped. Following its reading a committee of thirteen, including Ormond and Buckingham, was appointed to consider the petition and report to the king. Talbot was ordered to attend the meeting to identify his clients and to offer proposals for their relief.[7] Several days later, acting on Talbot's petition, the council made an interim order halting all grants of undisposed land in Ireland.[8]

On 21 January the committee heard Talbot plead for a hearing of his proposals as a means of affording relief for the Catholic proprietors. Ormond, alarmed at the prospect of the uprooting of the entire settlement, immediately opposed further consideration of the petition , arguing that it was better to maintain the settlement, despite its imperfections, than start the work all over again. But a majority opposed him and Talbot was permitted to plead the petitioners' cause.[9]

Their 'case', subsumed under twenty-three headings, was introduced with a distinctly Catholic interpretation of events between 1649 and 1660, in which the constant fidelity of the Irish Catholics to the Stuart crown was stressed. Talbot then pointed to their virtual exclusion from the Irish parliament of 1661, which, he asserted, should at any rate have been dissolved in December upon the death of the earl of Mountrath, one of the lords justices.

Talbot next complained about two important provisions in the Act of Settlement which effectively blocked the restoration of many Catholics, viz., that which prohibited the restoration of those who had lived in Irish quarters during the rebellion, and that which barred them from being restored to property in corporations. Talbot's next grievance concerned the shortness of time allotted to the hearing of claims to innocence. Here he committed a curious error, stating that the commissioners of the first court of claims conducted their hearings between February and July 1663. The Act of Explanation was denounced largely on the general grounds that it barred the future adjudication of innocence or the benefit of the articles of the peace of 1646 and of 1649.

Talbot then proceeded to complain of the distribution of Irish land to the adventurers and soldiers; the adventurers because the money subscribed by them had been employed against the crown, and, moreover, that they had obtained extra land as a result of the enactment of the doubling ordinances of 1643 and 1647; the soldiers because the land was allotted to them as a reward for services to the parliament. Talbot drew attention to the fact that the '49 officers had been satisfied for their services while serving the royalist cause under Ormond, yet the petitioners had lost their land for performing the same service. Many of the Cromwellian grantees, he said, had no justifiable claim to arrears at all; they had obtained Irish land as 'free gifts' and could 'pretend no equitable interest whatsoever within the rules of the Declaration . . . [of 30 November 1660]'.

The Catholic cause, said Talbot, had never been allowed a full and just hearing, and he touched on the fundamental reason for the petitioners' distress; that the settlement had been undertaken not by disinterested parties, but by the very people who had a personal interest in maintaining the Cromwellian settlement, which proceeded, he added, 'from those who are both judges and parties . . . [to it]'. Talbot concluded by urging the king to provide speedy relief for the petitioners and that an act of indemnity be passed covering all his Irish subjects. Appended to the plea was a '6th paper' which cited some imperfections and legal inconsistencies in the Acts of Settlement and Explanation, together with examples of individual cases in which these imperfections and inconsistencies had affected several of Talbot's clients.[10]

Following the presentation of Talbot's case all the documents connected with it were referred to the English solicitor-general, Sir Heneage Finch, who was instructed to present his opinion on the case. Finch, who had played an important role in the evolution of the entire Irish settlement, made his report on 1 February. He had been ordered to 'give an account of the two acts', a task which, understandably, he found rather daunting. 'In general,' he began, 'I may truly say that these acts were the performance of his majesty's declarations and promises at Breda, made to his Protestant subjects of Ireland, who were earlier in their public addresses to him than his subjects of

England were.' Finch then dealt briefly with the main points raised in the petition. He dismissed the claim that the Catholic cause had never been given a full and just hearing; 'They had many and many an audience, large and small', he said. He then questioned Talbot's authority to act as agent for the petitioners, referring to it as a style the king had 'never yet gave leave to any man to assume'. Finch made the telling point that some of the petitioners had already been fully restored to their estates, and mentioned by name Lords Barnewall and Dongan, Robert Nettervill and Mathew Plunket. Others, he said, had been partially restored, naming the earl of Westmeath, Lords Nettervill and Trimleston, Theobold Dillon and Sir Nicholas Plunket. Some, he added, never held an Irish estate.

When he turned to the 'case' of the petitioners, Finch began by heaping scorn on Talbot's claim that the Catholics of Ireland had remained consistently loyal to the crown throughout the rebellion. There was not a word in the petition, he said, which acknowledged that there had been an Irish rebellion, 'as if all Irishmen had been very dutiful subjects, and not a man among them had deserved to lose his estate'.

He was less convincing when he attempted to justify the Catholics' exclusion from the 1661 parliament. It was not true, he said, that no Catholics had been elected or admitted to vote in the elections. Many of the 'Irish' who had freeholds were admitted to vote, 'such as were all the men in Connacht'. No Catholic peers were excluded, he said, except those outlawed for rebellion; he failed to add that virtually all the Catholic lords had in fact been outlawed. As to the claim that Mountrath's death ought to have led to the dissolution of the Irish parliament, Finch referred to a ruling of the English judges that the parliament was 'still in being' notwithstanding Mountrath's death.

Concerning Talbot's objections about the barring of Catholics from corporations, Finch replied that the rule was not universal; the king had the power to allow individual exceptions. It was true that this power had been revoked in the Act of Explanation, but many Catholics had by that time been allowed back into the corporations.

Finch admitted that Talbot's next complaint—that to have lived on an estate in Irish quarters during the rebellion was enough to bar restoration—carried some merit. It seemed harsh, he said, but it was regarded as necessary because the rebellion had occurred twenty years before the passing of the Act of Settlement. The Catholics had murdered or driven out all of the Protestants and it was impossible to find witnesses to these events. It seemed reasonable to assume that no man could have lived quietly among the rebels without having complied with them; it was therefore taken as an act of delinquency. Anyhow, the rule was so moderated in the execution of the Act of Settlement that there was 'hardly one example to be showed in all Ireland where the commissioners condemned any man by that rule alone'.

When Finch referred to Talbot's complaint about the shortness of time in the hearing of claims to innocence, he pointed out that the commissioners sat for this purpose between January and August 1663, not, as Talbot maintained, between February and July. Finch then said that about 5,000 claims (not 8,000 as Talbot claimed) had been submitted to the first court of claims, but that many had been submitted several times and 'many were for estates in Connaught and many were only to have benefit of articles . . . [of the peace of 1646 and 1649]; so that a great part of the claims put in were far from being claims of innocence'. Lacking the full record of all the claims submitted to the court, it is not possible to gauge the accuracy of this response. However, in view of the fact that most of the claims heard by the commissioners were claims to innocence, Finch's statement must be regarded with caution.

His explanation as to why a majority of claimants were adjudged innocent was because, he said, 'none were heard but those who desired it, and they only desired it who had reason to be confident of success'. No man could justly complain of not being heard, he said, adding that there were several occasions when the commissioners wanted cases and were unable to persuade claimants to submit them.

Finch defended the Act of Explanation on the general grounds that the Catholics—after prolonged negotiations in which 'every paragraph was debated'—had consented to it. He asserted also that the Catholic agents opposed the resumption of hearings to claims of innocence because, first, the 'principal men amongst them, the nominees, could not hope to escape as innocents', and therefore never attempted to claim as such, replying instead on provisions for them in the Act of Settlement; and, second, because the 'principal men' did not want to see a new batch of 'obscure freeholders' being adjudged innocent, which would absorb the stock of reprisal land created by the one-third retrenchment, from which the nominees were to be satisfied. The Protestants, Finch continued, only wanted to end the clamour and be secure in their two-thirds. Thus, from a sense of mutual interest, an agreement had been reached in which 'an end was put to all further considerations, either of articles or innocence, yet now the Catholics exclaim against it'.

He evaded the issue when replying to Talbot's complaint that the adventurers and soldiers had been rewarded for their service to parliament; their settlement was not, he said, the effect of the Act of Explanation but derived from the Act of Settlement as it evolved from the Declaration of 30 November 1660. The Act of Explanation did not 'enlarge' that settlement but reduced it by a third. Finch employed the same argument in relation to the '49 officers, adding that the value of their security was far less than Talbot claimed. As to those 'new grantees' who had no claim to any kind of arrears under the Cromwellian settlement, Finch answered that in these cases the sole judge of their merit was the king.

To Talbot's charge that many of the adventurers were allotted land based on the doubling ordinances of 1643 and 1647, Finch responded by pointing out that the Act of Settlement had stipulated that no adventurer was to be satisfied except in proportion to the money he had actually subscribed, which in any case had been retrenched by a third.

The petitioners complained 'that soldiers have been satisfied who were not of the usurper's army at the time of his majesty's restoration; and some soldiers have been confirmed in gifts made to them by the usurpers'. But this was not true, he said, since no soldier was confirmed in his holdings who was not in actual possession on 7 May 1659. The force of Finch's logic falters when he remarked that it was a mistake to say, with the petitioners, that the soldiers were confirmed in the gifts made by the usurpers, 'for none are so unless those gifts were afterwards confirmed by his majesty, and in the said acts'.

Finch returned to the question of the time allowed to the Catholics in the negotiations on the Act of Explanation. The Catholics, he said, 'were so far from not being heard that they seemed to be fully satisfied with the passing of the act'. But even if the act had not fully satisfied their expectations, it was not because of the care exercized by the commissioners in the executation of it, 'for they do not offer anything in all their papers against them'.[11]

Finch summarized what he interpreted as the four aims of the petitioners: the alteration of the Acts of Settlement and Explanation; failing this, to alter particular clauses in the two acts; to have all undisposed land granted to them; and to have enacted an act of indemnity covering all Irish subjects.

As to the first aim, he acknowledged that the settlement was not without its inequalities, but the country had benefited generally. Ireland was 'improved and planted'; the Protestant religion established and the corporate towns secured in their hands; royal revenue had increased, as had trade; the land 'knew its owners'; money was in circulation.

Altering particular grants, Finch said, would have to be done piecemeal, with separate acts of parliament in each case; and where would this end? The granting of undisposed land to Catholics would also require an act of parliament because such lands were vested in the king. But he did not object strenuously to this proposal; the amount of undisposed land was small and if the king was inclined to grant it by right of prerogative, nobody would complain. He also had no serious objection to an act of indemnity covering all the king's Irish subjects, provided it did not lead to the general restoration of the Catholics or to an 'examination' of the entire settlement.[12]

During the course of the report Finch was obliged to respond to two cases cited by Talbot to illustrate the claim that various provisions in the Declaration of 30 November 1660 and the Act of Settlement had been voided by the Act of Explanation. One was the case of Philip Hore of Kilsallaghan, whose sons, daughters, and grandchildren had been declared innocent and were ordered restored by the provisions of the Act of Settlement, yet under the Act of Explanation Sir George Lane was granted part of Hore's estate and the decrees of innocence awarded to the Hore's rendered null and void 'as if there were no such decrees'.

Finch reviewed the whole history of the case, bringing it down to the time in June 1665 when Hore and Lane came to a private agreement by which the estate was to be divided between them. At this point Finch was interrupted by

Richard Talbot, who denied the existence of such an agreement or his involvement with it. Talbot's interruption prompted Finch to reply: 'Have a little patience Mr. Talbot, you yourself shall prove it'. Whereupon Lane was called in, produced a copy of the agreement with Talbot's signature affixed to it, and, according to an account (written many years later), 'baffled the petitioners in that matter, and having proved an agreement with Mr. Hore . . . [the] affair was cleared to the satisfaction of the king, and the committee, much contrary to the expectation of the petitioners'.[13] It is difficult to understand, given Talbot's role in drawing up the agreement, why he chose to cite the case at all.

Talbot's second case concerned the letters patent confirmed in the Act of Settlement to Patrick Sarsfield of Lucan, which, he said, were voided by a clause in the Act for the Enlargement of Time in the execution of the Act of Settlement in favour of Sir Theophilus Jones.[14] Finch's reply to this case was empirical; Jones had held the Sarsfield estate for a long time, had expended much money on improvements, yet had obtained nothing except possession during the life of Patrick Sarsfield.[15]

Finch concluded his report by advising the king to maintain the existing settlement and warning him that there were, in both England and Ireland, too many 'discontended spirits; many who still retain their old venom who remember when the government was once in their hands, and would be glad by any kind of approaches to return to it again. Nothing can so much gratify their malace', he said, 'as the countenance of such a petition'.

Several days later, when the debate had resumed, the legal foundation of the entire Irish settlement was called into question. It was objected that by the Adventurers' Act of 1642, and those acts dealing with Irish land which immediately followed, all grants of land in Ireland not confirmed by parliament were voided. The Irish settlement had never been confirmed by an English parliament.

Finch replied that under the Adventurers' Act no adventurer had legal title to a foot of land in Ireland. There should have been a declaration from parliament that Ireland was subdued before the settlement was undertaken. When Charles II was restored in 1660 it was decided that the settlement would be passed in an Irish parliament because no one doubted that 'an act of parliament in Ireland did bind Ireland'. The process of settling Ireland by an Irish act was chosen as the 'safer way'. It would be futile to attempt to alter the Irish settlement by an English act, Finch continued, because the consequences of this would be that Ireland would be 'always settling and never settled', since an English act 'do in truth bind Ireland . . . yet . . . binds Ireland no longer than till it be repealed in Ireland, so that all settlements in England will be unsettled by the next parliament in Ireland'. Finch regarded it as logically absurd to suppose that a parliament endued with legislative power could be disabled from acting legislatively. The Irish parliament, he said, had as much power to repeal the affect of any law in Ireland as the English parliament had in England. When asked to justify this opinion Finch used the argument from authority: 'I would justify it to be my opinion, and I did conceive it to be law', he replied. It was then objected that Ireland was a conquered country, in which case its parliament had no rights. This was true, Finch replied, but it was conquered by the king and not by parliament. The king, Finch said, was predictably 'very well pleased by this opinion', adding that he did 'know not whether it be good law', but was 'sure it is very good reason'.

Finch's assertion of (albeit limited) Irish parliamentary independence post-dates similar assertions made earlier in the century by, among others, the Catholic lawyer Patrick Darcy (in 1641) and by Sir William Domville (in 1660), but anticipates by eighteen years the more celebrated repudiation of the English parliamentary claim to legislate for Ireland in *The case of Ireland's being bound by acts of parliament in England, stated* (1698) by Domville's son-in-law William Molyneux, who drew heavily upon Domville's work.[16]

Despite the thrust of Finch's report, a majority of the committee remained committed to the petitioners' objectives, chiefly as a means of bringing Ormond down. But it now became necessary to circumvent the effect of the report by changing the procedure of the investigation. As a result, a committee of inquiry, superseding the previous one, was appointed by the king on 4 February 1671, one of whose members was Buckingham, but from which Ormond was conspicuously excluded. This committee was instructed to examine the documents connected with the Irish settlement 'from first to last', to compile a new report and an abstract of the whole settlement. But when they reported to the king on 13 June they found that the task had proved impossible to fulfil, largely because they lacked adequate data and sufficient legal authority to complete their mission. They recommended that a new committee, invested with such authority, be established. Accordingly, on August 1, the existing committee of inquiry, with the addition of Prince Rupert and Sir Thomas Chicheley, received a new commission with adequate legal powers to carry out its functions.[17] But the principal design of the investigation—the impeachment of Ormond—failed when charges against him, finally dismissed in 1673, involving illegal land transactions in Ireland, remained unsubstantiated. Richard Talbot, meanwhile, fearing involvement in some questionable legal activities surrounding the charges against Ormond, departed for Ireland. 'Rupert's committee' of inquiry continued its work temporarily, but there was now no hope of realizing its objectives.[18]

The Catholic cause was in jeopardy, however, for more trenchant reasons than the collapse of the case against Ormond. Anti-Catholic sentiment, relatively dormant for several years, was on the rise again in England, caused in part by the leniency being shown to Catholics at court. In Ireland, meanwhile, Berkeley had been replaced as lord lieutenant by the earl of Essex in August 1672. Under both men various long standing rules against the Catholics were relaxed; they were admitted to corporations and several were appointed justices of the peace.[19]

The measures connected with the inquiries into the land settlement, together with the relaxation of some of the anti-Catholic rules, provoked a strong Protestant reaction. Their fears soon became manifest in the English House of Commons, now grown increasingly critical of the pro-Catholic policies of the court. In March 1673 the Commons demanded, in a petition to the king, that the Acts of Settlement and Explanation be maintained, that Rupert's commission of inquiry be recalled, that no Catholic be admitted or continued in office in Ireland, military or civil, and that Richard Talbot be banished from Court.[20] In response, Charles temporized but finally bowed to the storm. In April he issued a proclamation which declared his intention to maintain the Irish settlement and, in July, dissolved Rupert's commission and returned all consideration of Irish affairs to the Irish committee within the privy council, which should, however, only establish the best means of disposing of such forfeited land in Ireland as could be discovered to be still vested in the crown.[21]

The following month Essex was informed by Shaftesbury that the king was still resolved to have 'a perfect account' of the lands in Ireland still vested in him. However, since the late commission of inquiry had 'given occasion of some umbrage to the parliament', Charles, Essex was told, had accepted a scheme advanced by Dr Robert Gorges, the duke of York's principal land agent in the second court of claims, in which it was proposed to undertake an inquiry into the land settlement in secret. Shaftesbury was assured by Gorges, who had been a sub-commissioner on Rupert's commission of inquiry, that in two months the whole province of Leinster could be 'perfected' with 'that secrecy that nobody should be alarmed'. The king was 'extremely pleased' with the plan, Shaftsbury added, but he instructed Essex to correspond only with him (Shaftsbury) when dealing with the matter.[22]

II

After the recall of Rupert's commission of inquiry in 1673, prospects for the restoration of Catholics who were still dispossessed of their estates became bleak indeed. Generally, only those who were to be restored in remainder, or by special provision in the Acts of Settlement or Explanation, could now hope to recover their land.

A useful case in point was the patent which gave Sir Theophilus Jones possession of the Sarsfield estate for the life of Patrick Sarsfield. In the event Patrick did not die until 1690, but a new twist in the case occurred in 1670 when William Sarsfield, Patrick's eldest son, 'privately stole away' and married Mary, the daughter of Charles II and Lucy Walter, and 'the sister of the duke of Monmouth, then fifteen years of age, without the consent . . . of her guardian', presumably her adoptive father, the earl of Carlingford.[23] As a result, Monmouth's influence was exerted on the king and an agreement was reached in 1674 whereby Jones's interest in the estate was purchased by the crown, in return for which Jones obtained a grant of £800 a year in concealed land which he could discover elsewhere. A similar amount was settled as a jointure on William's wife.

William died in 1675 and by his will the estate was left first to his son Charles and, failing him, to his younger brother Patrick, later earl of Lucan. The case became more complicated when William's widow, who had married an English civil servant named Fanshawe, attempted to prove the will a forgery, but the attempt had made little progress by 1688.[24] It is not certain when the entire estate in Dublin was back in the hands of the Sarsfields. There is a reference to Patrick the elder holding possession of 'the great house' from 1675, but the records are conflicting and another source suggests that Jones was still in possession of Lucan in 1678. There were complaints as late as 1684 that Jones was still detaining parts of the estate even though he had been fully reprised for his surrender of it. Jones appears to have surrendered the estate piecemeal fashion, giving up each time the equivalent he discovered in concealed land elsewhere. When Charles Sarsfield died in 1683 his uncle Patrick proved the will in the prerogative court. Jones died in 1685 and it can therefore probably be assumed that the Sarsfields were in full possession by that year.[25]

The granting to Jones of the right of discovery of concealed land can conveniently be cited as an example of one of the principal factors which continued to play a disruptive influence on the Irish land settlement after the rising of the second court of claims. We have seen how the king was determined, even after the recall of Rupert's commission of inquiry, to continue the investigation into the discovery of land still vested in the crown. The potential financial rewards were such that Charles was even willing to undertake this project in secret to avoid parliamentary 'umbrage'.

If the recall of Rupert's commission and the king's announced intention of maintaining the Acts of Settlement and Explanation had a calming affect on the Protestants, Charles's policy of granting individual commissions of inquiry for the discovery of crown land had the opposite effect, especially on the Catholics, who were the main victims of the procedure. Once such a commission was obtained, and crown title proved, the discoverer would then petition for a grant of the land in question. In some cases it was only necessary to establish a doubt of the validity of a title, following which a *custodiam* grant might be issued pending a final judgment. Restoration Ireland obviously offered a rich potential in this field, and numerous courtiers were engaged in it. On the day the second court of claims rose for good Robert Leigh expressed the opinion that there were still 'many concealed lands . . . in the king's power to dispose of by patents'. In 1675 he was still searching assiduously for such land for his English clients.[26]

Sir William Petty, who had a vested interest in protecting the vast estate he had acquired during the Interregnum, referred to the right of discovery as a 'principal trade in Ireland', and a 'calamity upon the nation,' and Essex, from the start of his viceroyalty, protested about the deleterious effects the practice was having on the country. In 1673 he complained that people were obtaining royal letters to pass land patents by pretending to have discovered crown title. Once the letter arrived in Ireland, he said, the plea was: 'let me have the benefit of my letter, and if it prove that his majesty has no title, the king has given nothing, and there is no hurt done'. But, Essex continued, this was not always the result:[27]

> the possessors of these lands, who, if poor, and not able to contest, have been necessitated to compound; nay, there are some cases . . . wherein patents have been granted for lands to which the king had no right at all; but yet the persons who had these grants being great men, and those whose lands were passed being mean, and not able to wage law with them, have been forced after many vexatious suits to submit, and part with their lands for 2 years' purchase. This having been the case of many men here. . . .

The following year, after several more had arrived, Essex again expressed his objection to these grants. He had been told by Shaftesbury, he said, that the king wanted an inspection of the distribution of Irish land. He had been careful to select people with 'great secrecy about the work', adding, however, that he regarded Dr Robert Gorges as 'no very extraordinary person'. The king's purpose was, he presumed, to discover concealed land that might form a common stock to be used for the aims of the Acts of Settlement and Explanation, and for providing additional revenue for the crown. But now, with the search for concealed land well advanced, and with no one 'in the least suspect what is doing', he had received several letters for grants of right of discovery, and he understood that more were being prepared. These letters, he said, were 'utterly incompatible with the other design'. The truth, he concluded, was that[28]

> the lands of Ireland have been a mere scramble, and the least done by way of orderly distribution of them as perhaps has ever been known, which makes men so unsettled in their estates and so unquiet in their possessions. And this has been a ground for projectors to work upon, which, considering Ireland as a plantation (for in reality it is little other), cannot but be so great a discouragement to all people from coming here, and . . . laying out money on improvements . . . I . . . wish that . . . there were an end to these discoveries, for better were it for the crown to be cheated of its right to diverse parcels of lands, than by perpetual inquisitions so to harass men's estates.

Petitions for right of discovery, however, continued to be submitted to the end of the reign. In 1682 a Robert Sanders petitioned for right of discovery to several thousand acres in Ireland, including over 1,600 in Dublin. He proposed to find royal title to Ballyscorning in Newcastle, restored to John Talbot of

Belgard; to 90 acres in Uppercross; and to Kilmashogue in Rathdown, then in the tenuous possession of Sir Maurice Eustace.[29]

Essex, while protesting about the ill effects these grants were having on the stability of the land settlement, may himself have contributed to the problem. In his attempt to dissuade the king from granting the Phoenix Park to the duchess of Cleveland he searched about for other lands in the country which could be used as a substitute for the duchess. 'I have already found above 39,000 acres', he said in 1673, 'which are in his majesty's dispose.'[30]

Essex may have had in mind, among others, Lord Dillon of Costello-Gallen, who died in 1673 leaving no sons. After his death Essex found many people 'offering at discoveries of several lands which he possessed, and did not of right belong to him. . . . I am confident, a great deal that he enjoyed, which by his decree [of innocence] he ought not to have. . . .' Essex asserted that some proprietors who now feared an inquiry had 'sheltered themselves' under Dillon's name to protect their estates. They were now 'labouring to get some other great men to patronize their estates, and will themselves become discoverers'. Dillon's estate, he added, was one of the 'greatest covers of concealed lands in the kingdom'.[31]

In 1678 the disquiet which many proprietors still felt about the safety of their land titles led Ormond, then starting his second viceroyalty, to propose a bill for the general and final settlement and security of Irish estates. The scheme would have empowered the king, by act of parliament, to issue a commission for securing defective land titles on the payment of fines to the crown. However, various interested parties—the '49 officers, the nominees, the duke of York—protested that their claims for full satisfaction would be forever frustrated if such a commission were established. The plan was therefore temporarily set aside. In 1684, however, the king was persuaded, mainly because of the money the crown would realize, to issue the commission without the sanction of parliament. The commission would have the power to bar the unsatisfied claims of the deficient soldiers, adventurers, and the nominees. An account of the nature and purpose of the commission, with a statement of the legal basis for its powers, was published the same year:[32]

> For many years after the closing of the court of claims, those who had favour in court got commissions of inquiry to look after concealed lands, and in the execution of such commissions there was much vexation and harassing to the subject; however, this rule was still observed, that they who found out such concealed lands thought they were due unto the ends of the acts [of Settlement and Explanation], for the acts had promised satisfaction to all . . . And therefore these favourite grantees bought up unsatisfied debentures . . . and so entered as it were regularly by satisfying so much of the public debt. But of late it had been held for law that all the periods of those acts were expired, and consequently that all concealed or forfeited land to be found was no longer in his majesty as a royal

> trustee to the uses of the acts, but in his own right, and therefore he has lately issued a commission (styled the Commission of Grace) to free the subject from such former vexatious inquiries, and to encourage those possessed under a doubtful title to purchase a confirmation at a moderate fine. . . . It were to be wished that a considerable part of such money were distributed to those Irish families as have been notoriously disappointed of the good intended them by the acts. . . .

This commission, dated 14 March 1684, explains that the possessors of certain undisposed lands, to which the king was entitled, were being disturbed 'on pretence that their titles are defective, and by discoveries that have endeavoured to be made thereof, and of commissions of inquiry that have been issued. . . .'[33] Instructions for the commissioners were issued in May, under which all lands in Ireland were to be classified under three headings, viz., those which had been held by the same proprietor since 23 October 1641, or who claimed from a proprietor who had been in possession on that date; second, the lands which were held under the terms of the Acts of Settlement and Explanation, or by letters patent from the king since the Restoration; finally, those lands being held without title.[34]

The death of Charles II in February 1685 put a legal end to the Commission of Grace. In April James was persuaded, reluctantly, to renew the commission, but it was designed to apply only to claimants who had applied for new patents under the first commission and had already lodged the money required. This commission expired after the letters patent had been issued. The second earl of Clarendon, who replaced Ormond in August 1685, urged that another commission, 'in the same manner as the last', be established:

> The truth is, one cannot discourse with any man of fortune, of either old or new interest, upon the affairs of this country, but they run into complaints of the unsettledness of things. . . . [If] the commission of grace were on foot again, that would settle us, and make our minds easy; would increase the king's revenue, and raise a considerable sum of money with which his majesty might gratify such hard cases among the old proprietors, as he shall think fit.

The following year, however, Clarendon had come to the belated conclusion that the centre of Irish political influence rested with Richard Talbot, now earl of Tyrconnell, and that it was not his objective to have the commission renewed, since, as it now appeared, his ultimate aim was not to have the existing settlement confirmed,

> but on the contrary quite shaken; that is, that all provisoes in the acts of settlement and explanation, whereby estates are settled upon any persons not directly pursuant to the king's Declaration [of 30 November 1660] . . .

> shall be liable to a new inquisition: that all lands by the acts of settlement were vested in the late king, as a royal trustee, and that therefore all subsequent grants made by his majesty, not in pursuance of the acts, must be made void. . . .

Two weeks later Clarendon announced that he had changed his opinion and was now opposed to a Commission of Grace, 'because my Lord Tyrconnell, and the Irish Catholics of the king's council . . . will oppose and obstruct it; which will render a commission ineffectual, and make it bring in very little'.[35]

The author of an anonymous pamphlet, published in 1689, declared that the Commission of Grace was finally perceived by the Protestants to be a 'snare', and that it was 'designed to make a narrow inspection into all men's title, and thereby to discover what advantage might be derived from it'. The commission was established, says the author, to 'prepare pretences of the Irish', and the assertion is made that the king's mistress, the duchess of Portsmouth, was active in promoting the commission because she received a proportion of the money obtained from the fines for the new letters patent.[36]

The disillusioned Clarendon was replaced by Tyrconnell, as lord deputy, in February 1687. Tyrconnell's appointment, while greeted with enthusiasm by the Catholics, had the opposite affect on a Protestant community already disturbed by the changes made the previous year by Tyrconnell, who had been sent to Ireland as lieutenant-general with powers independent of Clarendon, whereby many important posts in the army, the judiciary, and the administration, were transferred from Protestant to Catholic hands. It was now generally believed, despite assurances from the king to the contrary, that the land settlement was about to be altered. Shortly before his recall Clarendon remarked that he had no reason to believe that the king's mind had changed, 'for in almost every letter I have had . . . from him, he has declared the acts of settlement must not be touched, and that he will support the English interest; and yet certainly all proceedings look as if his majesty's mind were altered, and as if he intended a total alteration'.[37]

The fears of the Protestants tended to be corroborated by the activities of Catholics such as Bartholomew Russell of Seatown. Russell had been awarded a decree of innocence in 1663, but had been left to the regular law courts to recover his estate after his father's death. His Dublin estate (over 500 acres) was meanwhile in the possession of the see of Dublin, the archbishop, Michael Boyle, having obtained a *custodiam* grant. Bartholomew's father died in 1682, but Bartholomew delayed submitting a claim to the regular law courts until 1688, 'when the . . . earl of Tyrconnell was chief governor, and Popish judges sat upon the benches who gave judgment in his favour . . .[and] the archbishop was dispossessed by the said Bartholomew. . . .'[38]

Such events did little to reassure an already nervous Protestant community, which had in fact started, on a small scale, to leave the country shortly after James's accession. Clarendon noted in June 1686 that one ship had carried 120

Protestants to Chester, and that 'multitudes are preparing from all parts of the kingdom to be gone, as fast as they can get in their debts, and dispose of their stocks'.[39] As the tension rose the exodus increased, stimulated by a rumour, in late 1688, of an invasion followed by a general massacre of the Protestants.

James, meanwhile, having fled to France, made his way to Ireland in early 1689. That summer in Dublin Tyrconnell's long cherished dream of dismantling the land settlement was realized. A parliament was called and, with the Catholics holding a large majority in both houses, an act of repeal was passed, to which James grudgingly assented, by which landed property in the country was by law restored, as far as possible, to the situation as it existed before the rebellion of 1641. But the battle of the Boyne in July 1690 ended any chance that the repeal could be carried into effect, and in 1695 the Williamite parliament invalidated the proceedings of this Jacobite 'Patriot Parliament' of 1689. Orders were given to destroy the records of its proceedings.[40] The Acts of Settlement and Explanation again became the legal basis upon which land ownership in Ireland was to rest. They were to remain so for the next two centuries.

CHAPTER IX

Commercial Land Transactions, 1663–1688

The Books of Survey and Distribution record the ownership of Irish land in 1641 and the land assignments under the Restoration settlement, together with most of the grants awarded under the Commission of Grace of 1684–8 and the sale of land forfeited under the Williamite settlement. Apart from the grants issued under the Commission of Grace, they do not indicate the changes of land ownership which occurred as a result of commercial transactions negotiated after 1663. The available evidence suggests that such changes took place on a fairly wide scale and that the general trend, at least in Dublin, continued to be one of an increasing penetration by the Protestants into the proprietorship of the county. An examination of the grants issued under the Commission of Grace provide some indication of this trend.

Twenty proprietors obtained letters patent under the Commission for over 11,000 acres in Dublin; nine Protestants for some 3,200 acres; twelve Catholics for almost 8,000, most of it represented by the patent awarded to Henry Barnewall, Viscount Kingsland of Turvey for nearly 5,500 acres.[1]

Most of the Catholics who obtained letters patent for land in Dublin under the Commission of Grace were heirs of restored innocents. An exception was Robert Leigh, who in 1684 was granted two townlands that had been restored to Robert Nugent and Luke Hussey. Leigh may have purchased this land, or, more plausibly, have obtained it as a form of compensation for his aid in getting Nugent and Hussey restored. Another exception was William Clinch, who was given a patent for several hundred acres that had been restored to John and Thomas Holiday.

Most of the land in Dublin granted to Protestants under the Commission of Grace was obtained from restored Catholics. The one exception here was the patent issued to Richard Foster for an inherited estate in Coolock that had been held in 1641 by Charles Foster.[2]

Another patent under the Commission of Grace was awarded to Sir Joshua Allen, son of an English master-builder who had arrived in Ireland at the close of Elizabeth's reign and was later employed by Wentworth in building his great mansion near Naas in Kildare. Joshua was an astute business man, a prominent member of Dublin corporation, lord mayor in 1673. In about 1680 he purchased the manor of Stillorgan, which had been restored to James Wolverton. The latter had died in 1666 and his widow married Sir Brian O'Neill, later a justice of the king's bench under James II. It was O'Neill who sold Stillorgan to Allen. At about the same time Allen also purchased the nearby townland of Carrickmines (forfeited and never recovered by a branch of the Walsh family) from the earl of Meath, to whom it was granted in 1669. Taken together the two properties amounted to over 1,000 acres.[3]

Stillorgan was the most valuable, but not the only portion of the Wolverton estate in Dublin disposed of by O'Neill. A patent for 30 acres in Little Bray, to which James Woolverton had also been restored, was issued under the Commission of Grace to Jeremy Donovan, a Protestant member of a well known Old Irish family from Cork.[4] Two other patents for land in the county that had formerly comprised the restored Wolverton estate were awarded to William Williams, a brewer, and Anthony Piercy, who was to become lord mayor in 1699.[5]

One of the more significant shifts of land in the county from Catholic to Protestant hands occurred when Michael Boyle, archbishop of Dublin and lord chancellor, became the proprietor of Monkstown in Rathdown, which had been restored to Walter Cheevers. Although the evidence for the precise nature of the transaction is wanting, it is likely that Boyle purchased the estate—over 600 acres—from John Byrne, husband of Cheevers's only surviving child, following Cheevers's death in 1678. Boyle obtained a patent for Monkstown under the Commission of Grace in 1685.[6]

Sir William Davies, chief justice of the king's bench (from 1681), also obtained a patent under the Commission of Grace for the townland of St. Catherine's in Newcastle, on the western border of the county adjacent to Leixlip in Kildare. St. Catherine's had been restored in 1663 to Nicholas, eldest son of Sir Nicholas White of Leixlip. Nicholas died in 1664 and the estate was sold by Charles, his brother, to Davies in 1666.[7]

We have seen how, in 1678, Thomas, fourth Viscount Fizwilliam of Merrion, had redeemed the mortgages held by Richard Dixon, on the two townlands of Kiltiernan and Ballybetagh in Rathdown. The money for the redemption (£1,012) came, in fact, by agreement with Fitzwilliam, from a Christopher Johnson, who may have come from Durham. The same day Fitzwilliam sold the two parcels, for £419, to Johnson, who also purchased the nearby townland to Glenamuck, part of the forfeited estate of another branch of the Walsh family. Glenamuck, which had been granted under the Restoration settlement to Roger Jones, had been sold by him in 1670 to a Thomas Corker, who in turn had sold it to Johnson.[8] As a result of these transactions, Johnson became the proprietor of nearly 1,000 acres in the barony.

The sale of Glenamuck—like that of Carrickmines already noted—represents another example of the shift of land in the county after 1663 between Protestants. Several other examples are worth citing. In August 1667 the duke of Ormond sold over 1,100 acres in the county to James Margeston, archbishop of Armagh. This land, for which Margeston paid £3,640, comprised nearly the entire estate forfeited by Luke Nettervill of Corballis.[9] Another instance involved the sale by Sir George Rawdon, in 1680, of nearly 500 acres in Dublin, forfeited by Robert Preston, to Richard Coote, first Baron Clooney, younger brother of the first earl of Mountrath. Clooney, however, sold the same land to William Barton, who in turn transferred, in June 1684, to Clooney's son, the second baron. A month later Clooney sold the same land, for £1,510, to a Dublin merchant named Thomas Putland.[10]

There were of course transactions involving much smaller amounts of land. Dr John Westley, for example, who had obtained a patent on 2 June 1668 for 78 acres in Newcastle, sold the same land on 18 June to a Robert Bowyer.[11]

In attempting to deal with the commercial changes in land ownership which occurred in Dublin after 1663, it becomes appropriate to re-open the question of the duke of York's estate. Although he was granted some 7,400 acres in the county, it is clear that York was never able to gain effective control over all the land thus acquired. A comparison of the acreage figures entered in his letters patent with those in the records of the Williamite forfeitures reveals considerable discrepancies; many of the townlands in his letters patent are not recorded as having been forfeited by York. In some instances we find York, having obtained a patent for an entire townland, forfeiting only a small part of the estate.

By way of illustration we can cite the townland of Stevenstown (233 acres) in Balrothery, held in 1641 by Elizabeth, widow of Richard Finglas. Although York received a patent for Stevenstown, Elizabeth Finglas was adjudged innocent in the first court of claims and was ordered restored, for life, to 530 acres in Dublin, including Stevenstown, which she held as her jointure prior to 1641. The records of the Williamite confiscation show that York forfeited only 8 acres in Stevenstown.[12]

The contraction of York's estate in the county can also be illustrated by examining in some detail the Restoration history of the former estate of Nicholas Eustace of Confey, a patent for a considerable portion of which was issued to York in 1666. Nicholas Eustace, who died in 1652, had been awarded a posthumous decree of innocence. His son James had been declared nocent, but his grandson Thomas was declared innocent. Consequently, a savings clause appended to York's patent reserved to Thomas his right to restoration following the deaths of his father, mother, and grandmother.[13] In the event, however, it does not appear that Thomas derived much advantage from the savings clause, since most of the estate was still in the hands of York, and others, in 1688, although it is possible, if unlikely, that a parent or his grandmother was still alive in that year.

Part of the Eustace estate in Dublin was held in 1688 by Sir Edward Sutton, who in 1669 had 'discovered' that Thomas Eustace had submitted his claim to innocence on pretence that his father, who was in fact still alive, was dead. In 1670, on the strength of this discovery, Sutton was granted an interest in the estate for the life of James Eustace. Sutton soon learned, however, that his grant was worthless because York had a prior claim. But Sutton had meanwhile discovered another 'abuse' in the case. James Eustace, he claimed, had passed the estate to his son after the outbreak of the rebellion in 1641, thus rendering the conveyance invalid. As a result of this new discovery directions were given for a grant to Sutton of so much of the estate, excluding the portion allotted to York, that had been illegally conveyed by Thomas to James Eustace.[14] Sutton seems to have proven his case, since by 1688 he was holding 140 acres of the Eustace estate in Dublin, including Ballyhack in Castleknock and portions of two other townlands, Corrstown in the same barony and 7 acres in Monkstown in Rathdown. Oddly enough, Corrstown and the 7 acres in Monkstown were included in York's letters patent, and the names of York and Sutton are bracketed opposite these two denominations in the Restoration column of the Book of Survey and Distribution. Opposite Ballyhack the name of Sutton is bracketed with Thomas Eustace, but no symbol of title appears against Eustace's name.[15]

Another segment of the Eustace estate which was granted to York was Damastown (181 acres) in Castleknock. This townland had been included in the savings clause appended to York's patent. The proprietor in 1641 is entered in the Civil Survey as James Eustace, but as Thomas in the Book of Survey and Distribution, lending substance to Sutton's claim that the estate, or at least part of it, had been passed to Thomas after the outbreak of the rebellion. The Restoration column of the Book of Survey and Distribution bracket the names of York and Thomas Eustace, but once again no appropriate symbol appears opposite Eustace's name. Following York's name, however, an acreage figure of 99 acres is entered, and a Richard Crump forfeited exactly that amount in Damastown under the Williamite confiscation.[16] Moreover, Thomas Eustace is recorded in 1670 as having sold the 'castle town and lands of Damastown' to Leonard Hatfield, a lawyer and son of Ridley Hatfield, a former mayor of Dublin. But no acreage figure appears in the entry and it may be conjectured that York and Thomas Eustace divided the land between them by mutual agreement.[17] Neither York nor Eustace held any land in Damastown in 1688. At any rate, York, having been granted some 400 acres of the Eustace estate in Dublin, forfeited only about half that amount under the Williamite confiscation.

York had also sold, or otherwise disposed of, a considerable amount of his Dublin estate by 1688. He had, for example, obtained a patent for half the townland of Coldwells (115 acres) in Uppercross, which was forfeited under the Williamite confiscation by Sir Patrick Trant, an English-born Catholic Jacobite who had earlier purchased the great Clanmaliere estates in King's and Queen's counties from Lord Arlington.[18]

By far the greater amount of land in the country which York disposed of, however, went to his close friend Richard Talbot, who by 1688 had acquired, probably by purchase, over 1,000 acres of York's Dublin estate, including the manor of Balgriffin, forfeited and never recovered by the Bath family.[19]

York's estate had been so depleted that under the Williamite confiscation he forfeited only 4,531 acres in Dublin.[20] In the ninth book accompanying the inquiry commissioners report on Irish forfeitures, compiled in 1690, his estate in the county is described as containing 6,475 profitable acres.[21] J. G. Simms has pointed out, however, that it was the intention of the commissioners to give the English parliament the impression that it would be worth their while to appropriate the proceeds of the forfeited estates.[22] With this in mind, it is likely that they reported that the estate consisted of all the land contained in York's grant under the Restoration settlement, excepting only those he had disposed of prior to 1688. They apparently failed to deduct the land over which he was never able to gain effective control.

The 1,000 acres he acquired from the duke of York represented less than half of the total amount of land Richard Talbot accumulated in Dublin after 1663. In 1688 he was in possession of 285 acres in Castleknock that had been restored to Philip Hore;[23] we may assume that he obtained this property for his help in negotiating the compromise agreement between Hore and Sir George Lane in 1665. He had also acquired over 700 acres that had been restored to Christopher Barnewall, including his chief seat at Terenure. Talbot held Terenure for only a short time, however, selling it in 1672 for £4,000 to Edward Deane, brother of the regicide Colonel Richard Deane. Even after the sale, however, Talbot remained one of the more substantial proprietors in the county. He forfeited nearly 2,000 acres in Dublin under the Williamite confiscation.[24]

The sources relating to commercial transactions in Dublin between 1663 and 1688 will take us no further, although the suspicion remains that these activities occurred on a wider scale than the surviving evidence would suggest. The extant sources tend to support the view that the trend after 1663 was one of a continuing, though modest, penetration by the Protestants into the proprietorship of the county. Many of the Catholic commercial acquisitions of land after 1663 were from other Catholics. There is little evidence for the commercial acquisition by Catholics of the land of Protestants, even during the period between 1685 and 1688 when it might be expected that some panic selling of Protestant estates would have occurred. As a result, the land which the Protestants acquired from the Catholics by commercial means after 1663—at least 3,000 acres—represented an overall increase in the proportion of their holdings in Dublin by perhaps 2–3 per cent by 1688. The land records are too fragmentary, however, to warrant much certainty in this regard.

The general subject of commercial land transactions would not be complete without some mention of the question of mortgages, a topic touched on previously in several individual cases and in relation to the question of encumbered estates in the court of claims. The land records are littered with references to estates that were mortgaged, the majority of which seem to have been held by Protestants on land owned by Catholics. The process also seems to have accelerated after 1660, caused no doubt by the legal expenses incurred by Catholics in attempting to recover their estates.

Some of the mortgaged land was later forfeited under the Williamite confiscation and granted to the mortgagees. In 1686, for example, Sir Thomas Domville, son of the former Irish attorney-general, purchased a mortgage for £3,000 on James Talbot's manor of Templeogue. Two years later, finding the government under Tyrconnell 'very burdensome and oppressive', he fled to England, following which Talbot repossessed the estate. Soon after the 'happy rout of the Boyle', however, Domville returned, only to find Templeogue in a state of ruin. After expending £1,000 on repairs he then discovered that several others also had claims on the estate for unpaid debts, leaving him facing charges of over £6,500. He claimed that after 1689 Templeogue yielded barely £300 a year. Talbot was killed in the battle of Aughrim and his estate, which was forfeited under the Williamite confiscation, was granted to Domville in 1694.[25]

CHAPTER X

Conclusion

When dealing with the Restoration land settlement in Dublin it should always be born in mind that the county was in many ways atypical of the country generally. Although one of the smallest counties in Ireland, it had for centuries represented the most Anglicized region of the country; Dublin city was the strategic hub from which English influence radiated. The city had been the axis around which the boundary of the Pale had expanded or contracted. Moreover, the county contained a relatively high proportion of arable land. For these reasons the city had traditionally attracted to its orbit many prominent landed families. As a result, the struggle for the land of Dublin at the Restoration assumed an importance far out of proportion to its size.

One reflection of this importance can be found in the fact that the Catholic landlords of the county were restored to nearly two-thirds of their former holdings, a far higher proportion than was the case in the country generally. This success of the Catholics of Dublin can be attributed primarily to the quality of their political patronage, but other special factors should also be taken into account, one of which was the fact that the Old Irish had never represented an important element in the proprietorship of the county. Indeed, with the exception of a few individual cases, mainly in Connacht and Clare, the Old Irish landlords throughout the country were for all practical purposes eliminated under the Restoration settlement.

It should also be considered that at least ten Catholic proprietors managed to avoid the sequestration of their estates in the county under the Cromwellian settlement. Although considerable caution must be exercised here, the amount of unsequestered Catholic land may have reached as much as 4,000 acres.

Then there is the question of the large amount of land in the county that had been held during the Interregnum by the five regicides, perhaps as much as 20,000 acres. A good deal of this land must have been open to repossession by their former owners immediately at the Restoration. Although the regicides' estates were earmarked for the duke of York, it has already been observed that it does not appear that his final settlement was in fact composed primarily of such land.

Approximately three-fifths of the land in the county which the Catholics failed to recover under the Restoration settlement was granted to just fifteen prominent Protestants, most of whom were New English, but including

Ormond and the O'Connolly heirs. Also included, however, were several Restoration Protestants who only acquired their estates after 1660, Edward Vernon and Lord Fitzharding. They represented the vanguard in what was to become, by the end of the reign, a fairly substantial group of new planters in the county.

* * *

It is instructive to compare the results of the settlement in Dublin with that of Wicklow, a county whose history and geography stand in marked contrast to its contiguous northern neighbour.[1]

Wicklow's forested and mountainous terrain had for centuries acted as a barrier to the inroads of English influence, which in the mid-sixteenth century was largely confined to certain areas on the western slopes of the mountains leading to the plains of Kildare, and to various small enclaves along the fertile coastal strip, principally in the north, between Bray and Delgany and, in the south, to the shires of Arklow, held by the earls of Ormond. In most of the rest of Wicklow the Old Irish tribal society was still intact and, like medieval Wales, was regarded by the government as a wild frontier territory populated by barbarous clans who lived outside the royal jurisdiction and maintained a disturbing tradition of launching raids against the Pale. As late as 1579 it was noted that 'the sheriffs of the counties Dublin and Wexford have not often executed the writ in these mountains and woody countries...'[2]

Unlike Dublin the New English penetration in Wicklow began as a military operation when, in the mid-sixteenth century, a succession of attacks against the Old Irish were launched as a prelude to the construction of a series of forts to secure the region against the possibility of French intervention. Wicklow was divided into three administrative districts corresponding to the principal areas controlled by the major septs, the O'Byrnes, O'Tooles, and Kavanaghs. The Old Irish chiefs were dismissed and replaced by English captains to rule as seneschals from their forts in the name of the crown. Thus, the first grants of confiscated land were associated with the appointment of these military administrators, notably (in Elizabeth's reign), Francis Agard, Sir Jacques Wingfield, Sir Henry Harrington, Sir John Hoey, and Robert Pipho.[3]

There was, however, no comprehensive scheme of plantation; it was undertaken piecemeal fashion. The most significant forfeiture during Elizabeth's reign occurred in 1585 with the attainder of James Eustace, Viscount Baltinglas, for complicity in Desmond's rebellion. The Wicklow segment of this vast estate (some 11,000 acres on the Kildare border) was in 1587 granted (in reversion) to Sir Henry Harrington.[4]

On the death of Elizabeth, then, Wicklow remained one of the largest regions of Leinster still open to plantation on a broad scale. The Old Irish holdings were diminished but they still held large areas of the county, including most of the coastal strip between Delgany and Arklow town (the 'Birnes' Country') and in the mountainous central and southern regions. However, although the senior branch of the O'Byrnes supported the English in O'Neill's rebellion, and the junior branch had made peace with Mountjoy in 1601, in neither case did it lead to secure title.[5] The Old Irish grip on the land was uneasy and they were not long left unmolested.

The Spanish intervention at Kinsale in 1601 provided urgency to the process of confiscation, and indeed one of the first major grants of expropriated land in the county under James I was a direct result of that battle. This occurred in 1603 when, after the death of Phelim O'Toole, an inquisition found his estate at Powerscourt forfeited as a result of the complicity, twenty years before, of his son, Gerrett, in Desmond's rebellion. Powerscourt ('5 miles in length, and 4 in breadth') occupied a site of great strategic importance in the mountains south of Dublin in Rathdown barony, and it was primarily for this reason that it was first leased (in 1603), then granted (in 1609), to a soldier, Sir Richard Wingfield, marshall of the army (and a cousin of Sir Jacques), who played a vital role in the victory at Kinsale.[6]

The confiscation of most of what remained in Old Irish hands was carried out primarily in the 1620s and the 1630s as a consequence of a continuing government policy directed towards finding unencumbered royal title to Old Irish holdings. This involved the establishment of courts of inquisition operating in the interest of a relatively small group of avaricious land speculators, most of them English born, who were closely allied with a government intent on uprooting the native proprietors for its own political or strategic reasons. The operation of the courts are often obscure, but in general they were marked by deviousness and corruption; in the course of one legal struggle the O'Byrnes were imprisoned in Dublin Castle.[7] There was a legal transfer of ownership and no occupation on the Ulster model. Much of the land was unprofitable mountain and bog, but its proximity to the capital was an added inducement and explains why the county naturally attracted the interest of a number of prominent people who were already established in Dublin, among them Richard Bellings, Sir William Parsons, Sir Adam Loftus, and Lords Ranelagh and Meath.

Strafford, after his arrival as lord deputy in 1633, soon became engaged in the Irish land traffic, first in Kildare, later on a grand scale in Wicklow, where he became involved in the attempt to find royal title to the Birnes' Country. Much of his estate was purchased from previous undertakers; another portion, in the Birnes' Country, came by grant in 1640 after royal title was finally found. His investments were largely speculative (rents realized from the Old Irish occupiers) and the negotiations involved in his transactions are clouded in intrigue and virtually impossible to untangle. By the time of his recall in 1640 he had accumulated some 54,000 acres, or nearly 20 per cent of the land of the county, making him by far the greatest proprietor in Wicklow. However, the manner in which he exploited his office for personal profit and the ruthless and high-handed methods by which he acquired his estate were important factors which earned him the consolidated enmity of all the influential groups in

Ireland and accounts to a great extent not only for his eventual execution but also for the creation in Wicklow of an atmosphere which led to a ready response to the rebellion of 1641.[8]

At any rate, by 1641 the Catholic holdings were reduced to just under 100,000 acres, or 35 per cent of the land of the county. The Old Irish—47 of them—retained about 40,000, but much of it was unprofitable land in Ballinecur barony and in the uplands of the Birnes' Country. Only five individuals—a McPhelim, two O'Tooles and two O'Byrnes—held half this total. The remainder was in the hands of one New English and twenty-eight Old English Catholics, half of it by just four people, a Cheevers, a Talbot, an Esmond, and an Alen.

At the same time twenty-eight Protestants held over 135,000 acres, or about 40 per cent of the land. Over 90 per cent of this total was possessed by only seven New English individuals, Lords Strafford and Baltinglas (Thomas Roper), along with Calcott Chamber, Sir John Coke, Sir William Parsons, Kimbro Pipho, and Sir Edward Wingfield.

This was the position when the great rebellion erupted in October 1641. In the war that followed the Old Irish clans in Wicklow were completely tamed for the first time. The county was then allotted, under the terms of the Act of Satisfaction of 1653, for the satisfaction of the arrears of the Cromwellian '49 officers.[9] The following year a scheme was undertaken to transplant the entire Catholic population from the so-called 'five counties', a region composed of Dublin south of the Liffey river, along with Wicklow, Wexford, Kildare, and Carlow. This area was to be formed into an exclusively Protestant enclave. But faced with the loss of their tenants and servants, the proprietors petitioned the government against the measure and as a result the clearing of the Catholics was postponed and, eventually, unofficially abandoned.[10] There is no evidence of any large scale uprooting of the Catholic population. Unlike Dublin, however, no Catholic proprietor in the county escaped expropriation, which meant that nearly 100,000 acres[11] were forfeited under the Cromwellian settlement.

Unfortunately, the sources do not permit a satisfactory reading of the settlement, although we know that some of the forfeited land was granted to a small group of prominent Cromwellians. The vast Esmond estate, for example, which included over 11,000 acres in Wicklow, was given to Monck; Abraham Yarner, an army doctor, was granted 800 acres in Newcastle.[12] But these references are rare, and the truth seems to be that the plantation of the county, which was disrupted by vacillation in government policy, was far from complete by 1660.

Under the terms of the Act of Settlement of 1662 the forfeited land of Wicklow was assigned for the satisfaction of the arrears of the Restoration '49 officers;[13] thus it might be regarded as a kind of extension of the Cromwellian settlement. But in fact less than half (something over 46,000 acres) of the forfeited land seems to have been used for this purpose. The remainder was granted or leased to several dozen Cromwellian soldiers or prominent New English figures, among them Sir John Borlace (son of Sir John, lord justice,

1640–44), the earl of Mount-Alexander, Archbishop Michael Boyle, and William Flower, one of Ormond's retainers.[14]

Only fourteen Catholics were restored to just over 35,000 acres, or about 12 per cent of the total land area of the county, and representing 35 per cent of what seventy-six Catholics had held in 1641. Nearly 30,000 of this was restored to only five individuals, all of them well-connected members of the gentry of the Pale, Sir Richard Bellings, Sir Lawrence Esmond, James Alen of St. Wolstan's (Richard Talbot's client), Sir William Talbot (Richard's nephew), and John Walsh, Ormond's family lawyer. No O'Byrne or O'Toole was restored. Indeed, of the forty-seven Old Irish Catholic landlords who held estates in the county in 1641, only one regained his land. This was Edmund O'Meara, a physician to the earl of Clanrickarde, to whom we can no doubt attribute O'Meara's restoration.[15] Thus, Wicklow was virtually swept clear of Old Irish proprietors, and we see the racial character of the settlement vividly exposed.

The configuration of the Restoration proprietorship in Wicklow was, then, governed by two principle factors, the first of which was the topography of the county, which had historically shielded the Old Irish from English incursions. Largely because of this the Old Irish were able to retain large tracts of land well into the seventeenth century. But it also meant that the greater expropriations, when they came, were swift and wholesale, occurring mostly after about 1610. Hundreds of Irish proprietors forfeited *en masse*, leaving very large regions open to plantation. As a result, the new ownership became concentrated in far fewer hands than was the case in most other counties. This was eventually reflected in the Restoration settlement. The estates were large by Leinster standards, not to speak of Dublin.

Excluding the '49 officers, only five Restoration estates were under 100 acres and over half the county was held by ten proprietors; the church and twenty proprietors (four Catholics and sixteen Protestants) held between them over 70 per cent (202,000 acres) of the county. There were in total only fifty-nine individual landlords (excluding the '49 officers), fourteen Catholics and forty-five Protestants, as compared to Dublin's 194, with 105 Catholics and 89 Protestants, a county less than half the size of Wicklow. Moreover, there is considerable evidence that the allotments of the '49 officers were purchased in large blocks, probably starting during the Interregnum but certainly after the Restoration, by local landlords, or in some cases by the trustees of the officers. This had the effect of increasing the tendency toward the creation of large ranches, a characteristic which the county maintained until recent times.[16]

* * *

The Irish Restoration settlement was a compromise dictated by the circumstances attending the restoration of Charles II to the English throne in 1660. Charles owed his restoration largely to the Commonwealth army, part of the bargain being a commitment to maintain in substantive form the Cromwellian settlement of Ireland. Yet the king was obliged to reward numerous Catholic royalists from Ireland, many of whom had shared his exile, fought under his standards abroad, and expected to obtain toleration for their religion and the recovery of their estates. But although Charles doubtless felt sympathetic toward the plight of the Catholics, his policies were largely hostage to the Cromwellian interest, and he was by necessity forced, as Carte remarked, to regard the Irish settlement as 'an affair rather of policy than justice'.[17]

If the land settlement can be described as a 'compromise', in its final form it was a compromise which left the Protestants in a clearly dominant position, since the Catholics, by 1669, had recovered only about a third of the land they had held in 1641. Although their position improved somewhat after 1669, mainly as a result of purchases, crown grants or by the gradual recovery of their estates in the regular law courts, they held only about 22 per cent of the land in 1688. This percentage is distorted, however, by the high proportion (about half) in Connacht and Clare which was confirmed to the Catholics who had been transplanted under the Cromwellian settlement.[18]

The land question remained a dominant issue throughout Charles's reign. Like most compromises the settlement pleased neither side. The Catholics refused to accept it as final and were always searching for means to 'unravel' it at the first opportunity. Their case was stated as the settlement was nearing completion in *A Narrative of the Earl of Clarendon's Settlement and Sale of Ireland* (1669), which has been attributed to an exiled Catholic bishop, Nicholas French, who denounced the role played in the settlement by Clarendon and Ormond and called for a repeal of the Acts of Settlement and Explanation. French returned to the attack with the publication, in 1676, of *The Unkind Deserter of Loyal Men,* in which he accused Ormond of having abandoned the Catholics of Ireland in their time of trial and of joining with the enemies of the country for reasons of avarice.[19]

In James's reign a leading role in the agitation against the settlement was taken by Richard Nagle, author of the 'Coventry Letter' (1686), in which it is maintained that the Irish confiscations had been based on religion and not rebellion. This being the case, Nagle urged the king to refrain from issuing a proclamation confirming the settlement on the grounds that such an act would destroy all hopes for a restoration of the Catholic church, since the support of that church could only be realized if its members held land ('fortunes') in proportion to their numbers.[20]

Shortly before the end of the century the settlement was again attacked in a book apparently written by Hugh Reilly, Cavan-born Catholic lawyer, master in chancery and clerk of the council in Dublin ('After the abdication') in James II's reign, and a member of the Patriot Parliament of 1689.[21] The book, *Ireland's Case Briefly Stated* (1695), was indeed anything but brief; over half of it is devoted to a broad survey of the Restoration settlement, in the course of which Charles II is condemned for ingratitude to the Irish Catholics. Reilly's language maintains the strident verbosity so characteristic of seventeenth century political tracts, but he is at the same time often pithy and droll. He refers to the Act of Settlement as 'This idol, this great Diana of the Ephesians', and calls the Act of Explanation the 'dragon's tail'; the Cromwellians are denounced as 'the wildest sectaries and rankest fanatics ... who had nothing of Christianity but the name'. He accuses Charles of leaving the ensignmen to 'strave on' until he provided for them on 'Doomsday in the afternoon'. The settlement, Reilly says, was 'justice perverted in all its branches and degrees', and toward the end of the book states that no king 'since the creation of the universe has proved so bountiful to the worst rebels at the cost of his faithful subjects, as Charles the Second has done to the Cromwellians of Ireland'.[22]

In the early eighteenth century the Catholic cause was again enunciated in 'A light to the blind', which has in recent times been tentatively attributed to Colonel Nicholas Plunket, a brother of Luke, third earl of Fingall.[23] In highly vitriolic language ('Cromwellian scum', 'fanatic scabs') the author describes the settlement as the greatest injustice 'from the first day of the creation to the present time', primary responsibility for which he places on Clarendon, who is accused of savagery and corruption. But Ormond is not spared, nor is Charles, who is criticised for 'unnaturally preferring' the very people who destroyed the English monarchy.[24]

The Protestants had anticipated Charles's restoration as the best safeguard of the great shift in the balance of power that had resulted from the Cromwellian conquest. But they soon became dissatisfied with Charles's policies, which they viewed as being far too generous to the Catholics, and they resented having to surrender part of their holdings to a people they continued to regard as conquered rebels deserving of their fate. Petty drew a parallel between the Irish settlement and a match in which, he remarked cynically, the English had won a 'gamesters right' to their Irish estates.[25]

A restrained defence of the settlement appeared at the end of James's reign in a pamphlet, published anonymously, entitled *The State of Ireland with a Vindication of the Act of Settlement* (1688). In it the author, who was probably John Osborne, prime sergeant of Ireland between 1680 and 1686, proposes to refute both Nagle and French. He sets out to establish that there had in fact been a rebellion in Ireland and that the Restoration settlement was a just and reasonable consequence of it. 'The legality of the acts of settlement are not doubted, at least wise the British are satisfied to rest on them', he says. Nagle's proposals for breaking the settlement as a means of restoring the Catholic church are regarded by Osborne as a 'terrible consideration to the British in Ireland'.

French's *Narrative* is refuted first of all on factual grounds; later Osborne defends Clarendon's role in the settlement and charges French with a 'high touch of malice' and 'unparalleled impudence' in his attitude toward the former lord chancellor. Osborne asserted that the Catholics of Ireland had no reason to complain: 'they have been equally protected by the law; the free exercise of their religion has been connived at'. Moreover, he says, the Catholic lower classes favoured the existing settlement because they were better off economically than their ancestors; the restored Catholic landlords, he adds, 'found their lands in much better condition than when they lost them'. Osborne concludes his defence by offering the opinion of the Catholic earl of Castlehaven, 'that if the nuncio's party in the year 1646 had had all of Ireland it would have remained separate from England for ever'.[26]

Clause 57 of the Instructions proclaimed the Act of Settlement to be 'the positive and fundamental rule' for the settlement of Ireland, and indeed many Protestants referred to it as Ireland's 'magna carta'. But it was a hopeful analogy, a form of whistling-in-the-dark, for at no time between 1660 and 1688 did the proprietors of Ireland, especially the Cromwellian interest, maintain much fundamental faith in the security of their land titles. Thirteen years after the Restoration Essex remarked that he had 'always found that the generality of the English who enjoy their estates upon these new titles could not shake off their apprehensions of losing them again'.[27] The apprehensions were not, however, confined to the 'English'. In 1683 Edward Hussey, whose father, Luke, had been restored to his estate in Dublin as an innocent in 1663, petitioned the king for a patent (which Luke had neglected to obtain) because of the 'many difficulties and questions which daily arose touching the validity of the decrees of the court of claims'.[28]

The succession of James II naturally intensified the anxieties. In 1668 Clarendon referred to the 'melancholy apprehensions' of the landlords, and in his last work, *Treatise of Ireland* (1687), Petty pointed to the growing fears among the Protestants that the settlement was about to be altered, and he drew attention to falling land values and the start of a Protestant exodus to England.[29] The war of 1689–91 only confirmed these fears. The third major change in Irish land ownership during the seventeenth century was about to occur, and with it the Protestant ascendancy became fully and finally established.

APPENDIX A: LAND, LANDLORDS, AND NOMENCLATURE

The ensuing lists of proprietors and the acreage figures following their names have been extracted primarily from the Dublin volume of the Quit Rent set of Books of Survey and Distribution in the Public Record Office, Dublin. Two other sets have also been consulted for the same purpose, viz., the Headfort set, also in the Public Record Office, Dublin, and the Taylor set in the Royal Irish Academy.[1]

Complete accuracy cannot be claimed for the measurements appearing in these lists. The acreage figures entered in the Books of Survey and Distribution for most of the country, including Dublin, are based on Sir William Petty's Down Survey of 1654–9, which undermeasured the size of the country generally by 10–15 per cent. The Quit Rent set, which is the most complete of the various sets, return the land area of seventeenth century Dublin, including the detached barony of Uppercross (now incorporated into Kildare and Wicklow), as containing about 133,000 Irish acres, whereas in fact it contained roughly 146,000.[2] Petty thus undermeasured the county by about 10 per cent. Given the relatively primitive nature of the instruments employed in the survey, such inaccuracies are to be expected and they do not detract from Petty's remarkable achievement. Moreover, the general undermeasurement does not affect the relative proportion of land held by the landlords.

There are, however, various other difficulties which arise in dealing with the Books of Survey and Distribution. The entries are not always full or precise; groups of proprietors are often lumped together opposite townland names, especially in the 1641 column, with no distinction as to the size of the individual holdings. Unforfeited land is sometimes described only as 'Protestant land', with no proprietor indicated. In many of these instances the proprietors, or the size of their holdings, could be determined from the Down Survey barony maps or from the Civil Survey, but this was not always possible in the case of Newcastle barony (the largest in the county) because the entries for that barony did not survive. It was only possible in these circumstances to attempt to ascertain the 1641 proprietor or the amount of land he held by reference to the Restoration column of the Book of Survey and Distribution.

Determining the religious affiliation of some landlords also proved difficult, especially at the Restoration. The Books of Survey and Distribution contain references to the religious persuasion of most of the proprietors, but there is ample evidence that many Catholics attempted to regain their estates by claiming to be Protestants. In one case the same Dublin proprietor (William Warren) is entered in 1641 as a Catholic and as a Protestant at the Restoration.[3] It usually

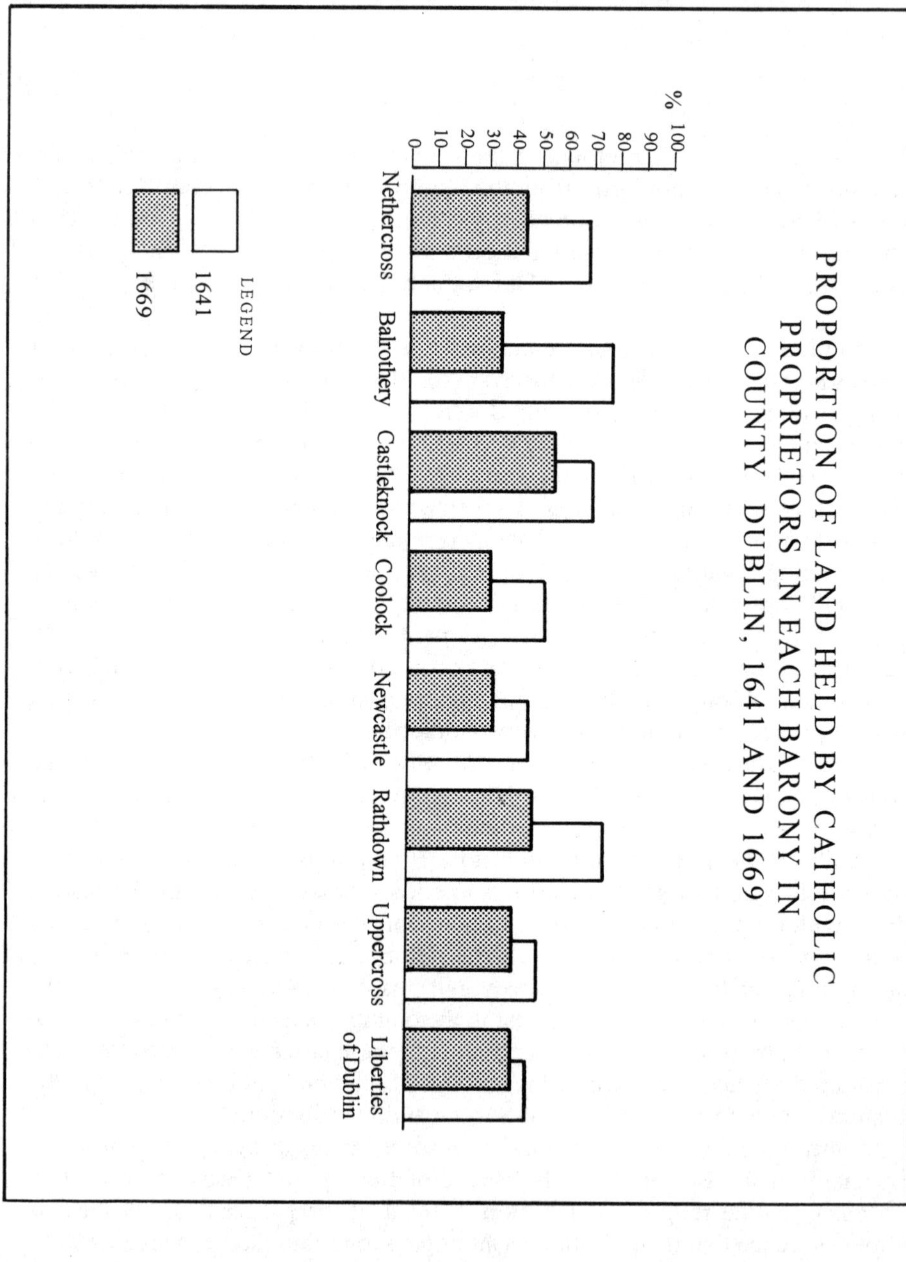

PROPORTION OF LAND HELD BY CATHOLIC PROPRIETORS IN EACH BARONY IN COUNTY DUBLIN, 1641 AND 1669

proved that the problem could be resolved by reference to other sources, in particular the records of the second court of claims. But in a small number of cases a decision as to the religious affiliation of a proprietor had *per force* to be based on the general weight of the evidence.

For the purpose of this study the term 'Old Irish' will be used to mean the indigenous population of Ireland prior to the Norman conquest. The term 'Old English' will refer to the descendants of those who colonized Ireland from the period of the original Norman conquest up to, approximately, the Reformation. The term 'New English' will be used to denote those colonists, or their descendants, who colonized Ireland from the period of the Reformation up to 1642.

Many of the New English acquired Irish land between 1642 and 1660 as a consequence of the forfeitures of the Catholic estates. Therefore, a distinction must be made between the New English and the 'Cromwellian' colonists, which term will be used to describe those English (or Scots) born individuals who first acquired Irish land between 1652 and 1660 by virtue of legislation enacted in England between 1642 and 1660. The term 'Cromwellian interest' (or 'occupant') will, however, be used in the broadest sense, that is, to denote all Protestants who had benefited from or shared an interest in, maintaining the Cromwellian settlement in whole or part. Within this broad category certain special distinctions, such as 'Cromwellian soldier', have been used in particular instances.

The classification of the landlords on the basis of the ethnic derivation of their surnames is a convenience which should be regarded with caution. It takes no account of the rather hybrid ethnic composition of either the original 'Norman' colonists or of the 'New English' planters of the sixteenth and seventeenth centuries. Nor does it take into account intermarriage or political and social ideology. Moreover, in some cases it is virtually impossible to determine whether a name is of Old English or Old Irish origin. Many of the Old Irish Anglicized their names. We can see this process in operation in the Book of Survey and Distribution where, for example, a Dublin family is entered by the mane of Meagh (O'Mea) in 1641 but as May at the Restoration.[4]

The designation 'Old English' is in fact a reversion to contemporary practice. The Old English were also known as the 'Later' or 'Newer Irish'.[5] The New English Protestants came to be known after the Restoration as the 'Old Protestants' as a means of distinguishing them from the Cromwellian planters, who were often referred to by contemporaries as the 'New interest' men. Despite these reservations the use of surnames as a guide in drawing these distinctions has considerable validity, especially when dealing with the Pale of the seventeenth century. At any rate there is no satisfactory alternative.[6] The 'Restoration proprietors', i.e., those English (or Scots) born individuals who can be identified as having first acquired land in Ireland between the Restoration and 1688, will be singled out by asterisk.

Modern spelling, capitalization, and punctuation of passages quoted have, with several obvious exceptions, been adopted. In the spelling of Old Irish names, or their Anglicized forms, I have generally relied on Edward MacLysaght's *A Guide to Irish Surnames* (2nd edition, Dublin, 1965). The spelling of place names has been based on the *Townland Index* of 1901. All acreage figures are expressed in Irish (or Plantation) measure (1 Irish acre equals 1.62 English). A map has been provided which shows the relative proportion of land held in the county by Protestants and Catholics in 1641 and 1669.

I. DUBLIN PROPRIETORS, 1641: CATHOLICS

1. *Old English Catholic Proprietors*

Name	*Acres*
Archbold, Garrett	229
Archbold, Maurice	150
Archbold, Richard	37
Archbold, William	190
Arthur, Benedict	4
Arthur, Robert	200
Aylmer, George	423
Aylmer, James	89
Aylmer, Thomas	86
Barnewall, Christopher (of Kellystown)	24
Barnewall, Christopher (of Castleknock)	496
Barnewall, James	1,061
Barnewall, Katherine	371
Barnewall, Mathew	752
Barnewall, Nicholas, Lord	5,754
Barnewall, Patrick	56
Barnewall, Peter	1,029
Barnewall, Richard	354
Barnewall, Sir Richard	127
Barnewall, Robert	830
Bates,—	1
Bath, James (of Drumcondra)	1,298
Bath, James (of Athcarne)	24
Bath, Margaret	54
Bath, Peter	
Bellings Sir Henry	1,500
Bellings, Lawrence	670
Begg, John	13
Begg, Mathew	415
Bermingham, James	245
Bermingham, Patrick	508
Blackney, George	742
Bowen, John	37
Brice, John	161
Caddell, John	163
Caddell, Richard	30
Cadwell,—	
Chamberian Robert	293
Cheevers, Walter	1,105
Chilliam, Christopher (of Gaffney)	40
Chilliam, Christopher (of Drogheda)	37
Chilliam, Patrick	168
Clarke, Symon	13
Clinch, William	7
Corbally, Robert	81
Cruise, Christopher	1,198
Cusack, Adam	46
Cusack, Patrick	100
Dalton, John	12
Deane, Nicholas	36
Delahide, Anthony	117
Delahide, John	225
Delahide, Thomas	310
Denn, John	170

Dillon, James	159	Harold, John	703
Dillon, Luke	80	Hollywood, Nicholas	1,957
Dillon Martin	253	Hore, Philip	1,176
Dillon, Robert	267	Humphrey, James	67
Dongan, Edward	417	Hussey, Luke	242
Dongan, Sir John	132	Hussey, Peter	445
Dowding, John	176	Jacob, Richard	313
Dunsany, Christopher, Lord	178	Jorden, John	128
Eustace, Alexander	519	Jorden Walter	11
Eustace, Anne	28	Kent, Christopher	2
Eustace, James	30	Locke, William	611
Eustace, Nicholas	443	Luttrell, Symon	2,743
Eustace, Oliver	166	Luttrell, Thomas	72
Eustace, Thomas	347	Martin, Nicholas	12
Fagan, Christopher	1,654	Merrion, Thomas, Viscount	1,739
Fagan, John	140	Mills, Ralph	248
Field,—		Moore, Andrew	8
Fingall, Christopher, earl of	35	Moore, Nicholas	12
Finglas, Elizabeth	508	Nettervill, James	58
Finglas, John (of Westpalstown)	753	Nettervill, Nicholas, Viscount	72
		Nettervill, Luke	1,340
Finglas, John (of Portraine)	367	Nottingham, Limerick	794
		Nugent, Andrew	241
Fitzrery, Robert	434	Nugent, Christopher	469
Fitzsimons, Marcus	150	Nugent, James	149
Fitzsimons, Richard	10	Peirce,—	
Fitzsimons, Thomas	617	Pentney, Richard	99
Fitzwilliam, Oliver	562	Plunket, Sir Christopher	383
Flemming, Thomas	12	Plunket, James	1,321
Font, John	8	Plunket, Mathew	136
Foster, George	88	Plunket, Thomas	1
Fox, Garrett	250	Plunket, Walter	451
Freene, William	197	Plunket, William	345
Gawdon, John	232	Preston, Robert	1,198
Goodman, James	459	Purcell, Ignatius	
Goodman, Rowland	30	Purcell, William	142
Gormanston, Nicholas, Viscount	735	Read, John	42
Gormley, Patrick	1	Reynolds, Patrick	60
Gough, Patrick	5	Rochfort, Henry	55
Gough, William	171	Rowse, John	80
Goulding, Christopher	71	Russell, Bartholomew	372
Goulding, Richard	416	Russell, Christopher	17
Hackett, George	83	Russell, Nicholas	167
Handcock, Christopher	15	Russell, Patrick	661

	Acres		
Russell, Thomas	60	Talbot, William	87
Sarsfield, William	1,394	Taylor, John	265
Segrave, Henry	826	Taylor, Thomas	560
Segrave, Richard	106	Travers, William	1,102
Shelton,—		Trimleston , Matthais, Lord	500
Sherlock, Patrick	848	Ussher, Orlando	78
Stephens,—		Ussher, Robert	245
Stoakes, George	67	Veldon, Christopher	33
Stoakes, William	138	Walsh, James (of Old Connaught)	697
Stronge, Katherine	218		
Talbot, Adam	1,438	Walsh, James (of Balally)	552
Talbot, Elizabeth	900		
Talbot, Sir Henry	503	Walsh, John	400
Talbot, Sir John (of Templeogue)	482	Walsh, Robert	360
		Walsh, Theobold	944
Talbot, John (of Robertstown)	349	Warren, William	238
		Westmeath, Richard, earl of	190
Talbot, John (of Malahide)	1,090	White, Sir Nicholas	326
		Wickam, Edward	70
			67,487

2. *New English Catholic Proprietors*

	Acres		
Alen, James	427	Alen, Mathew	823
Alen, John (of St. Wolstan's)	488	King George	593
		Wolverton, Christopher	80
Alen, John (of Landerstown)	262	Wolverton, William	917
			3,590

3. *Old Irish Catholic Proprietors*

	Acres		
Carbery, John	405	Dowde, John	133
Carbery, Richard	86	Duffe, Stephen	71
Connell, John	207	Kelly, Luke	23
Conran, Patrick	6	Kennedy, John	323
Conran, Thomas	640	Kennedy, Walter	130
Conran, Walter	200	Malone, Arthur	60
Conran, William	80	Meagh, James	229
Donell, David	423	Meagh, John	28
Dowde, Edward	223	Shield, Toby	4
			3,271

II. DUBLIN PROPRIETORS, 1641: PROTESTANTS

1. *Old English Protestant Proprietors*

	Acres		
Ball, Robert	55	Eustace, Walter	257
Barry, Edward	86	Fyan, Jane	18
Barry, Sir James	1,571	Grace, James	120
Barry, William	40	Howth, Nicholas, Lord	5,471
Brice, Richard	6	Mapus, Ignatius	140
Browne, Nicholas	167	Ormond, James, Earl of	1,248
Chilliam, James	32	Plunket, William	293
Cusack, Robert	157	Ussher, Sir William	756
Dillon, Robert	370	White, Thomas	159
			10,946

2. *New English Protestant Proprietors*

	Acres		
Adrian, Hubert	285	Loftus, Nicholas	103
Agar, John	970	Loftus, Sir Robert	473
Anderson, Lady	3	Lowther, Sir Gerard	4
Bagshaw, Edward	85	Meath, William, earl of	476
Bolton Sir Edward	1,484	Moore, Charles, Viscount	250
Burrowes, Alexander	101	Parsons, Sir William	1,710
Bulkeley, William	594	Percival, John	157
Bysse, John	1,085	Piers, Henry	7
Bysse, Robert	111	Piers, Lady	32
Dixon, Sir Robert	434	Radcliffe, Sir George	459
Exham, John	72	Ranelagh, Roger, Viscount	873
Foster, Charles	443	Reeves, Dorothy, Lady	65
Gazett, Edmund	30	Reeves, Sir William	240
Hackett, Lady	63	Smith, Morris	40
Hoey, Sir John	1,000	Turner, Christopher	125
Hooke, Thomas	5	Valentia, Henry, Lord	354
King, Sir Robert	25	Ware, Sir James	565
Kemp, John	88	Waterhouse, Thomas	20
Loftus, Sir Adam	7,639	Wingfield, Richard	210
Loftus, Dudley	52		20,732

3. *Old Irish Protestant Proprietors*

	Acres
Brady, Patrick	30
Donnellan, James	123
Kennedy, Robert	445
Thomond, Barnabas, earl of	1,052
	1,650

ABSTRACT OF LAND OWNERSHIP IN DUBLIN, 1641

	Acreage	*Per cent of total land area*
Old English Catholic proprietors	67,487	51
New English Catholic proprietors	3,590	3
Old Irish Catholic proprietors	3,271	2
Old English Protestant proprietors	10,946	8
New English Protestant proprietors	20,732	16
Old Irish Protestant proprietors	1,650	1
Others:		
(a) Church land	9,155	
(b) Crown land	267	
(c) Common land	1,617	
(d) Dublin city	993	
(e) Trinity College	552	
(f) Unidentified ownership	12,570	
	25,304	19

SUMMARY

Catholic Proprietors	74,348	56
Protestant proprietors	33,328	25
Others	25,304	19
	132,980	

I. DUBLIN PROPRIETORS, 1663–1669: CATHOLICS

1. *Old English Catholic Proprietors*

	Acres
Archbold, Gerald	229
Archbold, William	50
Arthur, Benedict	224
Arthur, John	200
Aylmer, Thomas	614
Barnewall, Christopher	1,402
Barnewall, James (of Dunbro)	797
Barnewall, James (of Bremore)	1,060
Barnewall, Jane	10
Barnewall, Nicholas, Lord	5,820
Barnewall, Sir Richard	44
Bellings, Sir Richard	1,550
Blackney, William	28
Blake, Patrick	36
Bowen, John	32
Cheevers, Walter	1,059
Clarke,—	13
Corbally, Robert	81
Denn, John	23
Denn, Thomas	120
Dillon, Anne	166
Dillon, James	177
Dillon, Martin	253
Dillon Robert	370
Dongan, William, Viscount	132
Dowding, Philip	170
Eustace, Thomas	184
Fagan, Christopher	1,996
Fagan, Richard	467
Fingall, Luke, earl of	35
Finglas, Elizabeth	254
Finglas, Mary	221
Finglas, Robert	364
Fitzrery, Robert	340
Fitzsimons, Marcus	371
Font, Thomas	8
Foster, John	88
Fox, Garrett	250
Glover, John	13
Gormanston, Jenico, Viscount	675
Gough, Ignatius	2
Gough, William	1
Hollywood, John	1,825
Hore, Philip	857
Humphrey, James	67
Hussey, Luke	660
Jacob, Richard	100
Jorden, John	164
Locke, John	776
Luttrell, Alice	234
Luttrell, Thomas	2,581
Lynes, Bartholomew	138
Mills, Ralph	143
Moore, Patrick	8
Nettervill, Nicholas, Viscount	36
Nottingham, Peter	797
Nugent, Levallin	25
Nugent, Richard	498
Nugent, Robert	425
Plunket, Anne	400
Plunket, Edward	178
Plunket, Luke	345
Plunket, Nicholas	1,462
Purcell, John	77
Read, John	42
Rowse, Richard	80
Russell, Bartholomew	463
Russell, Mathew	532
Sarsfield, Patrick	1,394
Segrave, John	848
Segrave, William	106
Stronge, Katherine	219
Talbot, Sir Henry	697
Talbot, John (of Belgard)	1,355
Talbot, John (of Malahide)	605
Taylor, Edward	290

Taylor, John	322	Walsh, Adam	40
Trimleston, Mathew, Lord	550	Walsh, John	697
Tyrconnell, Oliver, earl of	2,262	Walsh, Walter	229
Ussher, George	171	Warren, William	571
Ussher, Robert	253	White, Nicholas	326
Veldon, Christopher	10		43,787

2. *New English Catholic Proprietors*

	Acres
Alen, James	934
Wolverton, Christopher	122
Wolverton, James	933
	1,989

3. *Old Irish Catholic Proprietors*

	Acres		
Carbery, Richard	86	Dowde, Thomas	210
Carbery, Nicholas	41	Meagh, Mathew	220
Connell, John	207	Shield, Anne	4
Donnell, Richard	423		1,191

II. DUBLIN PROPRIETORS, 1663–1669: PROTESTANTS

1. *Old English Protestant Proprietors*

	Acres		
Ball, Robert	55	Fyan, Jane	18
Barry, Edward	86	Grace, James	119
Barry, Richard	244	Howth, William, Lord	5,312
Barry, William	40	Mapus, Ignatius	140
Brice, Richard	181	Mapus, Christopher	196
Browne, Richard	167	Mapus, Patrick	323
Cusack, Robert	157	Ormond, James, duke of	3,617
Denn, William	27	Plunket, Sir Walter	492
Dillon, Carey	34	Santry, James, Lord	1,743
Dowdall, Mathew	10	Tyrell, Sir Timothy	79
Eustace, Sir Maurice	703	Ussher, Sir William	756
Eustace, Walter	852	Walsh, John	400
			15,751

2. *New English Protestant Proprietors*

	Acres		
Adrian, Hubert	285	Lane, Sir George	820
Agar, William	811	Loftus, Sir Adam	7,639
Anderson, Lady	3	Loftus, Dudley	52
Archbold, Richard	75	Loftus, Nicholas	103
Bagshaw, Edward	85	Loftus, Robert	473
Bolton, Sir Edward	1,484	Lowther, Sir Gerard	4
Borr, John	552	Meath, Edward, earl of	1,108
Bulkeley, William	594	Mervin, Sir Audley	1,256
Burrowes, Alexander	101	Parsons, Sir Richard	1,710
Bysse, John	1,148	Piers, Sir Henry	7
Bysee, Edward	111	Piers, Martha	32
Cavan, Richard, earl of	50	Piercy, Anthony	38
Cork, Richard, earl of	120	Percival, Sir John	157
Dixon, Sir William	410	Piggot, Alexander	246
Domville, Sir William	514	Powerscourt, Folliot, Viscount	210
Drogheda, Henry, earl of	250	Radcliffe, Thomas	459
Exham , John	72	Ranelagh, Arthur, Viscount	1,063
Fitzharding, Chas, Viscount*	2,071	Rawdon, Sir George	1,055
Foster, Richard	443	Reeves, Dorothy, Lady	65
Gibbons, Thomas	24	Smith, Morris	138
Hackett, Lady	63	Staples, Alexander	613
Hilton, Robert	200	Sutton, Sir Edward	138
Holliday, John	113	Tallent, Oliver	60
Holliday, Thomas	100	Turner, James	125
Hooke, Thomas	5	Vernon, Edward*	593
Hoey, Sir John	940	Ware, Sir James	610
Hughes, John	154	Waterhouse, Thomas	20
Jones, Roger	692	Westly, Dr John	78
Jones, Sir Theophilus	46	White, Thomas	159
Kemp, John	88	Wybrant, Peter	20
Kingston, John, Lord	1,508		32,065

3. *Old Irish Protestant Proprietors*

	Acres		
Brady, Patrick	30	Kennedy, Sir Richard	446
Carberry, Richard	405	Kennedy, Walter	13
Donnellan, James	120	O'Connolly, Arthur & Martha	657
Duffe, Richard	11	Thomond, Henry, earl of	1,052
			2,734

ABSTRACT OF LAND OWNERSHIP IN DUBLIN, 1663–1669

	Acreage	*Per cent of land area*
Old English Catholic proprietors	43,787	33
New English Catholic proprietors	1,989	1
Old Irish Catholic proprietors	1,191	1
Old English Protestant proprietors	15,751	12
New English Protestant proprietors	32,065	24
Old Irish Protestant proprietors	2,734	2
Others:		
(a) Church land	12,294	
(b) Crown land	1,200	
(c) Common land	1,617	
(d) Dublin city	993	
(e) Trinity College	522	
(f) Duke of York	7,400	
(g) Unidentified ownership	11,437	
	35,463	27

SUMMARY

Catholic proprietors	46,967	35
Protestant proprietors	50,550	38
Others	35,463	27
	132,980	

LAND ACQUIRED IN DUBLIN BY COMMERCIAL MEANS, 1663–1688

I. *Protestants*

	Acres		*Acres*
Allen , Sir Joshua	1,002	Margetson, Archbishop James	1,113
Bowyer, Robert	78	Piercy, Anthony	183
Boyle, Archbishop Michael	600	Putland, Thomas	470
Davies, Sir William	146	Temple, Sir John	563
Deane, Edward	440	Witched, Thomas	229
Donovan, Jeremy	30	Williams, William	180
Johnson, Christopher*	960		5,994

II. *Catholics*

	Acres		Acres
Chamberlain, Michael	112	Leigh, Robert	342
Clinch, William	300	Sweetman, Edward	132
Crump, Richard	99	Talbot, Richard	1,641
Hackett, James	437	Trant, Sir Patrick*	116
			3,179

APPENDIX B: THE CLAIM SUBMITTED TO THE COURT OF CLAIMS ON 20 AUGUST 1663 BY PHILIP HORE, AND HIS TWO SONS, OF KILSALLAGHAN[1]

Philip Hore, late of Kilsallaghan, county Dublin, gentleman, and George Hore and Mathew Hore, second and third sons of the said Philip, claim the town and lands of Kilsallaghan, Dowmucky, Crostown, Stradbally, Cowleigh, Blackhall, Bewford, the Rath of Killossery, Chappellmidway, Ballboggane, Rahicastown; 13 houses and gardens and backsides, *cum pertinent'*, in Luske, Loghshill or Bullackesland, 2 houses, 2 gardens, 1 park and 1 orchard in New Street, Castleknock; and Irishtown, Castlecorragh, Rickinhead, part of Ballidowd; £12 chief rent in Killmartin; 8d chief rent in Ashtown; a mortgage in Paslostown. Denominations in the city and suburbs of Dublin: 5 houses, *cum pertinent'*, in Bull Lane; 1 house in Cork Hill or Corkow Lane; 1 house in Abbey Green; one house in the pavement leading to Young's Castle; 1 house, backside, and orchard in St. Bride's Street; 1 house, *cum pertinent'*, in St. Frances Street; 2 houses in Cork Street; one house in High Street. Lands also in the county of Meath: Clorterstown, Bulstown and Calestown. County Wexford: the manor of Skallrish; Kildowan and Carricks, Ballysholane, Crastestown, Craige Sallagh; 2 houses in St. Mary's Lane and Allen's Walls, town of Wexford, all which castles, manors, houses and royalties, etc., are in the possession of Sir George Lane, knight, and his under tenants.

Setting forth that Philip Hore of Kilsallaghan, county Dublin, deceased, the claimant Philip's father, was in his lifetime seized in fee of all and singular the premises, and being so seized did by his indenture bearing date 1 April 1630, in pursuance of certain articles of intermarriage, convey the same to James Bath of Athcarne, county Meath, esquire, and other feoffees, of part of the premises to the use of the said Philip, the feoffor, and Mary, his wife, for their lives; and of the residue of the premises to the use of the said Philip Hore, the feoffor, for life, the remainder of all and singular the premises to the use of the claimant Philip, son and heir apparent of the said Philip, the feoffor, for life, the remainder after the decease of the said Philip the younger to the use of the first son lawfully begotten of the said Philip, and the heirs males of the body of such first son; and for want of such issue, the remainder to the second and third sons of the said Philip the younger, and the heirs males of their bodies severally, successively and respectively, with divers other remainders over to the 4th and 5th sons of the said Philip the younger in like manner, with other remainders over, *pro ut per deed patet*.

By virtue whereof and of Statute of Uses the said Philip, the feoffor and Mary, his wife, became seized of the premises to them limited as aforesaid, and were in possession thereof on 22 October 1641, with the respective remainders over as aforesaid. That the said Philip and Mary, being so seized, about *anno* 1657 died so seized, after whose decease all and singular the premises remained and came to the claimant Philip for life, who accordingly entered and continued seized of the premises until he was thereout expulsed by the late usurpers, which is the claimant Philip's title.

The claimants George and Mathew set forth that the claimant Philip had issue Philip, his 1st son, who is dead without heirs males of his body, and that the claimants George and Mathew are the 2nd and 3rd sons of the said Philip the younger, lawfully begotten, and so are respectively entitled to the remainder so limited to them as aforesaid, and that they, being innocents, pray that the same may be decreed unto them by this court, is the scope of their claim.

Notes

PREFACE

1. Several recent studies have added to our understanding of the settlement. Harold O'Sullivan's thesis (Ph.D., University of Dublin, 1991), 'Land ownership changes in the county of Louth in the seventeenth century', has unravelled many of the technicalities concerned with the legal and administrative history of land tenure during the century. The pattern of land ownership distribution in county Dublin as it emerged in 1641 and under the Restoration settlement, including the disposal of suppressed and alienated church land, is summarized by W.J. Smyth, 'Exploring the social and cultural topographies of sixteenth and seventeenth-century county Dublin', Aalen, F. & Whelan, K. (ed.), *Dublin City and County: from prehistory to present* (Dublin, 1992), pp. 132–49.

CHAPTER I

1. *Cal. S.P. Ire., 1603–6*, p. 231. For a discussion of the terms 'Old Irish', 'Old English', and 'New English', see appendix A.
2. *Cal. pat. rolls Ire., Hen. VIII–Eliz.*, i. 54-5. Numerous references to both Alen and Brabazon can be found in B. Bradshaw, *The Dissolution of the Religious Orders in Ireland under Henry VIII* (Cambridge, 1974), and R.D. Edwards, *Church and State in Tudor Ireland* (Dublin, 1935).
3. *Cal. pat. rolls Ire., Hen. VIII-Eliz.*, i. 73–4, 77, 90; *Cal. fiants Ire., Hen. VIII*, nos. 91, 238, 314, 350, 374, 539; N. Donnelly, *History of Dublin Parishes* (Dublin, n.d.), iv. 98; B. Bradshaw, 'The opposition to the ecclesiastical legislation in the Irish Reformation parliament', *I.H.S.*, xvi (1969), 296–7; id., *Dissolution of Religious Orders in Ireland*, pp. 111, 128, 185, 239.
4. *State Papers, Henry VIII*, iii. 129; N.B. White (ed.), *Extents of Irish Monastic Possessions, 1540–41*, I.M.C. (Dublin, 1943), 59. This barony was known in the seventeenth century as Newcastle and Uppercross, but in the interest of clarity, and as a way of distinguishing it from the separate barony of Uppercross, it will henceforth be referred to simply as Newcastle.
5. *Cal. fiants Ire., Hen. VIII*, no. 547.
6. Ibid., no. 310, 460. Technically, Rathdown 'half barony', from the time in the early seventeenth century when the border of Dublin and Wicklow was officially delineated and the barony was bisected.
7. White, *Monastic Possessions*, p. 81; *State Papers Henry VIII*, ii. 384.
8. *Cal. pat. rolls Ire., Hen. VIII-Eliz.*, i. 57, 75; *Cal. Fiants Ire., Hen. VIII*, nos. 201, 525; *Cal. Fiants Ire., Eliz.*, no. 6425; Bradshaw, *Dissolution of the Religious Orders in Ireland*, pp. 28–9, 89–91, 122–3, 189.
9. A.J. Otway-Ruthven has estimated that at the end of the Middle Ages the church held nearly half of the land of modern geographical Dublin, which, she adds, was a much higher proportion than seems to have occurred elsewhere in the country. 'The mediaeval church lands of county Dublin,', J. Watt, *et al* (ed.), *Medieval Studies Presented to*

Aubrey Gwynn (Dublin, 1961), part I, p. 56.

10. White, *Monastic Possessions,* p. 1; *Cal. pat. rolls Ire., Hen. VIII-Eliz.*, i. 75; M.C. O'Conbhuidhe, 'The lands of St. Mary's Abbey, Dublin, at the dissolution of the abbey', *Reportorium Novum*, iii. no. 1 (1961–2); Otway-Ruthven, 'Mediaeval church lands of Co. Dublin', *supra*, p. 62.
11. *Cal. fiants Ire., Hen. VIII*, nos. 384, 386, 400–1, 449; M. Ronan, *The Reformation in Dublin, 1536–58* (London, 1926), 170–83.
12. *Cal. fiants Ire., Ed. VI*, no. 1083; *Cal. fiants Ire., Eliz.*, nos 1107, 1328, 1390, 1594, 2562–4, 2660, 2675, 5328.
13. *Cal. S.P. Ire., 1606–8*, pp. 133–4; *Cal. S.P. Ire., 1608–10*, pp. 207, 506; *Cal. S.P. Ire., 1611–14*, pp. 486–7; *Cal. pat. rolls Ire. Jas. I*, pp. 1, 186, 512. For Hamilton and Carroll see R.J. Hunter, 'The Ulster plantation in counties Armagh and Cavan, 1608–41' (M. Litt. thesis, Trinity College, Dublin, 1969), chp. 11. For Hamilton and Wakeman see T.M. Healy, *Stolen Waters* (London, 1913).
14. *Cal. pat. rolls Ire., Hen. VIII-Eliz.*, i. 109; *Cal. S.P. Ire., 1509–73*, pp. 165, 268, 277; *Cal. Carew MSS., 1589–1600*, p.188; *Cal. S.P. Ire., 1615–25*, pp. 83–4, 99.
15. *Cal. S.P. Ire., 1509–73*, p. 162.
16. A transcript of an inquisition of Bath's estate, taken in 1538, appears in Ainsworth, Reports, III. 674–5.
17. *Cal. fiants Ire., en. VIII*, no. 66; *Cal. S.P. Ire., 1509–73*, pp. 194, 228; T. O'Laidhin (ed.), *Sidney State Papers, 1565–70*, I.M.C. (Dublin, 1962), 7–9.
18. *Cal. S.P. Ire.*, 1574–85, p. 332.
19. *Cal. fiants Ire., Eliz.*, nos. 3745, 4126, 4129, 4925, 5260, 5509, 5911.
20. Ibid., no. 4134; *Cal. pat. rolls Ire., 18th–45th Eliz.*, ii. 36. Upon the death of Lady Baltinglas in 1610 Monkstown passed to her nephew, Henry Cheevers, whose son, Walter, was in possession in 1641. Donnelly, *History of Dublin Parishes*, i. 133, 134.
21. *Cal. fiants Ire., Eliz.*, no. 6033; *Cal. pat. rolls Ire., Jas. I*, p. 67.
22. *Cal fiants Ire., Eliz.*, nos. 4177, 4265.
23. E. McPharland, 'Rathfarnham Castle, Co. Dublin', *Country Life* (9 Sept. 1982), 734.
24. *Cal. S.P. Ire., 1588–92*, p. 534.
25. *Cal. pat. rolls Ire., Jas I*, p. 251.
26. Carte, *Ormond*, i. 382.
27. *Cal. fiants Ire., Eliz.*, no 6739; *Cal. S.P. Ire., 1606–8*, pp. 45–6.
28. H.F. Kearney, *Strafford in Ireland, 1633–41* (Manchester, 1959), 83. The seminal study of this subject is T. Ranger, 'Richard Boyle and the making of an Irish fortune, 1588–1614', *I.H.S.*, x (1957). See also N. Canny, *The Upstart Earl* (Cambridge, 1982).
29. *Cal. fiants Ire., Hen. VIII*, nos. 400, 446; *Cal. fiants Ire., Eliz.*, nos 2434–5; *Cal. pat. rolls Ire., Jas. I*, pp. 78–9.
30. A. Clarke, *The Old English In Ireland, 1625–42* (London, 1966), 192.
31. Ibid., pp. 205–7.
32. *Commons' jn. Ire., i. 299.*
33. R.C. Simington and J. MacLellan (ed.), 'Oireachtas Library, list of outlaws, 1641–1647', *Anal. Hib.*, no. 23 (1966). Another list of outlawries appears in B.L., Additional MS. 4772, ff. 38–87, which is printed in Gilbert, *Ir. Confed.*, iii. 340–86.
34. Incorrectly cited in *The Statutes of the Realm*, v (London, 1819), 168, as 16 Car. I, c. 33. It should read 17 Car. I. See the editor's note on p. 178, and J. Rushworth, *Historical Collections of private passages of state, 1618–48* (London, 1692), part iii, vol. 1, p. 557.
35. Ibid.
36. In the general treatment of the period 1641–52 I have relied on A. Clarke, *Old English in Ireland*, and P.J. Corish, chps. xi–xii, in Moody, T.W., Martin, F.X., Byrne, F.J. (ed.), *A New History of Ireland* iii, (Oxford, 1976).
37. Firth and Rait, *Acts*, ii. 598–603.

38. T. Barnard, 'Planters and policies in Cromwellian Ireland', *Past & Present, no. 61 (1973), 35, 37–8, 39.*
39. Firth and Rait, *Acts*, ii. 722–53.
40. R. Dunlop (ed.), *Ireland under the Commonwealth* (Manchester, 1913), ii. 355.
41. *Cromwellian Settlement*, p. 108; R.C. Simington, *The Transplantation to Connacht*, I.M.C. (Dublin, 1971), 84, 259; H.M.C., *Ormonde MSS.*, n.s., ii, 4-5; T.C.D., MS. 844, ff. 160–70.
42. Bodl., Carte MS. 60, f. 384.
43. P.R.O.I., Ferguson MS. xiii, pp. 73, 99–100; *Cal. S.P. Ire., 1660–2*, p. 74.
44. *Cal. S.P.Dom., 1649–50*, p. 305.
45. E. MacLysaght, 'Commonwealth state accounts: Ireland, 1650–1656', *Anal. Hib.*, no. 15 (1944), 245; Simington, *Transplantation to Connacht*, pp. 234, 245, 271.
46. C.S., pp. 44 (65), 71 (iii); Bodl., Carte MS. 154, f. 51. See also H. O'Sullivan, 'Land ownership changes in the county of Louth in the seventeenth century' (Ph.D., University of Dublin, 1991), i. 71.
47. Simington, *Transplantation to Connacht.*
48. See pp. 37–8.
49. Dunlop *Ireland under the Commonwealth*, ii. 387.
50. Russell and Prendergast, *Carte Manuscripts*, p. 146.
51. *Cal. S.P. Ire., 1660–2*,, p. 121; S. & D., pp. 55, 76.
52. B.M. O'Connell, *O'Connell Family Tracts*, no. 1 (Dublin, n.d.), 20.
53. S. & D., pp. 5, 7, 10, 17, 55, 101; R.I.A., S. & D. (Taylor set), Newcastle & Uppercross barony, p. 11.
54. Both are classified as Catholics in S. & D. (pp. 87, 89, 102) but as Protestants in the *C.S.* pp. 192 (45), 193 (47), 198 (55–6), 201 (61), 208 (73),. 212 (80), 247 (40). For a discussion of this problem see appendix A.
55. T. Birch (ed.), *A Collection of the State Papers of John Thurloe* (London, 1742), ii. 343; Dunlop, *Ireland under the Commonwealth*, ii. 197, 421; Simington, *Transplantation to Connacht*, pp. 85, 88, 89, 90, 172; Firth and Rait, *Acts*, ii. 599.
56. P.R.O.I., Ferguson MS. xiii, p. 87.
57. *Cal. S.P. Dom., 1649–50*, pp. 390, 396, 553; *Cal. S.P. Dom., 1650*, p. 547; *Cal. S.P. Dom., 1651*, pp. 500, 530; *Cal. S.P. Dom., 1651–2*, p. 13.
58. *C.S.*, p. 260 (1); *Calendar of Ancient Deeds and Muniments Preserved in the Pembroke Estate Office* (Dublin, 1891), 101 (314), 102 (316–17); *Common's jn.*, v. 114; *Lords' jn.*, ix. 86, 157; King's Inns, Dublin, Prendergast MS. xiv, pp. 427–31, 434–46, 463–5; *Cal. S.P. Dom., 1654*, p. 301; *Cal. S.P. Ire.*, 1647–60, p. 840. See Edmund Ludlow's amusing account of his voyage from Ireland to England in 1655, during which Fitzwilliam, a fellow traveller, assured Ludlow (who had just been arrested at Beaumaris on orders of the Irish council) of his willingness to use his 'utmost endeavours with His Highness the Lord Protector, as he thought fit to call him, on his behalf. Ludlow thanked Fitzwilliam ('a civil person, tho a papist') but viewed the episode as a 'strange revolution of affairs, that the interest of a gentleman who had been lieutenant-general in the army of the Irish rebels, should be so much greater than mine in the General of the army of the Commonwealth'. C.H Firth (ed.), *The Memoirs of Edmund Ludlow* (Oxford, 1894), i. 426–7. See also Fitzwilliam's reference to his estate in a letter to Henry Cromwell in 1657, and Richard Cromwell's favourable impression of Fitzwilliam in R.W. Ramsey, *Henry Cromwell* (London, 1933), 179, 236–7.
59. Clarendon, *Life: Continuation*, p. 59.
60. Firth and Rait, *Acts*, ii. 726–7, 736.
61. Dunlop *Ireland under the Commonwealth*, ii. 453, 519–20, 536, 608–9.
62. B.L., Additional Charter 32976; Harleian MS. 4784.
63. T.A. Larcom, *The History of the Survey of Ireland, commonly called the Down Survey,*

by Doctor William Petty, (Dublin, 1851), 381; Firth and Rait, *Acts*, ii. 753; *Cal. S.P. Ire.*, 1660–2, p. 436.

64. *C.S.*, p. 195 (50); Prendergast, *Restoration to Revolution*, p. 8; id., *Cromwellian Settlement*, p. 108.
65. J.T. Gilbert and Lady Gilbert (ed.), *Cal. Anc. Recs. Dublin* (Dublin, 1889–1944), iii. 479–80; *Cal. S.P. Ire.*, 1663–5, pp. 43–4.
66. Cal. S.P. Ire., 1660–2, p. 76; S. Pender (ed.), *A Census of Ireland, c. 1659*, I.M.C. (Dublin, 1939), 389.
67. *Cal. S.P. Ire., 1660–2*, p. 374; *C.S.*, p. 73 (114).
68. N.L.I., MS. 31, ff. 29–30, 85.
69. *Cal. S.P. Ire., 1660–2*, pp. 302–3; Lodge, *Peerage*, iv. 209; Clarke, *Old English in Ireland*, pp. 84, 182, 191, 200; *C.S.*, pp. 36 (54), 50 (76), 52–3 (79–80).
70. Prendergast, *Cromwellian Settlement*, p. 108; Firth and Rait, *Acts*, ii. 738.
71. *Cal. S.P. Ire., 1647–60*, pp. 643–5; W.H. Hardinge, 'On manuscript mapped and other townland surveys in Ireland of a public character. . .' *R.I.A. Trans*, xxiv, Antiquities (1873), 46; Bodl., Carte MS. 44, f. 474; *C.S.*, p. 222. For Cook read Hooke.
72. *Cal. S.P. Ire., 1660–2* p. 39.
73. P.R.O.I., Lodge MS. vi, ff. 432–3; Bodl., Carte MS. 44, f. 474; Ramsey, *Henry Cromwell*, p. 47; C. Hill, *God's Englishman* (New York, 1970), 96; C.H. Firth, *Cromwell's Army* (London, 3rd edn., 1921), 158; id., *Memoirs of Ludlow*, i. 394 (n); Firth and Rait, *Acts*, ii. 1134.
74. *Inq. Cancell. Hib. Report.*, i, (6) Car. II (Dublin).
75. *Cal. S.P. Ire., 1660–2*, p. 286.
76. Dunlop, *Ireland under the Commonwealth*, ii. 578; Firth and Rait, *Acts*, ii. 355–7.
77. As examples see *C.S.*, pp. 112 (52), 114–15 (55–7), 149 (121), and S. & D., pp. 20,40.
78. The author of *The State of the Papist and Protestant Proprieties in the Kingdom of Ireland* (London, 1689), maintains (p. 6) that the Catholics who proved their constant good affection to the parliament were restored to 100,000 acres. This, however, is a gross exaggeration and Petty probably came closer to the mark when he estimated that 40,000 acres were restored to twenty-six such people. C.H. Hull (ed.), *The Economic Writings of Sir William Petty* (Cambridge, 1899), i. 136; ii. 601.
79. *Mercurius Publicus*, no. 23 (24 May 1660), p. 357.
80. H.M.C., *Egmont MSS*, i, part 2, 600.
81. Bodl., Carte MS. 59, f. 465.
82. Pender, *Census of Ireland*, pp. 379, 381, 383, 384, 385, 386, 387, 388, 390, 391.
83. Barnard, 'Planters and politics in Cromwellian Ireland', *Past & Present*, no. 61 (1973), 65; R. Cox, *Hibernia Anglicana* (London, 1689–90), part ii, p. 3 ('A letter to the author of the history of Ireland. . .'); J.I. McGuire, 'The Dublin convention, the Protestant community and the emergence of an ecclesiastical settlement in 1660', in A. Cosgrove and J.I. McGuire (ed.), *Parliament & Community* (Historical Studies, xiv) Belfast, 1983.

CHAPTER II

1. Bodl., Carte MS. 48, f. 21v; Clarendon, *Life: Continuation*, pp. 27, 31.
2. W. Sachse (ed.), *The Diurnal of Thomas Rugg, 1659–1661* (Camden soc., 3rd ser., xci, 1961), 68; Bodl., Carte MS. 44, f. 665; T.C.D., MS. 808, ff. 155–155v.
3. Aungier to Ormond, 22 May 1660 (Bodl., Carte MS. 30, f. 667).
4. R. Steele (ed.), *Tudor and Stuart Proclamations* (Oxford, 1910), i, no. 3220 (England and Wales).
5. Bodl., Carte MS. 30, f. 626.
6. Gilbert, *Ir. Confed.*, vii. 188–9.
7. *Commons's jn.*, viii. 5–6.
8. *Lords' jn.*, xi. 109.

9. C. Hill, *God's Englishman*, p. 152.
10. Charles to Coote, 16 March 1659/60 (Bodl., Carte MS. 30, f. 551).
11. Sir Walter Scott (ed.), *Memoirs of the Court of Charles the Second by Count Grammont* (London, 1846), pp. 168, 206–10, 246–50. Macaulay depicted Talbot as, *inter alia*, a bully, a pimp, and a cold-hearted, scheming sycophant. *History of England from the accession of James II* (London, 3rd. edn., 1849), ii. 48, 50. For a sympathetic portrayal see P. Sergeant, *Little Jennings and Fighting Dick Talbot* (London, 1913).
12. Not to be confused with Nicholas Plunket of Dunsoghly, a member of a collateral branch of the family.
13. Lady Burghclere, *The Life of James first Duke of Ormonde* (London, 1912), ii. 24; C. McNeill, 'Reports on manuscripts in the Bodleian Library, Oxford', *Anal. Hib.*, no. 1 (1930), 131.
14. 12 Car. II, c. II, s. 25.
15. Gilbert, *Jacobite Narrative*, pp. 12–14.
16. 7 May marks the date on which the Rump of the Long Parliament reassembled. Steele, *Tudor and Stuart Proclamations*, i, no. 3108 (England and Wales). 5 June 1649 was the date on which the council of state gave orders for transporting Cromwell's troops to Ireland. B. Whitelock, *Memorials of English Affairs* (London, 1732), p. 406. For the '49 Officers see the Glossary of Terms.
17. My summary of the proposals advanced by the various agents is based on Carte, *Ormond*, iv. 26–30. Documents relating to the discussions on the settlement in 1660 can be found in B.L., Additional MS. 35850, ff. 114–55.
18. Carte, *Ormond*, iv. 31–2.
19. Clarendon, *Life: Continuation*, p. 56; Eustace to Sir George Lane, 17 April 1661 (N.L.I., MS. 8643/ 1).
20. *His Majesties Gracious Declaration for the Settlement of his Kingdom of Ireland . . .* (London, 1660), pp. 6–8, 9–11, 14–15, 17–19, 20–7.
21. The only exception to this principle occurred in cases in which an innocent Catholic, having been dispossessed of property in corporate towns for reasons of security, was required to accept other lands in the neighbourhood in lieu of being restored to his former property in the town. In these cases he was said to be restored *in specie*. The king, however, was empowered to exempt individual Catholics from the operation of this provision. Decl., s. 18. Individuals claiming restoration by proviso in the Declaration or Instructions were usually referred to generally as 'proviso-men', but a distinction was normally drawn between them and the nominees.
22. N.L.I., MS. 16974, p. 38. According to Sir George Lane, the Instructions were never passed under the great seal but were sent to Ireland under the king's privy signet and sign manual. Alterations in the Instructions continued to be made, however, after they had been transmitted to Ireland. Ibid., pp. 50, 51.
23. Inst., s. 11.
24. Prendergast, *Restoration to revolution*, p. 16; *Cal. S.P. Ire., 1660–2*, pp. 149, 306.
25. Steele, *Tudor and Stuart Proclamations*, ii, no. 640 (Ireland).
26. Aungier to Ormond, 27 April 1661 (Bodl., Carte MS. 31, f. 151).
27. Eustace to Sir George Lane, 17 April 1661 (N.L.I., MS. 8643/ 1).
28. Aungier maintained that 'very few or none' of the Catholics submitted claims to the commissioners. Aungier to Ormond, 27 April 1661 (Bodl., Carte MS. 31, f. 151). The evidence suggests, however, that a number of them did, in fact, submit claims. See S. & E., ff. 234, 305, 360; *Mercurius Hibernicus*, no. 3 (27 Jan. 1662/3), p. 18; no. 4 (4 Feb. 1662/3), p. 29; *Cal. S.P. Ire., 1660–2*, pp. 468, 470.
29. Since most of the Catholic lords had been indicted or outlawed, only one sat in the House of Lords when it first assembled in 1661. They were quietly admitted, however, by special agreement with the king, over the course of the life of the parliament. As a result,

they eventually came to represent over a third of the membership, leaving the number of Catholic and Protestant peers closely balanced. For this reason the Anglican bishops played an important role in the parliament, and it provides an explanation why the Old English Protestants supported the restoration of episcopacy, a point noted by T. Barnard, 'Planters and policies in Cromwellian Ireland', *Past & Present*, no. 61 (1973), 67 (n.) Because very few Catholics had been restored when the parliament assembled, the House of Commons was an exclusively Protestant body. F. O'Donoghue, 'Parliament in Ireland under Charles II', (M.A. thesis, University College, Dublin, 1970).

30. P.R.O.N.I., Annesley MSS., Misc. Books, no. 5, Lib. G, f. 69; N.L.I., MS. 16974, p. 54.
31. Recipients of such letters were called 'letterees'.
32. *Cal. S.P. Ire., 1660–2*, pp. 204, 309–10; *Cal. S.P. Ire., 1669–70*, p. 381; P.R.O., P.C. 2/55, ff. 395–6.
33. Sachse, *Diurnal of Thomas Rugg*, p. 144; *Cal. S.P. Ire., 1660–2*, p. 268; Steele, *Tudor and Stuart Proclamations*, ii, no. 624 (Ireland).
34. For references to members of the House of Commons being disturbed in their Dublin estates, see *Commons' jn., Ire.*, i. 499, 506, 525, 532.
35. Ibid., 434–5; Bodl., Carte MS. 44, f. 474.
36. *Commons' jn., Ire.*, i. 450, 451.
37. *Cal. S.P. Ire., 1663–5*, p. 305.
38. *Commons' jn., Ire.*, i. 496, 497, 504, 507, 572, 584; *Lords' jn., Ire.*, i. 299, 345.
39. *Cal. S.P. Ire., 1663–5*, p. 305.
40. 12 Car. II, c. 7; H.M.C., *Ormonde MSS.*, n.s. iii. 7; *Cal. S.P. Ire., 1660–2*, p. 447; Bodl., Carte MS. 42, f. 274.
41. *Cal. S.P. Ire., 1660–2*, pp. 214, 351–2.
42. Ibid., p. 344; Barnard, *Cromwellian Ireland*, pp. 82, 83. For Lane see F.E. Ball, 'Some notes on the households of the dukes of Ormond', *R.I.A. Proc.*, xxxviii, sec. C (1928–9), 2–4.
43. Bodl., Carte MS. 49, f. 75; H.M.C. *Hastings MSS.*, iv. 106; A. Bryant (ed.), *The Letters, Speeches and Declarations of King Charles II* (London, 1935), pp. 108–9.
44. P.R.O., P.C. 2/55, f. 293; T. Morrice (ed.), *A Collection of the State Letters of . . . Roger Boyle, the first Earl of Orrery . . .* (Dublin, 1743), i. 68–70; N.L.I., MS. 16974, pp. 56–8; H.M.C., *Hastings MSS.*, iv. 131. A full record of the discussions in council on the Act of Settlement during 1661–2 can be found in B.L., Additional MS. 35851, ff. 3–138; MS. 4781, ff. 35–301; P.R.O.N.I., Annesley MSS., Misc. Books, no. 5, Lib. G; and Pearse Street Library, Dublin, Gilbert Collection, MS. 198, ff. 147–75, and 219, ff. 256–740.
45. 14 & 15 Car. II, c. 2. T.C.D. MS. 587 contains a record of the discussions 'set down in the same order as they were delivered to his majesty. . .'
46. Mountmorres, *The History of the Principal Transactions of the Irish Parliament, from the year 1634 to 1666* (London, 1792), i. 397.
47. Preamble, ss. 1, 3–4. By s. 3 the land held by ten individuals, including Ormond and Sir George Lane, was exempt from the operation of the vesting clause.
48. Decl., ss. 25–7; Inst., s. 225.
49. Inst., s. 179.
50. Ibid.,ss. 170, 44.
51. Ibid., ss. 9, 130. S. 135, however, reserved the king's right to revoke letters patent issued after 30 November 1660.
52. *Collections for a History of Staffordshire* (Staffordshire Rec. Soc., 4th ser., ii, 1958), 32; D. Underdown, *Royalist Conspiracy in England, 1649–1660* (New Haven, Conn., 1960), pp. 46, 242; *Cal. S.P. Dom., 1655*, p. 575; *Cal. S.P. Dom., 1656–7*, p. 166; H.M.C., *Egmont MSS.*, i, part 2, 563–4; *The Case of John Vernon Depending Before the . . . House of Lords . . .* (n.d., n.p.), p. 1; J. O'Hart, *Irish Pedigrees* (New York, 1915), ii.

417–18; King's Inns, Dublin, Prendergast MS. xiii, pp. 847–9; *Cal. S.P. Ire., 1660–2*, pp. 60, 71; P.R.O.I., Lodge MS. vii, f. 4. The sources are conflicting as to the exact family relationship of Edward and John Vernon, but the weight of the evidence suggests that they were cousins.

53. Inst., s. 131; *Cal. S.P. Ire., 1663–5*, p. 336.
54. N.L.I., MS. 16974, p. 82.
55. Inst., ss. 195–7; *Cal. S.P. Ire., 1660–62*, p. 509; *Cal. S.P. Ire., 1663–5*, pp. 335–7, 425–7.
56. *D.N.B.*; Albemarle to Ormond, 24 Aug.. 1661 (Bodl., Carte MS. 31, f. 302); Inst., s. 98.
57. Inst., ss. 222–3. The matter was already under discussion. See *Cal. S.P. Ire., 1660–2*, p. 570.
58. Gilbert, *Contemp. Hist.*, i. 353–9; id., *Ir. Confed.*, i. 8.
59. H.M.C., *Ormonde MSS.*, n.s., ii. 6; *Commons' jn.*, ii. 300, 306, 360; iii. 674; iv. 150, 179, 192; vi. 184; W.H. Coates (ed.), *The Journal of Sir Simonds D'Ewes* (New Haven, Conn., 1942), pp. 63, 359; *Cal. S.P. Dom., 1649–50*, p. 80; *Cal. S.P. Dom., 1655–6*, p. 135; C.H. Firth and G. Davies, *A Regimental History of Cromwell's Army* (Oxford, 1940), i. 350; ii. 653–4; Bodl., Carte MS. 44, f. 474; T. O'Gorman, 'Notice of Owen O'Connolly', *R.S.A.I.J.*, vi, 4th ser. (1883–4), 52–60; P.B. O'Mordha, 'The MacMahons of Monaghan', *Clogher Record*, ii, no. 3 (1959), 493–7.
60. Inst, s. 147.
61. P.R.O., S.P. 63/307/4. I am indebted to Professor Ronald Hutton for providing me with the precise source for this information.
62. Inst., s. 194.
63. Ibid., ss. 102–5. The augmentation of the other seven sees provided for the following yearly episcopal incomes: Kildare, £700; Ossory, £400; Ferns and Leighlin, Cashell, and Limerick, £300; Clonfert and Killaloe, £200.
64. Clarendon, *Life: Continuation*, p. 56.
65. A.L. Rowse, *The Early Churchills* (London, 1956).
66. D. Witcombe, *Charles II and the Cavalier House of Commons, 1663–1674* (Manchester, 1966), p. 199; *Cal. S.P. Ire., 1663–5*, p. 87.
67. Lodge, *Peerage, v. 159; C.H. Firth,* The Last Years of the Protectorate London, 1909), ii. 67 (n); Carte, *Ormond*, v. 57; Cal. S.P. Ire., 1660–2, p. 226; *Lib. Mun. Pub. Hib.*, i, part 2, p. 56; H. Wheatley (ed.), *The Diary of Samuel Pepys* (London, 1895), vi. 109 (n); *Cal. Claren. S.P.*, iv. 22, 23, 323, 403, 536–7, 613, 644–5, 655.
68. E.S. de Beer (ed.), *The Diary of John Evelyn* (Oxford, 1955), iv. 360 (n); Firth and Davies, *Regimental History of Cromwell's Army*, ii. 577–9; Russell and Prendergast, *Carte Manuscripts*, pp. 189, 191–2.
69. M.F. Bond (ed.) *The Diaries and Papers of Sir Edward Dering, Second Baronet, 1644–1684* (London, 1976), 3, 6; D.B. Henning (ed.), *The Parliamentary Diary of Sir Edward Dering, 1670–1673* (New Haven, Conn., 1940), ix-xviii.
70. Bagwell, *Stuarts*, iii. 30, 46; *Cal. S.P. Dom., 1661–2*, p. 427.
71. F.E. Ball, 'Some notes on the Irish judiciary in the reign of Charles II, 1660–1685', *Jr. Cork Hist. and Arch. Soc.*, 2nd ser., vii (1901), 140–1; Bodl., Carte MS. 143, f. 215; *Cal. S.P. Ire., 1663–5*, pp. 589–90.
72. E. Foss, *The Judges of England* (London, 1848–64), vii 155–6; *Members of Parliament* (London, 1878), part 1, p. 526. Three of the commissioners, Dering, Cooke, and Broderick, obtained seats in the Irish parliament of 1661.
73. *Cal. S.P. Ire., 1663–5*, p. 107.
74. D.K.Rep. 19, p. 39; King's Inns, Dublin, Prendergast MS. v, p. 457: *Cal. Claren. S.P.*, v. 256, 260. Twenty one court attorneys were appointed on 2 October 1662. Steele, *Tudor and Stuart Proclamations*, ii, no. 690 (Ireland).
75. *Cal. Claren. S.P*, v. 280, 281, 283.

CHAPTER III

1. The number 829 is based on a tabulation of the figures which appear in the precis of the abstract of the decrees of the court in *D.K. Rep. 19* p. 41. The total entered for May is incorrect and should read 74. Some names appear more than once in the body of the abstract (for example, nos. 100, 103; 152, 218; 127, 599; 61, 784), while others whose claims were heard do not appear at all, the most conspicuous being the earl of Westmeath. For examples of claimants restored by means other than decrees of innocence, see nos. 615, 625 and 733. The number of nocent decisions awarded is not accurately rendered, the total of which, derived from other sources, was considerably more than the 115 as entered in the abstract. Some inaccuracies arose in the transcription, and in all doubtful cases comparison should be made with N.L.I., 19080, from which the printed version appears to have been taken. For the provenance of this document see p. 38 of *D.K. Rep. 19*. The same manuscript was transcribed by J.P. Prendergast and can be found in vol. v, pp. 791–1051 of his papers in the King's Inns, Dublin. Another manuscript copy of the abstract appears in B.L., Egerton MS. 789. A condensed version of this chapter appears in L. Arnold, 'The Irish court of claims of 1663', *I.H.S.*, xxiv (Nov. 1985).
2. Philip Hore, the plaintiff, was postponed and his father was declared nocent posthumously, but Hore's five brothers and sisters, along with his two sons and a brother-in-law, were all declared innocent. Bodl., Carte MS 67, f. 31.
3. Larcom, *History of the Down Survey*, pp. 43, 124.
4. See p. 67.
5. Ormond to Clarendon, 8 Feb. 1662/3 (Bodl. Carte MS, 143, f. 81).
6. J.P. Prendergast classified 168 of the claimants as Protestants. King's Inns, Dublin, Prendergast MS. v, pp. 416–19.
7. Bodl., Carte MS. 67, f. 13v.
8. S. & E., f. 12; *Cal. S.P. Ire., 1660–2*, p. 89; *Cal. S.P. Ire., 1663–5*, p. 143; S. & D., p. 26.
9. P.R.O.I., MS. 3538; S. &E., f. 18; *D.K. Rep. 19*, p. 45 (66).
10. *Cal. S.P. Ire., 1660–2*, pp. 121–2; *Cal. S.P. Ire., 1669–70*, pp. 585, 586. The *D.K. Rep.* 19, p. 42 (2), indicates that Richard Brice was declared an innocent Catholic, but the printed transcript of his decree makes it clear that he was restored as an innocent Protestant and that his father was a Catholic. *I.R.C.R.*, pp. 523–5.
11. F.E. Ball, *A History of the County Dublin* (Dublin, 1902–17), part 2, p. 74; W.A. Shaw (ed.), *Letters of denization and acts of naturalization for aliens in England and Ireland, 1603–1700*, Huguenot Society of London, xviii (Lymington, 1911), 328; R. Loeber, 'English and Irish sources for the history of Dutch economic activity in Ireland, 1600–1689', *Irish Economic and Social History*, viii (1981), 77; *D.K. Rep. 19*, p. 45 (60) S. & E., f. 17.
12. *Mercurius Hibernicus*, no. 11 (28 March 1663), p. 83; no. 12 (4 April 1663), p. 92; *Mercurius Publicus*, no. 15 (28 March 1663), pp. 239–40; no. 18 (4 April 1663). p. 277; Prendergast, *Cromwellian Settlement*, pp. 156–8; id., 'The Butlers, Lords Ikerrin, before the court of transplantation . . . and at the first and second court of claims . . . 1662–1666', *R.S.A.I.J.*, 4th ser., vii (1885–6), 599–600; Inst., s. 46.
13. S. & E., f. 63.
14. *Mercurius Hibernicus*, no. 10 (23 March 1662/3), p. 73.
15. G. Howard, *A Treatise on the Exchequer and Revenue of Ireland* (Dublin, 1776), ii. 149, 152; W. Betham, An Historical Account of the Acts of Settlement and Explanation (N.L.I., Joly MS 6), p. 94. Betham extracted entire passages from Howard.
16. *Mercurius Hibernicus*, no. 14 (14 April 1663). p. 113; *I.R.C.R., p. 525; Mercurius Publicus*, no 15 (21, 27 March 1662/3), pp. 237, 239. Harold O'Sullivan states that the claims of encumbrancers were 'normally' left to law. 'Land ownership changes in the county of Louth in the seventeenth century', i. 272.

17. *Mercurius Publicus*, no. 10 (17 Feb. 1662/3), p. 162.
18. Howard, *Treatise*, ii. 133–4; *H.M.C., Rep. 15*, app. i. 122. A transcript of an injunction from the commissioners to the sheriffs of county Meath ordering the restoration of an innocent claimant can be found among Sir William Beham's genealogical abstracts, P.R.O.I., BET, vol. 8, ff. 40–1.
19. *State of the Papist and Protestant Proprieties in the Kingdom of Ireland*, pp. 31–2; Howard *Treatise*, ii. 150, 165–6.
20. Delahide to Ormond, 7 Dec. 1663 (Bodl., Carte MS. 159, f. 143).
21. S. & E., f. 64; Bodl., Carte MS. 67, f. 14; *D.K. Rep. 19*, pp. 49 (135), 77 (707).
22. *Mercurius Hibernious*, no. 2 (22 Jan. 1662/3), p. 10; no. 5 (10 Feb. 1662/3), p. 33.
23. S. & E., ff. 24, 31, 101; Prendergast, *Restoration to Revolution*, p. 21; Butler, *Confiscation*, p. 185. See also Carte, *Ormond*, v. 118, for Sir Heneage Finch's reference to this legal principle in the case of the Sarsfields of Lucan.
24. Decl., s. 28.
25. Bodl., Carte MS. 67, f. 14v. The commissioners said later that they had had time to restore only about a sixth of the innocent transplanters. *I.R.C.R.*, p. 653.
26. S.& E., f. 4; *D.K. Rep. 19*, pp. 48 (111, 123), 64 (475). It was entered on the court record of John McNamara, who claimed an estate in county Clare, that he 'had a decree for lands in Connacht', an example of internal transplantation. S. & E., f. 274.
27. King's Inns, Dublin Prendergast MS. v, p. 353.
28. Kent Archives Office, Dering papers, MS. U, 350, f. 11; S. & E., ff. 215–16; Bodl., Carte MS. 67, ff. 14–14v.
29. *Mercurius Hibernicus* no. 3 (27 Jan. 1662/3), p. 18.
30. S. & E., ff. 240, 427.
31. Ibid., ff. 85–8, 132; *D.K. Rep. 19*, pp. 49 (152), 52 (218).
32. *Cal. S.P. Ire., 1663–5*, p. 154.
33. Ibid., pp. 48, 50, 56–7.
34. S. & E., f. 46; *D.K. Rep. 19*, p. 48 (124).
35. *Cal. S.P. Ire., 1663–5*, p. 231; Russell and Prendergast, *Carte Manuscripts*, p. 152; *The Historical Works of the Right Rev. Nicholas French* (Dublin, 1846), i. 90.
36. S. & E., ff. 16, 18, 392–8.
37. *D.K. Rep. 19*, p. 64 (468); Genealogical Office, Dublin, MS. 160, p. 137. A John Walsh of Shanganagh was in 1704 licensed, as a Catholic, to keep arms. 'Irish Catholics licensed to keep arms (1704)', *archivium Hibernicum*, iv (1915), 63.
38. Inst., s. 85; Steele, *Tudor and Stuart Proclamations*, ii, no. 689 (Ireland).
39. Bagwell, *Stuarts*, iii. 334–5.
40. *Cal. S.P. Ire., 1663–5*, pp. 166, 182.
41. Leigh to Williamson, 11 July 1663 (*Cal. S.P. Ire., 1663–5*, p. 167). For Leigh see H.F. Hore (ed.), 'A chorographic account of the southern part of the county of Wexford, written anno 1684; by Robert Leigh, esq., of Rosegarland, in that county', *R.S.A.I.J.*, ii (1858); E. MacLysaght, *Irish Families* (Dublin, 1957), p. 208; *Burke's Irish Family Records* (London, 1976), p. 716. Leigh has been described as a 'clerk in Arlington's [Bennett's] office attached to Williamson' in *c.*1666–8, but he was clearly acting in a similar capacity long before 1666. William Godolphin was an under-secretary to Bennett. J. Sainty, *Officials of the Secretaries of State, 1660–1782* (London, 1973), pp. 80, 87. No official schedule of court fees has come to light, so we can only conjecture what they may have been from a few oblique references to them. This seems to have been what Sir Thomas Blake was alluding to when in August 1663 he told his mother, Dame Ellinor, that her decree of innocence (obtained in July) would cost 'upwards of £40.' M. Blake, *Blake Family Records, 1600 to 1700* (London, 1905), p. 92. See also H. O'Sullivan, 'Landownership changes in the county of Louth in the seventeenth century', ii. G155–60.

42. *Cal. S.P. Ire., 1669–70*, pp. 458–9; *Cal. S.P. Ire., 1663–5*, p. 199; *D.K. Rep. 19*, p. 74 (648).
43. *Cal. S.P. Ire., 1663–5*, pp. 96, 158–9.
44. Lane to Bennett, 8 July 1663 (Ibid., p. 163).
45. Bodl., Clarendon MS. 80, f. 314, and Appendix B. The former indicates that Philip Hore and his '2 brothers' submitted the second claim, but this is an error and should read '2 sons'.
46. Lane to Clarendon, 8 Aug. 1663 (*Cal. Claren, SP.*, v. 325).
47. Bodl., Carte MS. 67. f. 31; Lane to Bennett, 12 Aug. 1663 (*Cal. S.P. Ire., 1663–5*, p. 199).
48. *Cal. S.P. Ire., 1663–5*, p. 31.
49. *Thorpe Catalogue of Books and Manuscripts* (London, 1834), p. 214. The document is undated.
50. *D.K. Rep. 19*, p. 83 (801).
51. *Cal. Claren, S.P.*, v. 327; *Cal. S.P. Ire., 1663–5*, pp. 230, 253–4, 315.
52. *D.K. Rep. 19*, p. 72 (614).
53. Ibid., p. 81 (766).
54. Ibid., p. 48 (132); S. & E., f. 63; King's Inns, Dublin, Prendergast MS. v, pp. 322–3.
55. *Cal. S.P. Ire., 1663–5*, pp. 73, 147–8, 153; *Cal. S.P. Ire., 1666–9*, p. 658; *D.K. Rep. 19*, p. 71 (598, 599); S. & E., ff. 468–70. Edward Smith should not be confused with Sir Edward Smith, one of the commissioners of the court of claims.
56. *Cal. S.P. Ire. 1660–62*, pp. 302–3, 331; H.M.C., *Egmont MSS.*, i, 285; *D.K.Rep. 19*, p. 42 (4).
57. S. & E., f.11.
58. *D.K. Rep. 19*, p. 45 (62); N.L.I., MS. 8033/1.
59. S. & E., f. 209; *Cal. S.P. Ire., 1647–60*, pp. 832–3; *D.K. Rep.* 19, p. 54(266).
60. *Cal. S.P. Ire., 1663–5*, p. 190; *D.K. Rep. 19*, pp. 51 (202), 83 (806); Bodl., Carte MS. 67, f. 31v; *Cal. S.P. Ire., 1669–70*, p. 465.
61. J. Kinston, 'Catholic families of the Pale', *Reportorium Novum*, ii (1958), 92–3; J. Love, 'Charles I and the Confederation of Kilkenny, 1643–9', *I.H.S.*, xiv (1964), 15; Gilbert, *Ir. Confed.*, iv. lxi–lxii; v. 198, 209; vi. 179–82; Carte, *Ormond*, v. 14; Clarendon, *Life: Continuation*, p. 59.
62. Inst., s. 11; *D.K. Rep. 19*, p. 46 (85); S. & E., f. 23.
63. Ormond to Clarendon; same to Bennett, 8 April 1663 (Bodl., Carte MS. 143, f. 117; 46, ff. 45–6); *I.R.C.R.*, p. 668.
64. Bodl., Carte MS. 32, ff. 366–7. Ormond, having informed the king of this problem, was given discretionary powers to enforce the decrees of the court. *Cal. S.P. Ire., 1663–5*, p. 74.
65. *D.K. Rep. 19*, p. 49 (151). For Eustace's grant see *Cal. Treas. Bks., 1681–5*, vii, part 2, 738. For Kilmacud read Kilmashogue.
66. Not to be confused with the regicide of the same name, nor with Dr Henry Jones, bishop of Meath, vice-chancellor of Dublin University throughout the Interregnum, a brother of Sir Theophilus and Colonel Michael Jones. Prendergast, *Cromwellian Settlement*, p. 315; Barnard, *Cromwellian Ireland*, pp 166, 178, 199, 211.
67. Bodl., Carte MS. 44, ff. 622–3.
68. Ibid., MS. 32, ff. 407, 644–644v.
69. *Cal. S.P. Ire., 1663–5*, p. 99; H.M.C., *Rep. 8*, app. i., sec ii, 512a, 541b.
70. Bodl., Carte MS. 32, ff. 579, 736; *D.K. Rep. 19*, pp. 70 (593), 72 (615).
71. H.M.C., *Ormonde MSS.*, n.s., iii. 62.
72. *Commons' jn., Ire.*, i. 553; *Lord's jn., Ire.*, i. 325.
73. Bodl., Carte MS. 60, ff. 201–201v; S. & E., f. 96; *Cal. Treas. Bks., 1676–9*, v. part 2, 884–5.

74. 14 & 15 Car. II, *c.*12.
75. See p. 179 (n.37). My treatment of this subject has been based largely on the late J.G. Simms's typescript (pp. 17–18), which he kindly allowed me to consult, of his introduction to the forthcoming publication, by the I.M.C., of the calendared version of the S. & E.
76. Most contemporaries put the number of unheard of claims at 7–8,000. See, for example, Lansdowne, *Petty-Southwell Correspondence, 1676–87* (London, 1928), p. 152; *Cal. SP. Ire., 1663–5*, p. 503; *Historical Works of Nicholas French*, i. 90; [H. Reilly], *Ireland's case briefly stated* (n.p., 1695), p. 104.
77. *Rules, Orders, and Directions . . . for the execution of the Act for the Settlement of Ireland . . .* (Dublin, 22 Oct. 1662).
78. Ibid., p. 3.
79. Ibid., p. 5, rule 5.
80. *The Abstract of the Claims of all persons claiming as Innocents in the City, County of the City, and County of Dublin* (Dublin, 1663). The names of the claimants (some 250), the majority of whom claimed property in the city, are entered alphabetically. It is worth noting (p. 1) that the commissioners originally intended to start the hearings on 10 Feb. 1663. I am grateful to professor Karl Bottigheimer for drawing my attention to this unique document, deposited in the B. L., shelf mark B.o.1.
81. Ibid., pp. 19–22.
82. *Commons' jn., Ire.*, i. 636.
83. Ibid., 625–6.
84. Ibid., 632, 634–5, 636–7.
85. *The Intelligencer*, no. 4 (21 Sept. 1663), p. 27.
86. Bodl., Carte MS. 67, ff. 37, 38, 42.
87. 'Order by the Court of Claims, July 1664', *R.S.A.I.J.*, iv, 4th ser., app. xii (1876–8), 309.
88. King's Inns, Dublin, Prendergast MS. v, pp. 447–8, 455.
89. Bodl., Carte MS. 44, f. 263.

CHAPTER IV

1. Ormond to Clarendon, 14 Jan. 1662/3; Ormond to Charles, 7 Feb. 1662/3 (Bodl., Carte MS. 143, ff.66, 79).
2. *Cal. S.P.Ire., 1663–5*, p. 11.
3. *Commons' jn., Ire.*, i. 614–31. Proposals cited are nos. 2–5, 15. By s. 25 of the Instructions of the Act of Settlement the lord lieutenant and council were empowered to issue further instructions and rules to the commissioners for their proceedings.
4. *Commons' jn., Ire .*, i. 640–1; *Cal. S.P.Ire., 1663–5*, pp. 29, 31–2, 35, 48–9; *Cal.Claren. S.P.*, v. 301; R. Hutton, *Charles II: King of England, Scotland, and Ireland* (Oxford, 1989), p. 207.
5. Churchill complained that the commissioners were being blamed for the plot 'as if we were more in fault for doing justice than they for opposing it.' *Cal. S.P.Ire., 1663–5*, p. 100.
6. P.R.O., P.C. 2/56, f. 315^v; 2/58, f. 122; H.M.C., *Ormonde MSS.*, n.s., iii. 104; Carte, *Ormond*, iv. 193.
7. Ibid., iv. 190.
8. Bodl., Carte MS. 44, f. 656.
9. Ormond to Clarendon, 16 Nov. 1663 (Bodl., Carte MS. 143, ff. 214–15); Scott, *Memoirs of the Court of Charles the Second by Count Grammont*, pp. 206, 207, 248.
10. Ormond to Orrery, 26 Feb. 1660/1 (Bodl. Carte MS. 48, f. 11); *I.R.C.R.*, P. 664.
11. *Diary* for 18 Sept. 1683.
12. D. Ogg, *England in the Reign of Charles II* (Oxford, 1955), i. 151–2.; Hutton, *Charles II*, pp. 19, 241, 259, 398.

13. St. Albans to Williamson, 11 Feb. 1663; Henrietta-Maria to Ormond, 26 March 1663 (*Cal. S.P.Ire., 1669–70*, pp. 443 – 4; Bodl., Carte MS. 214, ff. 454, 454^{v}).
14. *Cal. S.P.Ire., 1663–5*, pp. 42–4, 48, 56.
15. Sergeant, *Little Jennings and Fighting Dick Talbot*, i. 41.
16. D. Cregan, 'An Irish cavalier; Daniel O'Neill in exile and restoration, 1651–64', *Studia Hibernica*, no. 5 (1965), 64, 66, 67, 68–9, 70–1, 75.
17. *Diary* for 24 Oct. 1664.
18. Gilbert, *Ir. Confed.*, i. vi–viii; Robert Southwell's *Life* of Ormond in Mountmorres, *History of the Principal Transactions of the Irish Parliament*, i. 239.
19. Ogg, *England in the reign of Charles II*, i. 203, 339, 342; C. Giblin (ed.), 'Catalogue of material of Irish interest in the collection *Nunziatura di Fiandra*, Vatican archives', *Collectanea Hibernica*, no. 1 (1958), 101, 102, 109, 119, 120, 123, 124; M. Ashley, *Charles II: the man and the statesman* (N.Y. and Washington, 1971) pp. 167, 319–20; Bryant, *Letters Speeches and Declarations of King Charles II*, p. 118; *Cal. Claren. S.P.*, v. 49; W. Shaw (ed.), *The Knights of England* (London, 1906), ii. 242; B. Jennings (ed.), *Wild Geese in Spanish Flanders*, I.M.C. (Dublin, 1964), pp. 454, (2645).
20. *Cal. S.P.Ire., 1663–5*, p. 400; *Cal. Claren. S.P.*,v. 400, 403; Hutton, *Charles II*, pp. 77, 90, 231, 237.
21. Quoted in Bagwell, *Stuarts*, iii. 24(n).
22. Bodl., Carte MS. 68, f. 589.
23. Bodl., Carte MS. 31, f. 218; 32, ff. 353, 353^{v}; 44, f. 584.
24. Ormond to Eustace, 16 Nov. 1661 (Bodl., Carte MS. 31, ff. 358, 358^{v}); *Cal. S.P.Ire., 1660–2*, p. 184.
25. Bodl. Carte MS. 33, ff. 313–14, 315–16. The first report is dated 11 Feb. 1663/4, the second 7 May 1664.
26. Patrick Moore was probably the son of the man of the same name who had been one of Charles's secretaries of state when the exiled court was in Holland. Prendergast *Restoration to Revolution*, pp. 29–32. See also Sergeant, *Little Jennings and Fighting Dick Talbot*, i. 176(n). For some typical letters from Moore to Ormond see H.M.C., *Ormonde MSS.*, n.s., iii. 176, 179, 182.
27. *Cal. S.P.Ire., 1663–5*, p. 198; C. Giblin, 'Catalogue of material of Irish interest in the . . . Vatican archives', *Collectanea Hibernica*, no. 1 (1958), 107.
28. *Cal. S.P.Ire., 1663–5*, p. 279.
29. Catherine to Ormond, 26 Nov. 1662; Marquess of Sandez to Ormond, 23 Dec. 1663 (Bodl., Carte MS. 43, f. 287; *Cal. S.P.Ire., 1660–2*, p. 374.
30. *Cal. S.P.Ire., 1663–5*, p. 52; Sergeant, *Little Jennings and Fighting Dick Talbot*, i. 82–3, 85–6, 90–1, 104(n); Bagwell, *Stuarts*, iii. 99; Pepys, *Diary* for 17 Oct. 1662.
31. *Cal. S.P.Ire., 1660–2*, pp. 444, 470, 612; *Cal. S.P.Ire., 1663–5*, p. 59; *Cal. S.P.Ire., 1666–9*, pp. 683–5.
32. Eustace to Bennett, 31 Dec. 1662 (*Cal. S.P.Ire. 1660–2*, p. 670).
33. Ibid., pp. 612, 613, 614, 643, 663–4; *Cal. S.P.Ire., 1663–5*, pp. 3, 10, 17–18.
34. Inst., s. 47.
35. *Cal. S.P.Ire., 1663–5*, pp. 17, 19.
36. *Cal. Claren, S.P.*, v. 296.
37. Mount Alexander to Duchess of Ormond, 11 Jan. 1664/5 (Bodl., Carte MS. 34, f. 12).
38. *Cal. Claren, S.P.*, v. 325.
39. Lane to Bennett, 27 Aug. 1663 (*Cal. S.P.Ire. 1663–5*, p. 226).
40. Clarges to Ormond, 3 Nov. 1663; Ormond to Clarges, 18 Nov. 1663 (Bodl., Carte MS. 33, f. 214^{v}; 49, f. 246^{v}).
41. Lane to Clarendon, 8 Aug., 15 Oct., 9 Dec., 1663; 27 Jan., 13 Feb., 1664. (*Cal. Claren. S.P.*, v. 340, 344, 352–3, 363, 366, 371.
42. Carte *Ormond*, v. 118.

43. P.R.O., P.C. 2/57, ff. 43ᵛ, 140, 152, 154.
44. *Diary* for 18 Nov. 1664.
45. N.L.I., MS. 8644 / 2 / 7.
46. Bagwell, *Stuarts*, iii. 35–7; P.R.O.I., *D.K.Rep. 56*, app. iv. 344–5; *Cal. Claren. S.P.*, iv. 574, 597, 602, 617.
47. Leigh to Williamson, 20 June 1663 (*Cal. S.P.Ire., 1663–5*, p. 142).
48. Jones to Lane, 9 July 1664 (N.L.I., MS. 8643/7). The 'Irish' referred to by Jones were Thomas Luttrell, Nicholas White, James Alen, Peter Nottingham, and John Foster, all of whom had been restored to land in the region of Lucan.
49. Lodge, *Peerage*, iv. 215; King's Inns, Dublin, Prendergast MS. v. pp. 318–23; P.R.O., P.C. 2/57, f. 43.
50. Inst., s. 147.
51. *Cal. S.P.Ire., 1660–2*, p. 391; S. & E., f. 3; *D.K.Rep. 19*, p. 43 (27); *C.S.*, pp. 6 (5), 10 (12), 20 (26).
52. Underdown, *Royalist Conspiracy in England*, pp. 74, 115, 161.
53. *Cal. S.P.Ire., 1663–5*, pp. 59–60, 499–500; *Cal. S.P.Ire., 1669–70*, pp. 452, 496; Bodl. Carte MS. 165, ff. 110, 150ᵛ *Inq. Cancell. Hib Repert.*, i. 3–Car. II (Dublin).
54. Armorer died in 1686 and it is probable that the Hollywoods were back in possession shortly thereafter. In 1697 a Catholic priest was reported to be 'living at Mr. Hollywood's at Artaine'. *The State Letters of Henry Earl of Clarendon . . .* (Oxford and Dublin, 1765), i. 73; W. O'Riordan, 'A List of the priests, secular and regular, of the diocese of Dublin in the year 1697', *Reportorium Novum*, i (1955), 147.
55. *Cal. S.P.Ire., 1660–2*, p. 372.
56. Ibid., p. 478; *Cal. S.P.Ire., 1669–70*, pp. 447–8.
57. Vernon to Williamson, 6 June 1663 (*Cal. S.P.Ire., 1663–5*, p. 121).
58. Ibid., pp. 39, 95.
59. Ibid., p. 170; *Cal. S.P.Ire., 1669–70*, p. 463.
60. Charles to Ormond, 13 March 1663; Charles to commissioners, 19 May 1663 (*Cal. S.P.Ire., 1663–5*, pp. 39, 95).
61. Ormond to Bennett, 30 May 1663 (Bodl., Carte MS. 143, f. 133r); *Cal. S.P.Ire., 1663–5*, p. 109.
62. An abstract of Mountrath's will, together with a brief account of the events surrounding the case, and including a rather confused report of the decision of Ormond and the council, appears in Lodge, *Peerage*, ii. 76(n).
63. *D.K.Rep. 19*, p. 56 (312); *Mercurius Hibernicus*, no. 9 (10 March 1663/3), p. 66.
64. *Cal. S.P.Ire., 1663–47*, p. 388; *Cal. S.P.Ire., 1660–2*,. pp. 215, 331, 374–6; *Cal. S.P.Ire., 1666–9*, pp. 334–5; *Cal. S.P.Ire., 1669–70*, pp. 610–11.
65. Clarendon, *Life: Continuation*, p. 59.
66. Anglesea to Ormond, 1 Aug. 1663 (*H.M.C., Ormonde MSS.*, n.s., iii. 65).
67. Ormond to Bennett, 14 March 1663; Ormond to Clare, 18 Nov. 1663 (*Cal. S.P., Ire., 1663–4* ,p. 41; Bodl., Carte MS. 219, f. 37). Ormond said that his 'principal inducement to my endeavour to serve him [Tyrconnell] was that of his alliance with your lordship's [the Holles] family . . . ' Tyrconnell's brother-in-law, Denzil (now Lord) Holles, was at the Restoration appointed a member of the committee for Irish affairs in the English privy council. P.R.O., P.C. 2/55, f. 1ᵛ.
68. Albermarle to Ormond, 25 Aug. 1663 (Bodl., Carte MS. 33, f. 88). In the redemption of mortgages on forfeited estates the Act of Settlement assigned to the '49 officers, towards the satisfaction of their arrears, the value of such land over the amount of the mortgage. The holders of mortgages on undisposed forfeited land could claim ownership, as mortgagees with prior right of redemption, by paying to the '49 officers the difference between the current value of the estate and the amount of the mortgage. 14 & 15 Car. II, c. 2; Decl., s. 9; Inst., ss. 36–7.

69. Talbot to Bennett, 13 March 1663 (*Cal. S.P.Ire., 1663–5*, pp. 375–6).

CHAPTER V

1. Bodl. Carte MS. 31, f. 526; *Cal. Claren.S.P.*, v. 219, 320.
2. *Commons' jn., Ire.*, i. 503; *Lords' jn., Ire*, i. 303.
3. Bodl. Carte MS. 143, f. 36.
4. H.M.C., *Rep. 15*, app., vii. 165–6.
5. Bodl., Carte MS. 47, f. 107; *Commons' jn., Ire.*, i. 613–14. Ormond said that it was the case of James Alen of St. Wolstan's which led the Commons to cast out the Explanatory bill without commitment'. *Cal. Claren. S.P.*, v. 296
6. *Ormond*, iv. 191; H.M.C., *Ormond MSS.*, n.s., iii. 10.
7. Ormond to Clarendon, 13 June 1663; Ormond to Bennett, 20 June 1663 (Bodl. Carte MS. 143, f. 142/d; *Cal. S.P.Ire. 1663–5*, p. 140).
8. Daniel O'Neill to Ormond, 25 July 1663 (Bodl. Carte MS. 32, f. 732).
9. Ormond to Anglesey, 26 Dec. 1663 (H.M.C., *Ormonde MSS.*, n.s., iii, 130).
10. *Cal. S.P.Ire., 1663–5*, p. 237.
11. John Walsh to Ormond (?), n.d. (Bodl. Carte MS. 44, f. 238).
12. Carte, *Ormond*, iv. 204–6. Vol. 44 of the Carte manuscripts contains the proposals cited. They can also be found in N.L.I., MS. 16974, pp. 151–5, and in the Gilbert collection, Pearse Street Library, Dublin, MS. 198, ff. 181–256.
13. Clarendon, *Life: Continuation*, p. 64.
14. Reference to a preliminary, written agreement, signed at Anglesey's house in London on 6 July 1665, appears in Lansdowne, *Petty-Southwell Correspondence*, pp. 259, 262.
15. Aungier to Ormond, 13 July 1661 (Bodl., Carte MS. 31, ff. 242, 244).
16. *Ormond* iv. 88. There is no evidence of this in the relevant volume of the records of the privy council, P.R.O., P.C. 2/55.
17. Bodl. Carte MS. 44, ff. 542, 546, 548; H.M.C., *Ormonde MSS.*, n.s., iii. 104, 112.
18. 16 Car. I, c. 33, s. 1.
19. Firth and Raitt, *Acts*, ii. 724.
20. Decl., s. 6.
21. The citation should read 18 Car. I, c. 37. See p. 166 (n.34).
22. *Cal. S.P.Ire., 1663–5*, p. 270.
23. Inst., s. 126.
24. Inst., s. 9.
25. Inst., s. 6.
26. Domville to Ormond, 13, 17, 20 Aug. 1664 (Bodl., Carte MS. 33, ff. 534, 534^{v} 535, 546, 546^{v} 557, 557^{v}). See also *Cal. S.P.Ire., 1663–5*, pp. 236–41, 269–73, 415–24,.
27. P.R.O., P.C. 2/55, ff. 138–9; Bodl., Carte MSS. 68, ff. 14–20^{v}; 44, ff. 143, 143^{v}. Domville has raised some of these legal points in 1661. *Cal. S.P.Ire., 1660–2*, pp. 419–21, 433–6.
28. In March 1662 Ormond thanked Domville for his observations on the Act of Settlement. They were received, he said with 'great satisfaction'. He wanted Domville to 'put those you have made into such a method as may most readily guide [the commissioners] . . .' Ormond to Domville, 25 March 1662 (Bodl., Carte MS. 49, f. 115). In 1666, when it appeared that an illness might prove fatal to Lord Chancellor Boyle, Ormond wrote to Bennett (now Lord Arlington) stating that if Boyle died 'no man has more of my vote for succeeding him at the seal than Sir William Domville'. In the event, Ormond had anticipated Boyle's death by thirty-six years, but the incident illustrates the high regard in which Domville was held by the lord lieutenant. Ormond to Arlington, 30 Oct. 1666. (*Cal. S.P.Ire., 1666–9*, p. 228).
29. 17 & 18 Car. II, c. 2. Royal assent 23 Dec. 1665. The atmosphere in the House of Commons during the debate on the final passage of the bill was described as 'most

virulent, the members confronting each other with swords half drawn . . . ' *Cal. S.P.Ire., 1663–5*, p. 699; Hutton, *Charles II*, p. 236.
30. 'On manuscript mapped and other townland surveys in Ireland of a public character . . . ', *R.I.A. Transactions* (Antiquities), xxiv (1873), 30.
31. S. 7.
32. Adams to Bull, 27 Feb. 1667 (Russell and Prendergast, *Carte Manuscripts*, pp. 168–9).
33. Lansdowne (ed.), *The Petty Papers* (London, 1927), i. 53.
34. *London Gazette*, no. 28 (15–19 Feb. 1665–6), p. 2.
35. Bodl., Carte MS. 44, f. 615; *Cal. S.P.Ire., 1666–9*, pp. 101–2.
36. *Cal. S.P.Ire., 1660–2*, pp. 270–1.
37. Ss. 1–3, 70, 187. Most of the decrees of innocence awarded after 2 July 1669 were, by s. 188, confirmed, but recipients were required to pay a year's rent from their restored estates for the benefit of the ensignmen.
38. Ss. 148. 152, 157.
39. S. 136.
40. S. 97.
41. Ss. 67–8.
42. Ss. 106, 143, 193, 228. See p. 169 (n 21).
43. Ss. 121. 126. The date on which Ormond and the council reached a decision concerning Mountrath's will appears under s. 126.
44. Ss. 184–5; *I.R.C.R.*, pp. 67–8 (50), 74 (3).
45. *Cal. S.P.Ire., 1660–2*, p. 502.
46. Inst., s. 165.
47. S. 45.
48. *Ormond*, iv. 216.
49. Ss. 107–8, 110.
50. S. 75.
51. S. 223.
52. S. 191; *Cal. S.P.Ire., 1660–2*, p. 661.
53. Ss. 148–9.
54. S. 55.
55. H.M.C., *Ormonde MSS.*, n.s., iii. 84.
56. S. 3.
57. *Historical Works of Nicholas French*, i. 90 (n); Lansdowne, *Petty-Southwell Correspondence*, p. 259.
58. The names of all the commissioners, sub-commissioners, and general registrars of the courts of claims, including the abortive one of 1661, can be found in R. C. Simington, 'The office of general registrar to the courts of claims, A.D., 1661–1669', *Anal. Hib.*, no. 16 (1946), 384–5.

CHAPTER VI

1. N.L.I., MS. 31, f. 3; *Cal. S.P.Ire., 1666–69*, p. 369. The court was allotted two years from the first day of its hearings to execute the provisions of the Act of Explanation, but the time period could be enlarged, at the discretion of the lord lieutenant, for additional periods of up to one year. S. 160. Certain powers of the commissioners were extended beyond 2 January 1669. In late 1668 an order from the English privy council, noting that there would be 'some occasion to employ you longer in Ireland', extended the powers of the commissioners beyond January 2 in order to settle the quit rents on some of the unprofitable land in the country. P.R.O., P.C. 2/61, f. 66v
2. *Cal. S.P.Ire., 1666–9*, pp. 35–9. Rules cited are nos. 1–3, 12, 15, 17, 19, 22. All claims and petitions were originally to have been submitted within thirty days of the date of the

publication of the rules, but on February 17 new rules were issued which generally extended the date to early March. Ibid., p. 40.

3. Ibid., rules no. 7, 24–7, 31.
4. *Restoration to Revolution*, p. 34.
5. N.L.I., MS. 31, ff. 7–9, 17, 27, 28, 71, 85–6, 166, 199, 201.
6. Ibid., ff. 144, 166.
7. Ibid., ff. 104–5, 177, 184, 188–9.
8. Ibid., p. 172. Some evidence of court procedure can be deduced from the fact that on April 10 Gormanston appeared as plaintiff in four separate cases. Ibid., pp. 179, 181, 187.
9. *Cal. S.P.Ire., 1666–9*, pp. 317, 542–3, 657–8; *Cal. S.P.Ire., 1669–70*, pp. 610–11.
10. *Cal. S.P.Ire., 1666–9*, p. 658.
11. King's Inns, Dublin, Prendergast MS. viii, pp. 559–60.
12. *I.R.C.R.*, pp. 208–9(6)
13. *Clarendon, Life: Continuation*, p. 63.
14. Ormond to Clarendon, 11 Oct. 1662 (Bodl., Carte MS. 143, f. 14).
15. R. Gorges, *The Story of a Family through Eleven Centuries . . . being a History of the Family of Gorges* (Boston, Mass., 1944), pp. 215–17; Barnard, *Cromwellian Ireland*, p. 208(n); Ramsey, *Henry Cromwell*, p. 63.
16. Clarendon to Ormond, 27 Jan. 1662/3 (Bodl., Carte MS. 217, f. 471).
17. D. Brunton & D. H. Pennington, *Members of the Long Parliament* (Hamden, Conn., 1968), pp. 23, 241; W. C. Abbot (ed.), *The Writings and Speeches of Oliver Cromwell* (Cambridge, Mass., 1937–47), iii. 483; *Lib. Mun. Pub . Hib.*, i, part 2, 75; *Return of Members of Parliament* (London, 1878), part i (England), 488, 500, 508(n), 514; part ii (Ireland), 621, 639; D. Underdown, *Pridge's Purge* (Oxford, 1971), p. 396.
18. *Cal. S.P.Ire., 1663–5*, pp. 116, 141, 266–7, 303, 428; *Commons;' jn., Ire.*, i. 667.
19. *Cal. S.P.Ire., 1663–5.*, p. 116; *The Intelligencer*, no. 4 (21 Sept. 1663), p. 27.
20. Ball, *Judges*, i. 348–9; Gorges, *History of Gorges Family*, p. 217.
21. Bodl., Care MS. 68, f. 140; H.M.C., *Rep. 8*, app. i (sec. 2), 279b.
22. Bodl., Carte MS. 49, f. 492; *Cal. S.P.Ire., 1666–9*, p. 574.
23. Ibid., pp. 494–6, 528–9, 563.
24. Bodl., Carte MS. 215, ff. 462, 465, 477, 478; W. S. Churchill, *Marlborough, his Life and Times* (London, 1933), i. 48–9.
25. *Cal. S.P.Ire., 1666–9*, p. 574.
26. Bodl. Clarendon MS. 83, ff. 356–8. The manuscript is undated but the internal evidence suggests that the date assigned to it (Feb., 1666) by the editors of the calendered version is approximately correct. *Cal. Claren. S.P.* v. 534.
27. Bodl. Clarendon MS. 75, f. 442. The manuscript is incorrectly dated, in a contemporary hand, as 1661. It can be assigned to the years 1666–7. A figure of 5,768 acres in Castleknock barony is entered (p. 5) against Hewson's name in the Taylor set of S. & D., R.I.A.
28. N.L.I., MS. 31, ff. 205, 210, 214, 231, 241, 245, 247–8.
29. *Cal. S.P.Ire., 1666–9*, p. 300.
30. N.L.I., MS. 10991/A1; Bodl., Carte MS. 60, ff. 201, 201ᵛ; *C.S.*, p. 272(18); *Cal. S.P.Dom., Oct. 1, 1683–April 30, 1684*, pp. 345–7. The name Kilmashogue has been incorrectly identified at one point in the last citation as 'Kilmacud'.
31. *Cal. S.P.Ire., 1666–9*, pp. 312–13.
32. Ss. 103–5.
33. *I.R.C.R.*, p. 140(17).
34. *Cal. S.P. Ire., 1666–9*, p. 37, rule 15.
35. N.L.I., MS. 10993/1/3, f. 1.
36. *Cal. S.P. Ire., 1669–70*, p. 242.

37. J. B. Leslie (ed.), 'Calendar of leases and deeds of St. Patrick's Cathedral, Dublin, 1660–89', *R.S.A.I.J.*, 7th serv., iv (1934), 199, 201, 202.
38. N.L.I., MS. 10993/1/3, f. 3.
39. R. C. Simington and J. MacLellan, 'Oireachtas Library list of outlaws, 1641–1647', *Annal. Hib.*, no. 23 (1966), 338. Robert Chamberlain's name does not appear in *D.K. Rep. 19*, but it is recorded in another source that he was declared nocent in the first court of claims. See *Mercurius Publicus*, no. 10 (28 Feb. 1662–3), p. 162. Yet Robert Chamberlain was described in 1669 as a 'Protestant compounder'. R.I.A., S. & D. (Taylor set), Castleknock barony, p. 3.
40. N.L.I., MS. 10993/2/1; 3; Pender, *Census of Ireland*, p. 390.
41. N.L.I., MS. 10933/1/3, f. 7; *D.K. Rep. 19*, p. 68 (549), where it should be noted that no land is entered as being restored to Eleanor Bermingham.
42. P.R.O.I., Lodge MS. vii, f. 252; *I.R.C.R.*, pp. 183–4 (10).
43. N.L.I., MS. 10993/2/6.
44. The savings clauses appended to the letters patent issued under the Acts of Settlement and Explanation are printed in *I.R.C.R.*, pp. 281–328.
45. N.L.I., MS. 31, ff. 13, 21–2, 80, 156–7; S. & E., ff. 25, 56; *I.R.C.R.*, pp. 158 (33), 302.
46. *C.S.*, p. 273 (20); N.L.I., MS. 31, f. 173; P.R.O.I., Lodge MS. viii, ff. 48–9; *I.R.C.R.*, pp. 58 (44), 283.
47. N.L.I., MS. 31, f. 211; MS. 816, ff. 10, 36–8; Ball, *History of County Dublin*, part 4, pp. 93–4.

CHAPTER VII

1. *I.R.C.R*, p. 277 (16).
2. Ibid., p. 242 (36); Prendergast, *Cromwellian Settlement*, p. 153.Provision for most transplanters was not taken into consideration until 1675, when commissioners were appointed to determine their cases. *Cal. S.P. Dom., 1675–6*, pp. 307–9. An index of the names of those who obtained certificates for letters patent under this commission appears in *I.R.C.R.*, pp. 580–7.
3. *D.K. Rep. 19*, p. 51 (191); *Cal. S.P. Ire., 1660–2*, p. 381.
4. *D.K. Rep. 19*, pp. 44 (35), 56 (307).
5. *I.R.C.R.*, pp. 276 (12), 277 (16).
6. *Cal. S.P.Dom., 1673–5*, p. 9.
7. R. C. Simington (ed.), *Books of Survey and Distribution*, I.M.C., Co. Roscommon, i (Dublin, 1949), IV.
8. *I.R.C.R.*, p. 78 (10).
9. Ibid., p. 208 (6).
10. Ibid., pp. 48 (44), 126 (44).
11. *I.R.C.R.*, pp. 130 (10), 204 (1).
12. *D.K.Rep. 19*, p. 54 (272); S. & E., f. 213; *Cal. S.P.Ire., 1660–2*, p. 391; *Cal. S.P.Ire., 1663–5*, p. 279; *Cal. S.P.Ire., 1669–70*, p. 477; *C.S.*, pp. 25–8 (35–7, 39–40); S. & D., pp. 72. 74.
13. *D.K.Rep. 19*, pp. 46 (70), 65 (496); S. & E., f. 21.
14. *I.R.C.R.*, p. 186 (12); *D.K.Rep. 19*, p. 77 (711).
15. *I.R.C.R.*, p. 61 (39); S. & D., p. 79; *C.S.*, p. 47 (71); S. & E., f. 253.
16. *I.R.C.R.*, p. 166 (48); *D.K.Rep. 19*, p. 43 (27); *C.S.* p. 6 (5), 10 (12), 20 (26); S. & E., f. 3. A.
17. *I.R.C.R.*, p. 228 (10).
18. Ibid., p. 66 (16); *C.S.*, pp. 268–9 (13, 14).
19. *I.R.C.R.*, p. 72 (11).
20. Ibid., p. 74 (3).
21. Ibid., pp. 178 (37), 211 (6). Roger Jones is not certainly identified, but was probably the

man described as an attorney and a sub-commissioner to the trustees of the '49 officers in the second court of claims. N.L.I., MSS. 816, ff. 28–9; 31, p. 33 The earl of Meath held a mortgage on the Walsh estate, the benefit of the redemption of which was claimed by the '49 officers. This lends credence to the suggestion as to Jones's identity. *By his majesty's commissioners for executing the act of settlement . . . a list of mortgages, etc. within the '49 security appointed to be canted 26 November 1667*, (R.I.A., 3/B/55).

22. Bodl., Carte MS. 44, f. 474; G.E.C., *Baronetage*, ii. 251; *Cal. S.P.Ire., 1663–5*, pp. 289–90, 428; *Commons' jn., Ire.*, i. 667; T. W. Moody & J. G. Simms (ed.), *The Bishopric of Derry and the Irish Society of London, 1602–1705*, I.M.C. (Dublin, 1968), i. 198.
23. *I.R.C.R.*, pp. 55 (38), 176 (34), 282, 306; S. & E., ff. 566–7; *Ing. Cancell. Hib. Repert.*, i. (16, 23) Jac. II (Dublin); *D.K.Rep 19*, pp. 50 (164), 83 (804). In the last citation Jane Talbot's name is incorrectly printed as 'James'.
24. *I.R.C.R.*, p. 94 (21).
25. Titles to all the townlands in Eustace's patent of 1662 were challenged, but Kilmashogue was the main prize.
26. N.L.I., MS 10991 / A / 1; B.L., Additional MS. 4760, f. 250; *Cal. Treas. Bks., 1676–9*, v, part 2, pp. 884–5; *Cal. S.P.Dom., 1678*, pp. 98–100; *Cal. Treas Bks., 1681–5*, vii, part 1, p. 346; part 2, p. 1392; *Cal. S.P.Dom, Oct. 1 1683–April 30, 1684*, pp. 173, 242, 345–7; C. MacNeill, 'Reports on the Rawlinson collection . . . in the Bodleian Library, Oxford', *Anal Hib.*, no. 1 (1930), 114, 155; *H.M.C., Rep. 14*, app., part vii, 32. In the sources cited the name Kilmashogue has sometimes been incorrectly identified as 'Kilmacud'.
27. *I.R.C .R.*, p. 184 (33); *Cal. S.P.Ire., 1666–9*, pp. 39, 154.
28. *I.R.C.R.*, p. 206 (18).
29. S. & D., p. 40; J. Warburton, J. Whitelaw, R. Walsh, *History of the City of Dublin* (London, 1818), ii, app. ix, lxvi; G. Meige, *the Present State of His Majesty's Dominion in Ireland* (London, 1717), p. 46.
30. S. & D., p. 43; J. T. Gilbert, *A History of the City of Dublin* (Dublin, 1861), i. 147; Ball, *Judges*, ii. 189–90; *The Irish Builder* (15 Nov. 1891), pp. 261–2.
31. *I.R.C.R.*, p. 179 (1); *Cal. S.P.Ire., 1669–70*, p. 667.
32. *I.R.C.R.*, pp. 72 (24), 187 (19), 189 (1), 190 (13).
33. Ibid., pp. 285–6.
34. *D.K.Rep. 19*, pp. 47 (95), 51 (182).
35. *I.R.C.R.*, pp. 140 (17), 158 (33).
36. Ball, *A History of the County Dublin*, part 1, p. 64; J. Leslie (ed.), 'Calendar of leases and deeds of St. Patrick's Cathedral, Dublin, 1660–89', *R.S.A.I.J.*, 7th ser., iv (1934), 184.
37. A. J. Otway-Ruthven, 'The mediaeval church lands of county Dublin', J. Watt, *et al* (ed.), *Medieval Studies Presented to Aubrey Gwynn*, part 1, pp. 65–6.
38. C. L. Falkiner, *Illustrations of Irish History and Topography, mainly of the Seventeenth Century* (London, 1904), pp. 44–9; S. & D. (pp. 39–40) enters at least seventeen proprietors for Kilmainham parish in 1641.
39. *Cal. S.P.Ire., 1660–2*, p. 661.
40. P.R.O.I., Lodge MS. vii, f. 360.
41. *Cal. S.P.Ire., 1663–5*, pp. 93, 105.
42. H.M.C., *Ormonde MSS.*, n.s., iii. 193–4.
43. P.R.O., P.C. 2/63, f. 52. A Thomas Musgrave deeded 5 acres in Kilmainham to the crown in 1670. P.R.O.I., Lodge MS. vii, f. 306.
44. P.R.O.I., Lodge MS. vii, f. 214; Bodl., Carte MS. 165, f. 98v; H.M.C., *Ormonde MSS.*, n.s., iii. 294.
45. Falkiner, *Illustrations*, pp. 56–9. An account of the money expended on the park up to 1669 appears in H.M.C., *Ormonde MSS.*, n.s., iii. 293–5.
46. S. 191.
47. *Cal. S.P.Ire., 1669–70*, pp. 109–10, 174, 262; *Cal. S.P.Dom., 1693*, pp. 56–7; McNeill,

'Reports on the Rawlinson collection . . . in the Bodleian . . . ', *Anal.Hib.*, no. 1 (1930), 155.

48. P.R.O., P.C. 2/62, ff. 124, 163[v], 170[v]; McNeill, 'Reports on the Rawlinson collection ... in the Bodleian ... ', *supra*, 107 (n), 110.
49. Pearse Street Library, Dublin, MS. 159 (Gilbert collection), Thomas Willson, An account of the foundation of the Royal Hospital ... [1711?], pp. 8–17, 48–9, 52; W. Strickland, 'The Royal Hospital at Kilmainham and its Architect', *R.S.A.I.J.*, xiii (1923), 101–4; E. McParland, 'Royal Hospital, Kilmainham, Co. Dublin', *Country Life* (May 9, 16, 1985), pp. 1260–3, 1320–4.
50 Falkiner, *Illustrations*, p. 58; *Lib. Mun. Pub. Hib.*, part 2, p. 91.

CHAPTER VIII

1. H.M.C., *Ormonde MSS.*, n.s., iii. 186.
2. Ormond told his son that he had seen a report that Buckingham was 'putting for the lieutenancy of Ireland and was so far persuaded of obtaining it that he was naming officers for his attendance.' Ormond to Ossory, 25 Feb. 1667/8 (Bodl., Carte MS. 48, f. 254[v]).
3. *Commons' jn.*, ix. 10.
4. Broderick to Ormond, 14 Dec. 1667 (Bodl. Carte MS. 36, f. 31). For Lady Ranelagh, a daughter of the first Earl of Cork, see N. Canny, *The Upstart Earl.*
5. Sir John Nicholas to Sir Edward Nicholas, 21 April 1668 (B. L., Egerton MS. 2539, f. 204). For Ormond's removal from office in 1669 see J. C. Beckett, 'The Irish viceroyalty in the Restoration period', *Royal Historical Soc. Transactions*, 5th ser., xx (1970), and J. McGuire, 'Why was Ormond dismissed in 1669?, *I.H.S.*, xviii (1973).
6. *Cal. S.P.Ire., 1669–70*, p. 313.
7. *Cal. S.P.Dom., 1671*, pp. 30, 595.
8. P.R.O., P.C. 2/62, f. 188.
9. Carte, *Ormond*, iv. 453–5.
10. N.L.I., MS. 16974, pp. 5–13.
11. Carte, *Ormond*, v. 106–17. Sir Edward Dering, who with the other commissioners of the court of claims was in attendance at the hearing, noted that the 'substance of the complaint was to magnify the king's Declaration [of 30 November 1660] and to arraign the Acts of Settlement and Explanation'. Dering added that the commissioners were 'only hearers' since 'nothing [was] said by the complainants against the execution of the acts'. B. D. Henning, *Parliamentary Diary of Sir Edward Dering*, pp. 68–69.
12. Carte, *Ormond*, v. 119–21.
13. Ibid., pp. 117–18; Cox, *Hibernicia Anglicana*, part 2, p. 11 ('A letter to the author of the history of Ireland . . . ').
14. 14 & 15 Car. II, c. 12, s. 5.
15. Carte, *Ormond*, v. 118.
16. Ibid., pp. 122–3; J. G. Simms, *William Molyneux of Dublin* (Dublin, 1982), chp. viii. A full contemporary record of the review of the settlement appears in the Gilbert Collection, Pearce Street Library, Dublin, MS. 198, ff. 35–115.
17. N.L.I., MS. 16974, pp. 35, 40, 43–7; *Cal. S.P.Dom., 1671*, pp. 358, 410.
18. Carte, *Ormond*, iv. 470, 471. Richard Talbot went into exile in France in late 1673. He was back in Ireland in 1678 but was imprisoned as a result of the accusations of Titus Oates. Released (after eight months) largely through the good offices of Ormond, who had meanwhile begun his second viceroyalty, he returned to France where he remained until 1683, by which time the reaction against Oates had produced a more favourable political climate, permitting Talbot to return to Ireland later the same year. Sergeant, *Little Jennings*, i. 256, 266, 271–3, 284.
19. Bagwell, *Stuarts*, iii. 113. As early as 1663 Ormond complained about the large number

of Catholics who were restored to corporations on the king's orders. Ibid., p. 335.

20. *Commons' jn.*, ix. 276–7.
21. P.R.O., P.C. 2/64, ff. 1, 53.
22. Shaftesbury to Essex, 14 August 1673 (B. L. Stowe MS. 202, f. 293).
23. P.R.O.I., MS. 2778, f. 2.
24. *Cal. S.P.Dom., 1660–85*, addenda, pp. 483–5; P.R.O., P.C. 2/66, f. 76.
25. P.R.O.I., *D.K.Rep. 56*, app. iv, pp. 344–6, 380; *Cal. S.P.Dom., 1678*, p. 499; *Cal. S.P.Dom., Oct 1 1683–April 30 1684*, pp. 294–5.
26. *Cal. S.P.Ire., 1666–9*, p. 679. Leigh told Sir Joseph Williamson that he had made 'several discoveries . . . but I see so many others concerned in the like, and the lord lieutenant so averse to them all, that I judge it not seasonable as yet to put you on the like.' Leigh to Williamson, 27 March 1675 (*Cal. S.P.Dom., 1675–6*, p. 41).
27. Hull, *Economic Writings of Petty*, i. 195; O. Airy (ed.), *Essex Papers* (London, Camden Soc., n.s., xlvii, 1890), i. 98
28. Airy, *Essex Papers*, i. 200–2.
29. *Cal. Treas.Bks., 1681–5*, vii part 1, p. 433.
30. Airy, *Essex Papers*, i. 122; Bagwell, *Stuarts*, iii. 111–12.
31. *Letters written by . . . Essex . . . in . . . 1675* (London, 1770), pp. 16–17. For details on the history of concealed land in Ireland see T. Ranger, 'Richard Boyle and the making of an Irish fortune, 1588–1614', *I.H.S.*, x (1957).
32. Russell and Prendergast, *Carte Manuscripts*, pp. 91–2.
33. *Abstracts*, p. 3.
34. *Cal. S.P.Dom., May 1, 1684–Feb. 5, 1685*, pp. 16–18.
35. *State Letters of Henry Earl of Clarendon*, i. 94, 222, 358, 381. Clarendon said that in August 1686 Tyrconnell proposed that the Cromwellian planters be compelled to sell their estates to the crown, the money for which would come from a parliamentary grant. H.M.C., *Ormonde MSS.*, n.s., vii. 448–9.
36. *A full and Impartial Account of all the Secret Consults . . . of the Romish Party in Ireland* (London, 1689), pp. 40–1.
37. *The State Letters of Henry Earl of Clarendon . . .*, ii. 36.
38. *I.R.C.R.*, p. 359 (57).
39. *The State Letters of Henry Earl of Clarendon . . .*, i. 277.
40. J. G. Simms, *The Jacobite Parliament of 1689* (Dundalk, 1966), p 4.

CHAPTER IX

1. *Abstract*, pp. 16–17. The letters patent under the Commission of Grace are not always entered in both the S. & D., and the *Abstract*. See, for example, John Nugent's patent for half the townland of Corbally (55 acres) in Coolock on p. 49 of the *Abstract*. This patent does not appear against his name opposite Corbally on p. 90 of the S. & D. See also p. 48 of the S. & D., where the names of Christopher and Francis Wolverton are entered as having a patent under the Commission of Grace for 122 acres in Little Newtown in Rathdown. No such patent is to be found in the *Abstract*.
2. *Abstract*, p. 15.
3. Ibid., p. 31; T. U. Sadleir, 'Ladytown and the Allens', *Jr. County Kildare Archaelogical Soc.*, ix (1918–21), 61–3; F. E. Ball, 'Stillorgan Park and its history', *R.S.A.I.J.*, 5th ser., viii (1898), 25–6; id, *A History of the County Dublin*, part 1, pp. 120–1; id., *Judges*, i. 364; Gilbert, *History of the City of Dublin*, i. 351–2.
4. *Abstract*, p. 19; Simms, *The Jacobite Parliament of 1689*, p. 6.
5. *Abstract*, pp. 35–6; Gilbert, *Cal. Anc. Recs. Dublin*, iv. 494, 531.
6. *Abstract*, p. 38; Ball, *A History of the County Dublin*, part 1, pp. 10, 14.
7. *Abstract*, p. 39.
8. P.R.O.I. Lodge MS. viii, ff. 48–9; N.L.I., MS. 14908, f. 63; *Inq. Cancell. Hib. Repert*, i

(17), Jac, II (Dublin); W. Playfair, *British Family Antiquity* (London, 1811), ix. 234.
9. P.R.O.I., Lodge MS. vii, 252; *I.R.C.R.* p. 126 (44); *Inq. Cancell Hib. Repert*, i (11), Jac. II (Dublin).
10. P.R.O.I., Lodge MS. viii, f. 187.
11. *I.R.C.R.*, p. 179 (1).
12. Ibid., pp. 72 (24), 375 (38); *C.S.*, p. 6 (5); *D.K.Rep 19*, p. 43 (27); S. & E., f. 3; S. & D., p. 54.
13. *I.R.C.R.*, p. 285.
14. *Cal. S.P.Ire., 1663–5*, p. 389; *Cal. S.P.Ire., 1666–9*, p. 708; *Cal. S.P.Ire., 1669–70*, p. 215.
15. S. & D., pp. 49, 101.
16. *I.R.C.R.*, pp. 72 (24), 285, 360 (33). For Danestown read Damastown on p. 360; *C.S.* p. 225 (6); S. & D., p. 99.
17. P.R.O.I., Lodge MS. vii, f. 308.
18. *I.R.C.R.*, pp. 189 (1), 362 (53); S. & D., p. 27; Simms, *Williamite Confiscation*, p. 17.
19. *I.R.C.R.* p. 72 (24). The seventh owner of Balgriffin, since its forfeiture in the sixteenth century by John Burnell, was John Forster, who purchased the estate in 1702–3 following the Williamite confiscation. Simms, *Williamite Confiscation*, p. 185; S. & D., p. 96.
20. Simms, *Williamite Confiscation*, p. 179.
21. T.C.D., MS. 744, ff. 250, 255.
22. Simms, *Williamite Confiscation*, p. 176.
23. *I.R.C.R.*, p. 378 (1); S. & D., p. 102 (Lower Castleknock).
24. *I.R.C.R., p. 372 (52); Simms,* Williamite confiscation, p. 182.
25. N.L.I., MS. 9382, ff. 16–20; S. & D., p. 29.

CHAPTER X

1. County Wicklow was created in 1577 but 'seems not to have functioned and ceased to exist some time after 1586, a somewhat larger county of that name being recreated in 1606.' Until 1606 most of Wicklow was regarded as part of Dublin, and indeed long after that date there continued to be confusion over the exact border, official documents sometimes using such terms (in 1637) as 'Co. Dublin and Wicklow or one of them.' K. W. Nicholls, 'Counties, 1542–1613', in T. W. Moody, *et al* (ed.), *New History of Ireland* (Oxford, 1984), ix. 108 (45); P.R.O.I., Lodge MS. v, f. 419.
2. J. Hogan & N. O'Farrell (ed.), *Walsingham Letter Book or Register of Ireland, May 1578 to December 1579*, I.M.C. (Dublin, 1959), p. 65.
3. N. Canny, *The Elizabethan Conquest of Ireland: a pattern established*, 1565–76 (Sussex, 1976), pp. 34, 54; *Cal. pat. rolls Ire., Hen. VIII–Eliz.*, i. 445; *Cal. fiants Ire., Eliz.*, nos. 741, 848, 1415, 2854, 3266, 3707, 6033, 6071, 6083; *Cal. S.P.Ire., 1509–73*, p. 296.
4. 27 Eliz., c. 1; *Cal. fiants Ire., Eliz.*, no. 5081.
5. H. F. Kearney, *Strafford in Ireland*, p. 175.
6. *Cal. pat rolls, Ire., Jas. I*, pp. 17, 141; J. J. Silke, *Kinsale: the Spanish intervention in Ireland at the end of the Elizabethan wars* (Liverpool, 1970), pp. 143, 144.
7. Kearney, *Strafford*, p. 175.
8. Ibid. chp. 12.
9. Dunlop, *Ireland under the Crommonwealth*, ii. 579.
10. Prendergast, *Cromwellian Settlement*, pp. 269–71; Dunlop, *Ireland under the Commonwealth*, ii. 486.
11. This figure does not include Strafford's estate, which was not forfeited.
12. *Cal. S.P.Ire., 1647–60*, p. 802; Dunlop, *Ireland under the Commonwealth*, ii. 694–5; *I.R.C.R.*, p. 70 (5).
13. Decl., s. 9.
14. *I.R.C.R.*, pp. 123 (42), 134 (24), 140 (17), 181 (46), 254 (27).

15. P. Logan, 'Dermot and Edmund O'Meara, father and son', *Jr. Irish Medical Assoc.*, xliii (Nov. 1958), pp. 312–15; *Cal. S.P.Ire., 1663–5*, pp. 144, 469.
16. As examples see P.R.O.I., Lodge MS. vii, f. 558; *I.R.C.R.*, p. 138 (12). In 1880 three lords owned 26 per cent of Wicklow and half the county was held by nine proprietors. T. W. Moody, *Davitt and Irish Revolution, 1846–82* (Oxford, 1982), p. 445 (n).
17. Carte, *Ormond*, iv. 84.
18. Simms, *Jacobite Ireland*, pp. 3–4; id., *Williamite Confiscation*, p. 195.
19. *Historical Works of Nicholas French.*
20. Text in Gilbert, *Jacobite Narrative*, pp. 192–201. Petty said that the foundation of the Coventry Letter was the 'care and culture of Catholic religion; the giving it such growth, vigour and authority by wealth and acres, as may persuade a Successor to be friends with them upon fair and equal terms.' Lansdowne, *Petty-Southwell Correspondence*, p. 264.
21. W. Harris (ed.), *The Whole Works of Sir James Ware* (Dublin, 1764), ii (The Writers of Ireland), 252–3; *Cal. S.P.Dom, Jan. 1686–May 1687*, pp. 139, 207; *Lib. Mun. Pub. Hib.*, i, part 2, p. 83; J. D'Alton, *King James's Irish Army List* (Dublin, 1878), ii. 752; T. Davis, *The Patriot Parliament of 1689* (London, 1843), 159.
22. Pp. 85, 89, 108, 118, 127–8.
23. P. Kelly, '"A light to the blind": the voice of the dispossessed élite in the generation after the defeat at Limerick', *I.H.S.*, xxiv (1985), 442. J. G. Simms suggested that the author was Nicholas Plunket of Dunsoghly. Gilbert, *Jacobite Narrative*, intro., vii–viii.
24. Ibid., pp. 5, 15, 35.
25. Hull, *Economic Writings of Petty*, i. 154.
26. Pp. 26, 28, 30, 35–43, 46–50. A contemporary draft of this pamphlet, entitled A Defense of the Present Settlement of Ireland, can be found in the library of Trinity College, Dublin, MS. 747. For a description see T. W. Moody, 'Ulster Plantation papers, 1608–12', *Anal. Hib.*, no. 8 (1938), 181.
27. Airy, *Essex Papers*, p. 50.
28. P.R.O.I., Lodge MS. viii, ff. 190–1.
29. *The State Letters of Henry Earl of Clarendon . . .*, i. 94; Economic Writings of Petty, ii. 578–9, 583.

APPENDIX A

1. For a discussion of the various sets of Books of Survey and Distribution see G. Tallon, 'Books of Survey and Distribution, Co. Westmeath: a comparative survey', *Anal. Hib.*, no 28 (1978).
2. Nearly 10,000 acres are described as unprofitable, or about 7 per cent of the total land area of the county. W.J. Smyth maintains that the Civil Survey estimate of the acreage of Dublin as a whole is 'defective' by about 30 per cent, which seems high. 'Exploring the social and cultural topographies of sixteenth and seventeenth-century county Dublin', in F. Aalen & K. Whelan, *Dublin City and County*, p. 135. Dublin is described as containing 123,784 acres in *A Geographical Description of Ireland* (2nd edt., London, 1720), p. 4. The figure is based on Petty's maps. The sources will not permit a very accurate reading of the number of acres in Uppercross barony, lying west across the mountains between Kildare and Wicklow, the borders of which were not clearly defined in the mid-seventeenth century. The weight of the evidence suggests, however, that it contained somewhat over 6,000 acres. See *CS.*, pp 295–6.
3. P. 103.
4. Pp. 36, 37.
6. Prendergast, *Restoration to Revolution*, p. viii; C. Lennon, 'Richard Stanihurst (1547–1618) and Old English identity', *I.H.S.*, xxi (1978), 141.
6. For a general discussion to his problem see Clarke, *Old English*, chp. 1; R. Loeber, 'English and Irish sources for the history of Dutch economic activity in Ireland,

1660–1689', *Irish Economic and Social History*, viii (1981), 76–7, 79–80, and J.C. Beckett, *Confrontations: studies in Irish history* (London, 1972), p. 63 (n). Edmund Hore, a nineteenth century antiquarian, used the term 'old Strongbownian' to describe the Old English. *Jr. Assoc. for the Preservation of the Memorials of the Dead*, v, no. 3 (1903), 499.

APPENDIX B

1. Transcribed from S. & E., ff. 551–3.

Bibliography

I. MANUSCRIPTS

Public Library, Armagh

Submissions and Evidence, court of claims, 1663.

Public Record Office, Belfast

Annesley MSS., Miscellaneous Books, no. 5, Lib. G. Papers relating to the discussions on the settlement of Ireland, 1661–2.

Books of Survey and Distribution (Annesley set).

Genealogical Office, Dublin

MSS. 160, 179. Genealogies of Dublin proprietors.

King's Inns, Dublin

Prendergast MSS. Collections concerning the Cromwellian, Restoration, and Revolution settlement of Ireland, vols. v, viii, xiii.

National Library of Ireland, Dublin

Ainsworth Reports on manuscripts in private custody: (i) Bath papers.

Joly MS. 6. Sir William Betham, An Historical Account of the Acts of Settlement and Explanation.

MS. 31. Book of Orders of the commissioners of the second court of claims, 1666.

MS. 816. Entry of warrants from the commissioners of the court of claims, 1661–6.

MS. 8033. Fingall papers.

MSS. 8643–4. Lane papers.

MS. 9382. Domville papers.

MSS. 10991, 10993. Muschamp papers.

MS. 14908. Copies of grants and deeds, 1677–1690.

MS. 16974. Copies of privy council transactions and petitions concerning Ireland prepared for Sir George Lane, 1660–76.

MS. 19080. Abstracts of decrees of the court of claims, 1663.

Pearse Street Public Library, Dublin

Gilbert MS. 159. Thomas Willson's History of the Royal Hospital, Kilmainham, *c.*1711.

Gilbert MS. 198. Documents relating to the Irish land settlement, 1660–1675.

Gilbert MS. 208. Documents relating to the Commission for Defective titles, 1684.

Gilbert MS. 219. Documents relating to the discussions on the settlement of Ireland, 1660–61.

Public Record Office, Dublin

Books of Survey and Distribution (Quit Rent and Headfort sets)

Ferguson MS. xiii. Abstracts of equity exchequer orders.

John Lodge's summaries of entries on the Irish Chancery rolls, vols. vi–viii.

MS. 3538. Transcript of decree of innocence awarded to Thomas and Bridget Holliday, 1663.

MS. 2778. Sarsfield-Vesey papers.

MS.BET, ser. x, vol. 8. Sir William Betham's genealogical abstracts. Transcript of an injunction from the commissioners of the court of claims, 1663.

Royal Irish Academy, Dublin

Books of Survey and Distribution (Taylor set)

Trinity College, Dublin

MS. 587. Papers relating to the discussions on the settlement of Ireland, 1660–62

MS. 744. Ninth Book accompanying the report of the parliamentary commission on forfeitures, 1689

MS. 808. Petition of the Irish General Convention to the king, 1660.

MS. 844. Transplanters' dispensation records, 1654.

MS. 747. [John Osborne], A Defense of the Present Settlement of Ireland, *c.*1688.

MS. 810. Depositions, 1642–54 (co. Dublin).

British Library, London

Additional Charter 32976. Lease by Richard Cromwell of lands in Ireland, 1658.

Additional MS. 22548. Letter of Henrietta-Maria to Ormond, *c.*1662.

Additional MS. 35850. Papers relating to the discussions in council on the settlement of Ireland, 1660.

Additional MS. 35851. Papers relating to the discussions in council on the settlement of Ireland, 1661–2.

Additional MS. 4760. Order in council concerning the estate of Nicholas Harold, 1676.

Additional MS. 4772. List of Irish outlawries, 1641–2.

Additional MS. 4781. Papers relating to the discussions in council on the settlement of Ireland, 1661–2.

Egerton MS. 789. Abstracts of decrees of innocence in the court of claims, 1663.

Egerton MS. 2539. Letter of John Nicholas to Sir Edward Nicholas, 1668.

Harleian MS. 4784. Survey of Edward Roberts's lands in Ireland, 1659.

Stowe MS. 202. Letter of the earl of Shaftesbury to the Earl of Essex, 1673.

Public Record Office, London

Privy Council Registers, 2/55–66.

State papers relating to Ireland, 63/307/4.

Kent Archives Office, Maidstone

MS. U 350. Dering papers.

John Rylands Library, Manchester

MS. 507 (Crawford Irish 125). Transcriptions of documents relating to the court of claims, 1666–8.

Bodleian Library, Oxford

Carte MSS.

Clarendon MS. 75. Abstract of the regicides' estates claimed by the duke of York, *c.*1666.

Clarendon MS. 80. Papers relating to the case of Philip Hore of Kilsallaghan.

Clarendon MS. 83. Abstract of the duke of York's claim, *c.*1666–7.

II. PRINTED MATERIAL

1. *Record Publications*

[Calendar of Irish] patent rolls, James I (Dublin, 1830).

Calendar of patent and close rolls of Chancery in Ireland, Henry VIII to 18th Elizabeth, ed. J. Morrin (Dublin, 1861).

Calendar of State Papers, Domestic; Ireland.

[Calendar of] State Papers, Henry VIII (London, 1830–52), 11 vols.
Calendar of Treasury Books, v, viii (London, 1911, 1916).
Index to the Townlands of Ireland, 1901 (Dublin, 1904).
Inquisitionum in Officio Rotulorum Cancellariae Hiberniae Asservatorum Repertorium (Dublin, 1826–9), 2 vols.
Lascelles, R., *Liber Munerum Publicorum Hiberniae* (London, 1852), 2 vols.
Public Record Office of Ireland, Reports of the Deputy Keeper: 7th–9th, 11th-13th, 15th–18th, 21st *Reports*, appendixes (Calendar of fiants, Ireland, Henry VIII-Elizabeth), 1875–89.
19th *Report*, appendix v (Abstract of decrees of the court of claims for the trial of innocents), 1887.
56th *Report*, appendix iv A (Memorandum of Sarsfield-Vesey collection), 1931.
Reports of the commissioners appointed by his majesty to execute the measures recommended in an address of the House of Commons respecting the public records of Ireland; with supplements and appendixes (Dublin, 1811–25), 3 vols.

2. *Records of Parliament*

Brunton, D., and Pennington, D. H., *Members of the Long Parliament* (London, 1954).
Cobbett's Parliamentary History of England, iv (London, 1808).
Dunlop, R., *Ireland Under the Commonwealth* (Manchester, 1913), 2 vols.
Firth, C. H., and Rait, R. S., *Acts and Ordinances of the Interregnum, 1642–60* (London, 1911), 3 vols.
The Journals of the House of Commons.
The Journals of the House of Commons of the Kingdom of Ireland (Dublin, 1796).
The Journals of the House of Lords.
The Journals of the House of Lords of the Kingdom of Ireland (Dublin, 1779).
Mountmorres, H. R. M., Viscount, *The History of the Principal Transactions of the Irish Parliament from the year 1634 to 1666* (Dublin, 1792), 2 vols.
Return of Members of Parliament (London, 1879), 3 vols.
Statutes of the Realm (London, 1810–28), 11 vols.
Statutes at large passed in the Parliaments held in Ireland (Dublin, 1786), 20 vols.

3. *Publications of the Irish Manuscripts Commission*

Analecta Hibernica
No. 1 (Report of Bodl. Rawlinson MS. A. 482), 1930.
No. 8 (Ulster Plantation papers, 1608–12), 1938.
No. 15 (Commonwealth State accounts: Ireland, 1650–6), 1944.
No. 16 (Office of general registrar to the courts of claims, 1661–9), 1946.
No. 23 (List of outlaws, 1641–7), 1966.
No. 28 (Books of Survey and Distribution: a comparative survey). 1978.
Hogan, J., and O'Farrell, N. (ed.), *Walsingham Letter Book or Register of Ireland, May 1578 to December 1579* (1959).
Jennings, B. (ed.), *Wild Geese in Spanish Flanders* (1964).
Moody, T. W., and Simms, J. G. (ed.), *The Bishopic of Derry and the Irish Society of London, 1602–1705*, i (1968–83), 2 vols.
O'Laidhin, T. (ed.), *Sidney State Papers, 1565–70*, (1962).
Pender, S. (ed.), *A Census of Ireland, circa 1659* (1939).
Simington, R. C. (ed.), *Books of Survey and Distribution*, i. Co. Roscommon (1949).
—— (ed.), *The Civil Survey, A. D. 1654–1656*, vii, Co. Dublin (1945).

—— (ed.), *The Transplantation to Connacht, 1654–58* (1970).
White, N. B. (ed.), *Extents of Irish Monastic Possessions, 1540–41* (1943).

4. *Publications of the Historical Manuscripts Commission*

Eighth report, appendix , part i (Ormonde MSS.), 1881.
Fifteenth report, appendix, part i (Dartmouth MSS.), 1896; appendix, part vii (Ailesbury MSS.), 1898.
Ormonde MSS., ii-iii, new series, 1903–1904.
Egmont MSS., i, 1905.
Hastings MSS., iv, 1947.
Report on the manuscripts of the Marquis of Ormonde, ii, 1899.

5. *Other Documentary Material*

Abbott, W. C. (ed.), *The Writings and Speeches of Oliver Cromwell* (Cambridge, Mass., 1937–47), 4 vols.
The abstract of the claims of all persons claiming as innocents in the city, county of the city, and county of Dublin (Dublin, 1663).
Airy, O. (ed.), *Essex Papers*, i, Camden Soc., new series, xlvii (1890).
Birch, T., (ed.), *A Collection of State Papers of John Thurloe* (London, 1742), 7 vols.
Blake, M., *Blake Family Records* (London, 1902–5), 2 vols.
Bryant, A. (ed.), *The Letters, Speeches and Declarations of King Charles II* (London, 1935).
Burke's Irish Family Records (London, 1976).
Burtchaell, G. D., and Sadleir, T. U. (ed.), *Alumni Dublinenses* (Dublin, 1935).
Calendar of Ancient Deeds and Muniments preserved in the Pembroke estate office (Dublin, 1891).
Calendar of the Carew Manuscripts preserved in the Archepiscopal Library at Lambeth, 1515–74 (London, 1867–73), 6 vols.
Collections for a History of Staffordshire, Staffordshire Record Soc., 4th ser., ii (1958).
A Geographical Description of the Kingdom of Ireland (London, 1720).
Giblin, C. (ed.), 'Catalogue of material of Irish interest in the Collection *Nuziatura di Fiandra*, Vatican archives', *Collectanea Hibernica*, no. 1 (1958).
Gilbert, J. T., and Lady Gilbert (ed.), *Calendar of the Ancient Records of Dublin* (Dublin, 1889–1944), 19 vols.
Hatchell, G. (ed.), *Abstract of grants of lands and other hereditaments under the Commission of Grace, 36–37 Charles II, and 1–4 James II, 1684–1688* (Dublin, 1839).
Henning, B. D., (ed.), *The Parliamentary Diary of Sir Edward Dering* (New Haven, Conn., 1940).
By his majesty's commissioners for executing the Act of Settlement . . . ; a list of mortgages, etc. within the '49 security appointed to be canted 26 November, 1667.
His majesties Gracious Declaration of the settlement of his Kingdom of Ireland and satisfaction of the several interests of adventurers, soldiers, and other his subjects there (London, 1660).
Jacob, G., *A New Law Dictionary* (London, 1729).
Lansdowne, *The Petty Papers* (London, 1927), 2 vols.
The Petty-Southwell Correspondence, 1676–87 (London, 1928).
Larcom, T. A., *The history of the Survey of Ireland, commonly called the Down Survey, by Doctor William Petty* (Dublin, 1851).
Leslie, J. B. (ed.), 'Calendar of leases and deeds of St. Patrick's Cathedral, Dublin, 1660–89', *R.S.A.I.J.*, 7th ser., iv (1934).

Letters written by ... Arthur Capel, earl of Essex ... in the year 1675 (London, 1770).
Loeber, R., 'English and Irish sources for the history of Dutch economic activity in Ireland, 1660–1689', *Irish Economic and Social History*, viii (1981).
MacLysaght, E., *A Guide to Irish Surnames* (2nd edt., Dublin, 1965).
——*Irish Families* (Dublin, 1957).
Morrice, T. (ed.), *A collection of the State Letters of ... Roger Boyle, ... earl of Orrery ...* (Dublin, 1743), 2 vols.
O'Connell, B. M., *O'Connell Family Tracts*, no. 1 (n.p., n.d.).
Ogle, O. (*et al*, ed.), *Calendar of Clarendon State Papers* (Oxford, 1869–1970), 5 vols.
O'Hart, J. (ed.), *Irish Pedigrees* (New York, 1915).
'Order by the court of claims', *R.S.A.I.J.*, 4th ser., app. xii, iv (1876–8).
O'Riordan, W., 'A list of the priests, secular and regular, of the diocese of Dublin in the year 1697', *Reportorium Novum*, i (1955).
Pike, C. (ed.), *Selections from the Correspondence of Arthur Capel, earl of Essex, 1675–1677*, Camden Soc., 3rd ser., xxiv (London, 1913).
Playfair, W., *British Family Antiquity* (London, 1809–11), 9 vols.
Rules, orders and directions agreed upon by his majesties commissioners appointed for the execution of the Act of Settlement ... for regulating proceedings in the court... (Dublin, 1662).
Rules, orders, and directions appointed by his majesties commissioners for executing the Act of Settlement and the Act of Explanation ... (Dublin, 1666).
Rushworth, J., *Historical Collections of private passages of state, 1618–48* (London, 1682–1701), 6 vols.
Russell, C. W., and Prendergast, J.P., *The Carte Manuscripts in the Bodleian Library, Oxford* (London, 1871).
Sainty, J., *Officials of the Secretaries of State, 1660–1782* (London, 1973).
Shaw, W. (ed.), *The Knights of England* (London, 1906), 2 vols.
Letters of denization and acts of naturalization for aliens in England and Ireland, 1603–1700, Huguenot Soc. of London, xviii (Lymington, 1911).
The State Letters of Henry Earl of Clarendon ... (Oxford and Dublin, 1765), 2 vols.
Steele, R. (ed.), *Tudor and Stuart Proclamations* (Oxford, 1910), 2 vols.
Thorpe Catalogue of books and manuscripts (London, 1834).
Whitaker, T. D., *The Life and Correspondence of Sir George Radcliffe* (London, 1810).

6. *Newspapers*

The Intelligencer (1663).
The London Gazette (1666).
Mercurius Publicus (1660–3).
Mercurius Hibernicus (1663).

7. *Contemporary and near-contemporary works*

Bond, M. F. (ed.), *The Diaries and Papers of Sir Edward Dering, second baronet, 1644–1684* (London, 1976).
Clarendon, *The Life of Edward earl of Clarendon ... containing a Continuation of ... his History of the Grand Rebellion from the Restoration to ...1667* (Dublin, 1760).
Coates, W.H. (ed.), *The Journal of Sir Simonds D'Ewes* (New Haven, Conn., 1942).
Cox, R., *Hibernia Anglicana* (London, 1689–90), 2 parts.
DeBeer, E. S. (ed.), *The Diary of John Evelyn* (Oxford, 1955), 6 vols.
Firth, C. H. (ed.), *The Memoirs of Edmund Ludlow* (Oxford, 1894), 2 vols.

[French, N.], *A Narrative of the earl of Clarendon's Settlement and Sale of Ireland* (Louvain, 1668).

A full and impartial account of all the secret consults . . . of the Romish party in Ireland, from 1660 to . . . 1689 (London, 1689).

Gilbert, J. T. (ed.), *A Contemporary History of Affairs in Ireland, from A.D. 1641 to 1652* (Dublin, 1879), 3 vols.

—— *The History of the Irish Confederation and the War in Ireland, 1641–1653* (Dublin, 1882–91), 7 vols.

—— *A Jacobite Narrative of the War in Ireland, 1688–91* (Dublin, 1892; facsimily edn, with intro. by J. G. Simms, Shannon, 1971).

The Historical Work of the Right Rev. Nicholas French (Dublin, 1846,), 2 vols.

Hore, H. F. (ed.), 'A chorographic account of the southern part of the county of Wexford, written anno 1684: by Robert Leigh, esq. of Rosegarland in that county', R.S.A.I.J., n.s., ii (1858).

Hull, C. H. (ed.), *The Economic Writings of Sir William Petty* (Cambridge, 1899), 2 vols.

[Reilly, H.], *Ireland's case briefly stated* (n.p., 1695).

Sachse, W. (ed.), *The Diurnal of Thomas Rugg, 1659–1661*, Camden Soc., 3rd ser., xci (London, 1961).

Scott, Sir W. (ed.), *Memoirs of the Court of Charles the Second by Count Grammont* (London, 1846).

State of the Papist and Protestant proprieties in the Kingdom of Ireland (London, 1689).

Wheatley, H. (ed.), *The Diary of Samuel Pepys* (London, 1893–9), 10 vols.

Whitelock, B., *Memorials of English Affairs* (London, 1732).

8. *Later Works*

Arnold, L. J., 'The Cromwellian Settlement of Co. Dublin, 1652–1660', *R.S.A.I.J.*, 101 (1971).

—— 'The Irish court of claims of 1663', *I.H.S.*, xxiv (Nov. 1985).

Ashley, M., *Charles II, the man and the statesman* (London, 1971).

Bagwell, R., *Ireland under the Stuarts* (London, 1909–16), 3 vols.

Ball, F. E., *A History of the County Dublin* (Dublin, 1902–20), 6 parts.

—— *The Judges in Ireland, 1221-1921* (London, 1926), 2 vols.

—— 'Some notes on the households of the dukes of Ormond', *R.I.A. Proceedings*, xxxvii (1928).

—— 'Some notes on the Irish judiciary in the reign of Charles II, 1660–1685', *Journal of the Cork Historical and Archeological Society*, 2nd ser., vii (1901).

—— 'Stillorgan Park and its history', *R.S.A.I.J.*, 5th ser., viii (1898).

Barnard, T., *Cromwellian Ireland* (Oxford, 1975).

—— 'Planters and policies in Cromwellian Ireland', *Past & Present*, no. 61 (1973).

Beckett, J. C., 'The Irish viceroyalty in the Restoration period', *Royal Historical Society Transactions*, 5th ser., xx (1970).

—— 'The Confederation of Kilkenny reviewed' *Confrontations: studies in Irish history* (London, 1972).

—— *The Cavalier Duke: a life of James Butler, 1st duke of Ormond* (Belfast, 1990).

Bottigheimer, K. S., *English Money and Irish Land* (Oxford, 1971).

—— 'The Restoration land settlement in Ireland: a structural view', *I.H.S.*, xviii (1972).

Bradshaw, B., *The Dissolution of the Religious Orders in Ireland under Henry VIII* (Cambridge, 1974).

—— 'The opposition to the ecclesiastical legislation in the Irish Reformation parliament', *I.H.S.*, xvi (1969).

Burghclere, Lady, *The Life of James first duke of Ormonde* (London, 1912), 2 vols.
Butler, W. F. T., *Confiscation in Irish History* (Dublin, 1917).
Canny, N., *The Elizabethan Conquest of Ireland: a pattern established, 1565–76* (Sussex, 1976).
—— *The Upstart Earl* (Cambridge, 1982).
Carte, T., *Life of James, first duke of Ormond* (Oxford, 1851), 6 vols.
The case of John Vernon depending before the most honourable the House of Lords . . . (n.p., n.d., *c*.1730).
Childers, E., & Stewart, R., *The Story of the Royal Hospital, Kilmainham* (London, 1921).
Churchill, W. S., *Marborough, his Life and Times* (London, 1933–8), 2 vols.
Clarke, A., *The Old English in Ireland, 1625–42* (London, 1966).
Cokayne, G. E. (ed.), *Complete Baronetage* (Exeter, 1900–9), 6 vols.
—— *Complete Peerage* (London, 1910–40), 13 vols.
Cregan, D., 'An Irish Cavalier: Daniel O'Neill in exile and restoration, 1651–64', *Studia Hibernica*, no. 5 (1965).
D'Alton, J., *The History of the County of Dublin* (Dublin, 1838).
—— *King James's Irish Army List* (Dublin, 1878), 2 vols.
Davis, T., *The Patriot Parliament of 1689* (London, 1843).
Donnelly, N., *History of Dublin Parishes* (Dublin, n,d., *c*.1908–17), 4 parts.
Edwards, R. D., *Church and State in Tudor Ireland* (Dublin, 1935).
—— 'The Irish Reformation Parliament of Henry VIII,1536–7', *Historical Studies*, vii (1968).
Falkiner, C. L., *Illustrations of Irish History and Topography, mainly of the Seventeenth Century* (London, 1904).
Firth, C. H., *Cromwell's Army* (London, 3rd edt., 1921).
—— *The Last years of the Protectorate* (London, 1909), 2 vols.
—— and Davies, G., *A Regimental History of Cromwell's Army* (Oxford, 1940).
Fitzgerald, Lord, 'Leixlip Castle', *Journal of the County Kildare Archaeological Soc.*, ii (1896–9).
Foss, E., *The Judges of England* (London, 1848–64), 9 vols.
Fraser, A., *Royal Charles: Charles II and the Restoration* (New York, 1979).
Gilbert, J. T., *A History of the City of Dublin* (Dublin, 1861), 3 vols.
Gorges, R., *The Story of a Family through Eleven Centuries . . . being a history of the Family of Gorges* (Boston, Mass., 1944).
Hardinge, W. H., 'On manuscript mapped and other townland surveys in Ireland of a public character, embracing the Gross, Civil, and Down Surveys, from 1640 to 1688', *R.I.A. Transactions* (Antiquities), xxiv (1873).
Harris, W. (ed.), *The Whole Works of Sir James Ware* (Dublin, 1764), 2 vols.
Hill, C., *God's Englishman* (New York, 1970).
Howard, G., *A Treatise on the Exchequer and Revenue of Ireland* (Dublin, 1776), 2 vols.
Hunter, R. J., 'The Ulster Plantation in the counties of Armagh and Cavan, 1608–41', M. Litt, University of Dublin, 1969.
Hutton, R., *Charles the Second: King of England, Scotland, and Ireland* (Oxford, 1989).
'Irish Catholics licensed to keep arms', *Archivium Hibernicum*, iv (1915).
Journal of the Association for the Preservation of the Memorials of the Dead, v, no. 3 (1903).
Kearney, H. F., *Strafford in Ireland, 1633–41* (Manchester, 1959).
Kelly, P., '"A light to the blind": the voice of the dispossessed élite in the generation after the defeat at Limerick', *I.H.S.*, xxiv (1985).
Kingston, J., 'Catholic families of the Pale', *Reportorium Novum*, ii (1958).
Lennon, C., 'Richard Stanihurst (1547–1618) and Old English identity', *I.H.S.*, xxi (1978).
Lodge, J., *The Peerage of Ireland*, ed. M. Archdall (Dublin, 1789), 7 vols.

Love, J., 'Charles I and the Confederation of Kilkenny, 1643–9', *I.H.S.*, xiv (1964).
Macaulay, T. B., *The History of England from the Accession of James II* (London, 3rd edt., 1849–61), 5 vols.
McGuire, J., 'Why was Ormond dismissed in 1669?', *I.H.S.*, xviii (1973).
—— 'The Dublin Convention, the Protestant community and the emergence of an ecclesiastical settlement in 1660'., McGuire, J., & Cosgrove, A. (ed.), *Parliament & Community*, Historical Studies, xiv (Belfast, 1983).
McPharland, E., 'Rathfarnham Castle, Co. Dublin', *Country Life* (9 Sept. 1982).
—— 'Royal Hospital, Kilmainham, Co. Dublin', *Country Life* (May 9, 16, 1985).
Meige, G., *The Present State of His Majesty's Dominions in Ireland* (London, 1717).
Moody, T. W., Martin, F. X., Byrne, F. J. (ed.), *A New History of Ireland*, vol. iii (Oxford, 1976).
—— *Davitt and Irish Revolution*, 1846–82 (Oxford, 1982).
O'Conbhuidhe, M. C., 'The lands of St. Mary's Abbey, Dublin, at the dissolution of the abbey', *Reportorium Novum*, iii (1961–2).
O'Donoghue, F., 'Parliament in Ireland under Charles II', M.A. thesis, University College, Dublin, 1970.
Ogg, D., *England in the reign of Charles II* (Oxford, 2nd edt., 1955), 2 vols.
O'Gorman, T., 'Notice . . . of Owen O'Connelly', *R.S.A.I.J*, 4th ser., vi (1883–4).
O'Mordha, P. B., 'The MacMahons, of Monaghan', *Clogher Record*, ii, no. 3 (1959).
O'Sullivan, H., 'Land ownership changes in the county of Louth in the seventeenth century', Ph.D., University of Dublin, 1991 .
Otway–Ruthven, A. J., 'The mediaeval church lands of county Dublin', J. Watt, *et al* (ed.), *Medieval Studies Presented to Aubrey Gwynn, S.J.* (Dublin, 1961).
Prendergast, J. P., 'The Butlers, Lords Ikerrin, before the court of transplantation . . . and . . . the first and second court of claims . . . 1662–1666', *R.S.A.I.J.*, 4th ser., vii (1885–6).
—— *The Cromwellian Settlement of Ireland* (London, 3rd edt., 1870).
—— *Ireland from the Restoration to the Revolution, 1660 to 1690* (London, 1887).
Ramsey, R. W., *Henry Cromwell* (London, 1933).
Ranger, T., 'Richard Boyle and the making of an Irish fortune, 1588–1614', *I.H.S.*, x (1957).
Ronan, M., *The Reformation in Dublin, 1536–58* (London, 1926).
Rowse, A. L., *The Early Churchills* (London, 1956).
Sadlier, T. U., 'Ladytown and the Allens', *Journal of the County Kildare Archaeological Society*, ix (1918–21).
Sergeant, P. W., *Little Jennings and Fighting Dick Talbot* (London, 1913), 2 vols.
Silke, J., *Kinsale: the Spanish intervention in Ireland at the end of the Elizabethan wars* (Liverpool, 1970).
Simms, J. G., *Colonial Nationalism, 1689–1776* (Cork, 1976).
—— *The Jacobite Parliament of 1689* (Dundalk, 1966).
—— *William Molyneux of Dublin* (Dublin, 1982).
—— *The Williamite Confiscation in Ireland, 1690–1703*, (London, 1956).
Smyth, W. J., 'Exploring the social and cultural topographies of sixteenth and seventeenth-century Dublin', Aalen, F., & Whelan, K. (ed.), *Dublin City and County; from prehistory to the present* (Dublin, 1992).
Strickland W., 'The Royal Hospital at Kilmainham and its architect', *R.S.A.I.J.*, xiii (1923).
Underdown, D., *Pride's Purge* (Oxford, 1971).
—— *Royalist Conspiracy in England, 1649–1660* (New Haven, Conn., 1960).
Warburton, J., Whitelaw, J., Walsh, R., *History of the City of Dublin* (London, 1818), 2 vols.
Whitcombe, D. T., *Charles II and the Cavalier House of Commons, 1663–1674* (Manchester, 1966).

III. MAPS

Down Survey barony and parish maps, county Dublin (N.L.I., Reeves collection).

A survey of part of Newtown and Kilmainham left out of the Phoenix Park by making the wall straight. Admeasured by Thomas Taylor, 1671 (N.L.I.)

Ordnance Survey Maps, county Dublin (1835 edt., six inches to one mile).

William Duncan's map of county Dublin, 1821.

Index

References to the lists of landowners in Appendix A (pp 152–61) are not included. Unless otherwise noted, all place names are located in the county or city of Dublin.